Also by Mike Ayers

One Last Song

SHARING
IN THE
GROOVE

SHARING IN THE GROOVE

THE UNTOLD STORY OF THE
'90s JAM BAND EXPLOSION
AND THE SCENE THAT FOLLOWED

MIKE AYERS

ST. MARTIN'S PRESS
NEW YORK

First published in the United States by St. Martin's Press,
an imprint of St. Martin's Publishing Group

Printed in the United States of America. For information, address St. Martin's Publishing Group, 120 Broadway, New York, NY 10271.

www.stmartins.com

Endpaper photograph by Keith Griner / Getty Images

The Library of Congress Cataloging-in-Publication Data is available upon request.

ISBN 978-1-250-28745-8 (hardcover)
ISBN 978-1-250-28746-5 (ebook)

Our books may be purchased in bulk for promotional, educational, or business use. Please contact your local bookseller or the Macmillan Corporate and Premium Sales Department at 1-800-221-7945, extension 5442, or by email at MacmillanSpecialMarkets@macmillan.com.

First Edition: 2025

10 9 8 7 6 5 4 3 2 1

Contents

Cast

John Alagía—Producer, *Remember Two Things*
Sam Altman—Drums, The Disco Biscuits
Vinnie Amico—Drums, moe.
Trey Anastasio—Guitar, vocals, Phish
Sam Ankerson—Promotions Manager, Strangefolk
Michael Barbiero—Producer, *Four, Gov't Mule*
Chris Barron—Lead Singer, Spin Doctors
John Bell—Guitar, vocals, Widespread Panic
Andy Bernstein—Author, *The Pharmer's Almanac*; Co-founder, HeadCount.org
Jon Bevo—Keyboards, vocals, God Street Wine
Jim Bickerstaff—Assistant Engineer, *Widespread Panic*
Kerry Black—Co-founder, Superfly Presents
David Blackmon—Fiddle, Bluegrass Underground
Chris Bowman—Talent Booker, Trax
Hunter Brown—Guitar, Sound Tribe Sector 9
Marc Brownstein—Bass, vocals, The Disco Biscuits
Dean Budnick—Founder, Jambands.com
Oteil Burbridge—Bass, Aquarium Rescue Unit
Matt Busch—Tour Merchandiser, God Street Wine; Tour Manager, Gov't Mule
Eric Carter—Guitar, vocals, Bloodkin
Michael Caplan—Senior Vice President of A&R, Epic Records
Patrick Clifford—Vice President of A&R, A&M Records
Danny Clinch—Photographer
Billy Cohen—Lyricist, dreamspeak; Staff Member, Music Unlimited
Brian Cohen—Vice President of Marketing, Elektra Records
Aaron Comess—Drums, Spin Doctors

Jeff Cook—Senior Vice President of Promotion and Marketing, Capricorn Records
Grant Cowell—Road Manager, Blues Traveler
Shelly Culbertson—Internet and Ticketing Manager, Phish
Joel Cummins—Keyboards, vocals, Umphrey's McGee
Peter Denenberg—Producer, *Pocket Full of Kryptonite*
Karl Denson—Saxophone, vocals, The Greyboy Allstars, Karl Denson's Tiny Universe
Rob Derhak—Bass, vocals, moe.
Doug Derryberry—Engineer, *Recently* EP; Mixer, *Live at Red Rocks*
Cody Dickinson—Drums, North Mississippi Allstars
Sue Drew—Vice President of A&R, Elektra Records
DJ Logic—Musician
Mary Dugas—Operations Management, Widespread Panic
Steve Eichner—Photographer
Benjy Eisen—Journalist
Ben Ellman—Saxophone, Galactic
Drew Emmitt—Mandolin, guitar, vocals, Leftover Salmon
Alan Evans—Drums, Moon Boot Lover, Soulive
Lo Faber—Guitar, vocals, God Street Wine
Brett Fairbrother—Manager, Strangefolk
Rick Farman—Co-founder, Superfly Presents
Jon Fishman—Drums, vocals, Phish
Béla Fleck—Banjo, Béla Fleck & the Flecktones
Steve Fleming—Bouncer, Uptown Lounge; Sound Engineer, Georgia Theatre
Bruce Flohr—Senior Vice President of A&R, RCA Records
Dave Frey—Manager, Blues Traveler
Andy Gadiel—Founder, Andy Gadiel's Phish Page; Co-founder, Jambase.com
Andre Gardner—Tour Manager, Strangefolk
Chuck Garvey—Guitar, vocals, moe.
Reid Genauer—Rhythm guitar, vocals, Strangefolk
Mike Gordon—Bass, vocals, Phish
David Graham—Manager, Blues Traveler
Tom Gruber—Founder, Music Unlimited
Jon "The Barber" Gutwillig—Guitar, vocals, The Disco Biscuits

Kevin Halpin—Producer, *A Picture of Nectar*
Scotty Hard—Producer, *Combustication*, *The Dropper*
Philip Harvey—Live Sound Engineer, Medeski Martin & Wood
Warren Haynes—Guitar, vocals, The Allman Brothers Band, Gov't Mule
Vince Herman—Guitar, vocals, Leftover Salmon
Jimmy Herring—Guitar, Aquarium Rescue Unit
Brendan Hill—Drums, Blues Traveler
Ken "Ranch Man" Hoff—Owner, Arrowhead Ranch
Kyle Hollingsworth—Keyboards, vocals, The String Cheese Incident
Gordon Hookailo—Producer, *Junta*
Mikey Houser—Guitar, vocals, Widespread Panic
Ben "Junta" Hunter—Manager, Phish
Peter Jackson—Drum Technician, Production Manager, Widespread Panic
Jamie Janover—Musician
Nancy Jeffries—Senior Vice President, A&R, Elektra Records
Michael Kang—Mandolin, vocals, The String Cheese Incident
John Keane—Producer/Engineer, Widespread Panic
Chan Kinchla—Guitar, Blues Traveler
Eric Krasno—Guitar, Soulive, Lettuce
Russ Lawton—Drums, Trey Anastasio Band
Cheryl Liguori—Manager, Wetlands; Co-founder, Fox Theatre
Steve Lillywhite—Producer, *Under the Table and Dreaming, Crash, Before These Crowded Streets, Billy Breathes*
Jim Loughlin—Drums/Percussion, moe.
Mike Luba—Manager, The String Cheese Incident
Aron Magner—Keyboards, piano, The Disco Biscuits
Jono Manson—Guitar, vocals, Joey Miserable and the Worms
Al Marks—Executive Director, Artist Development, A&M Records
Tom Marshall—Lyricist, Phish
Billy Martin—Drums, Medeski Martin & Wood
Dave Matthews—Guitar, vocals, Dave Matthews Band
Aaron Maxwell—Guitar, vocals, God Street Wine
Cree McCree—Journalist
Page McConnell—Piano, keyboards, vocals, Phish
Jim McGuinn—Program Director, WEQX, Manchester, Vermont

John Medeski—Keyboards, piano, Medeski Martin & Wood
Robert Mercurio—Bass, Galactic
Rob Mitchum—Journalist
John Moore—Tour Marketing and A&R, Mammoth Records
Stanton Moore—Drums, Galactic
Kevin Morris—Founder, SCI Fidelity Records
Keith Moseley—Bass, The String Cheese Incident
Matt Mundy—Mandolin, Aquarium Rescue Unit
Zak Najor—Drums, The Greyboy Allstars
Todd Nance—Drums, Widespread Panic
Bill Nershi—Guitar, vocals, The String Cheese Incident
Zach Newton—Front-of-House Engineer, Aquarium Rescue Unit
Tye North—Bass, Leftover Salmon
Domingo "Sunny" Ortiz—Percussion, Widespread Panic
Jon O'Leary—Co-founder, Fox Theatre; Front-of-House Engineer, The String Cheese Incident
Tom "Tomo" Osander—Drums, God Street Wine
Joan Osborne—Singer-songwriter
Elgin Park—Guitar, The Greyboy Allstars
Liz Penta—Manager, Medeski Martin & Wood
David Phipps—Bass, Sound Tribe Sector 9
Dan Pifer—Bass, God Street Wine
Steve "The Dude of Life" Pollak—Musician
John Popper—Vocals, harmonica, Blues Traveler
David Precheur—Tour Manager, Blues Traveler
Chris Rabold—Live Sound Mixer, Production Manager, Widespread Panic
Scott "bullethead" Reilly—Manager, God Street Wine
Ted Rockwell—Founder, *Everyday Companion*
Michael Rothschild—Founder, Landslide Records
Anne Rothwell—Founder, Club Metronome
Brad Sands—Tour Manager, Phish
Eric Schenkman—Guitar, Spin Doctors
Al Schnier—Guitar, vocals, moe.
Dave Schools—Bass, vocals, Widespread Panic
Ray Schwartz—Drums, moe.

Pete Shapiro—Owner, Wetlands
John Siket—Engineer, *Crash, Billy Breathes, Tin Cans & Car Tires, Story of the Ghost, Farmhouse*
Jeff Sipe—Drums, Aquarium Rescue Unit
Luke Smith—Drums, Strangefolk
Dirk Stalnecker—Production Assistant, Blues Traveler; Tour Manager, Widespread Panic
Jeremy Stein—Manager, The String Cheese Incident
Chris Stillwell—Bass, The Greyboy Allstars
Don Strasburg—Co-founder, Fox Theatre
Luc Suèr—Monitor Engineer, Medeski Martin & Wood
Dave Swanson—Sound Engineer, Blues Traveler
Shawn Sweeney—Owner, The Front
Michael Travis—Drums, The String Cheese Incident
Jon Topper—Manager, moe.
Jane Tower—Operations Manager, Dave Matthews Band
Jon Trafton—Guitar, vocals, Strangefolk
Derek Trucks—Guitar, Derek Trucks Band, The Allman Brothers Band
Mark Vann—Banjo, Leftover Salmon
Zach Velmer—Drums, Sound Tribe Sector 9
Rich Vink—Sound Engineer, Blues Traveler
Kristin Wallace—Tour Manager, Medeski Martin & Wood
Robert Walter—Keyboards, The Greyboy Allstars, Robert Walter's 20th Congress
Jim Walsh—Publicist
Dave Watts—Co-founder, Shockra; Drums, The Motet
Russ "In the Bus" Weis—Environmental Director, Wetlands; Office Manager, Strangefolk
Michael Weiss—Road Crew, God Street Wine
Fred Wesley—Trombone, James Brown, Maceo Parker
Buck Williams—Manager, Widespread Panic
Keller Williams—Musician
Chris Wood—Bass, Medeski Martin & Wood
Steve Young—Sound Engineer, moe.

1

It's Not Horrible, but I'm Stoned

David Graham (Manager, Blues Traveler): Princeton is the forgotten center of rock and roll.

David Precheur (Tour Manager, Blues Traveler): Let's go back to when I was very young. Nine, ten, eleven, living in Princeton, New Jersey. My father was a doctor. My mom, a stay-at-home mom. Princeton's a very well-to-do town. My mom was a socialite, she loved to hang with people. My dad was like, "I can't stand people." And so they found a balance. We lived on the edge of town, on a few acres. And I lived on this road and when you rode that a mile up the street, there was this abandoned bridge that went over Stony Brook, which is a little creek that runs through Princeton. There was another kid playing down there. And it was Bob Sheehan, the [Blues Traveler] bass player.

Chris Barron (Lead Singer, Spin Doctors): I went to high school with John Popper, who was an amazing instrumentalist and a deeply talented improviser. In high school, we played a lot of music together—improvisational music. I used to drive his car until we were lost. Then we would find somewhere cool to pull over, get stoned, and play music until we were lost. Just singing . . . I'd be playing guitar and sometimes he'd play harmonica and we'd sing together and improvise that way . . . making up songs and stuff. It wasn't easy to record things back then either, so there's no recordings of any of this stuff.

There wasn't any expectation of it being documented, you know? It was all just kind of disappearing into the ether.

Chan Kinchla (Guitar, Blues Traveler): All the kids in Princeton High School were all into the Grateful Dead, Led Zeppelin, Allman Brothers—all these great classic rock bands. That's what everyone was listening to at parties.

Brendan Hill (Drums, Blues Traveler): Princeton High School . . . I was a freshman in 1983. I had already been playing drums in the middle school band. The high school jazz band was basically called Studio Band. The movie *Whiplash* is actually about our Studio Band, and our teacher Tony Biancosino, or Dr. B as we used to call him. So we used to compete at the Berklee Jazz high school jazz competition every year. There would be this very intense lead-up to that competition. John was part of that student band. I ended up in a basement band with my older brother, Sebastian, who played bass. And we had a guitar player, David Stern. We started this group up in middle school and we were just jamming Police covers, Romantics, whatever we could emulate. And so as soon as I got into high school, Dr. B was looking for a special instrument, to make us win next year's competition. Dr. B was walking down the hall and John was sitting by his locker, just playing harmonica in the hallway, and Dr. B said, "That's it! Something different!" So he grabbed John and said, "Come on in here with me." And he brought him into our band's practice, and gave him a microphone and just said, "Play along with us." And John was like, "Well, what key is it?" Luckily, he had that harp. The song was "Joint Venture" and there's a lot of opportunity to solo over that. The excitement in that room . . . not only because it was different from a saxophone or trumpet solo, it was just palpable. You could just feel it. That's gonna give us that special edge. Immediately after that, I was taken aback and obviously got very excited about John's sound.

Chan Kinchla: John was the celebrity of the music department. I would skip class, get baked, and go sit in the rehearsal rooms and just play rock and roll. I didn't know theory or anything, so I was very much a periphery to the music program.

John Popper (Vocals, harmonica, Blues Traveler): When I first started being in a band with Brendan, his older brother on the bass, this was the very, very beginning of what would become Blues Traveler. They would do '80s songs, like The Police and David Bowie—there wasn't really much use for harmonica in that band. So we decided once his brother went off to college to call ourselves "Blues Band," because the original songs we were writing had a harmonica. I was very much into the Blues Brothers and all that, and playing a harmonica just lent itself to that. We were being very pragmatic: "This is what we are, we're a blues band." But we didn't know what we were doing. I would always say that if Muddy Waters was like a little white kid in Jersey, in the '80s, he'd sound a lot more like us.

Chan Kinchla: We all grew up on Classic Rock radio. That's what the radio was in the '80s. And we were all listening to all of that. Allman Brothers, Led Zeppelin, Grateful Dead—there's a lot of jamming going on. That's what I was all into after I got out of my New Wave, early punk rock phase. Classic Rock radio in the '80s definitely played a part in exposing us to that.

Tom Marshall (Lyricist, Phish): I think my parents were worried that I was starting to hang out with the wrong crowd and sent me to private school. I am almost positive that was the same motivation why Trey [Anastasio] got sent to private school. Boom, we were both in private school. I couldn't imagine a more musical grade. We were a hundred people—fifty girls, fifty boys. There were, I think, six bands in our grade. And Trey was in all of them, as a drummer.

Lo Faber (Vocals, guitars, God Street Wine): I knew Trey Anastasio slightly. He played drums for all the musicals at the PDS [Princeton Day School] orchestra—wearing a tux, playing drums.

Tom Marshall: Many of our friends played instruments and wrote original songs and recorded them in homemade studios. He left in tenth grade and went to Taft. We lost touch and then randomly both met again at Mercer County Community College where we were forced to go since we were both kicked out of college after our freshman year for different reasons. It was great—we just picked up where we had left off three years earlier. We built a mini-studio in his dad's basement, got tremendously stoned nightly, and recorded lots of music, like "Divided Sky," "Letter to Jimmy Page," "Antelope," etc.

Chan Kinchla: Bobby knew of him, but not as a musician—just as Trey Anastasio. Bobby, for a while, was in the Princeton Day School.

Lo Faber: I didn't know Blues Traveler, except Bobby Sheehan, their bassist. We actually had a band—me, Bobby, and Tomo, the drummer from God Street Wine—we had a band together for, I don't know, a couple months. Bobby actually left this gorgeous acoustic bass amp at my house and then we had another band with another bassist, but we used Bobby's amp for a year.

David Precheur: We're going to Princeton Day School and the superintendent of Princeton Day School said to my mother, "This school is not made for a person like Dave Precheur." So, Princeton High School, the public school, was kind of a hip place. And I moved over there and as soon as I moved over there, I was coming home with great weed. I said to Bob, "If you want to save some money, move over to Princeton High School." I don't know high schools around the country, but that place was cool as shit! Everybody was a Deadhead, everybody hung out and smoked cigarettes in front of the school, we had keg parties in the middle of the week. It was just *chill*. The administration left us alone. You went to class, or you didn't. Your parents weren't blowing 50 to 60K a year for your education. Immediately with the drinking crowd, we meet Chan, the guitarist. Chan's like a football guy—a very smart football guy. Chan became a buddy and he was a godawful guitarist when he started. But like any good guitarist will tell you, just practice and practice and practice.

Chan Kinchla: My buddy, who I grew up across the street with, we were best friends from the age of four. I was like eleven and I went over to his house and he had gotten a guitar. So I picked it up and immediately was like, "This is amazing." For the next two weeks, I'd go to his house not to play with him, but just to play his guitar. Finally he just gave it to me.

David Precheur: I have my own John Popper story, whether he remembers or not. It was the first day, Princeton High School, definitely my junior year. And I was sitting out front of the auditorium on the steps, which is completely hidden from the administration. And I was smoking a joint before school. The morning assembly on Wednesdays, it was mandatory. But I never went into it. So I'm smoking this joint and all of a sudden, there's a hand on my shoulder. And it's the assistant superintendent, Mr. Van Arsdale. He said, "Mr. Precheur." And like a total fucking pro move, I flicked that joint into the bushes.

He said, "The assembly is starting. You're going, right?"

"Yes, Mr. Van."

"I'll go with you," he said.

The place is fucking packed. Every seat is taken, and literally with his hand on my shoulder, he walks me up to the front row. Everybody in school kind of knew I was the stoner Deadhead, troublemaker kid. He sat me front and center and sat down right next to me. We have a few minutes left and they said the Princeton jazz band is going to play us a song. They play a song. It's not horrible, but I'm stoned. And then they said there's time for one more song and this one is gonna feature Mr. John Popper. And I saw this rather large student walk out. He's a year older than me. And he has this lunchbox—he opens it up. It's all painted psychedelic, and I'm like, "What is going on?" He pulls out a harmonica and I'm like, "Oh god . . . is this fat kid gonna play fucking harmonica? This is horrifying." The band starts and John starts to play. And I'm like, "Holy shit!" It wasn't spectacular, but better than any other harmonica I had heard in my life. And I get up and introduce myself and John's like, "I know who you are." I said, "Dude. Seriously. What are we going to do with this?" And he said, "We?" Then he goes, "Can I get some weed?"

Brendan Hill: My brother was a couple years older than me, so he graduated in '85. And that meant we needed a new bass player. At that point, we'd gone through a couple of different guitar players and we heard about this guy Chan, who was kind of a jock. We had him come in and it was perfect because Chan loved the same music that we loved, like Zeppelin, The Clash, Bowie. Chan knew this guy who was a Deadhead—he was a bass player, and his name was Bobby. And so he joined maybe February or March of '87, which was my senior year. John had already graduated and moved to New York at that point, but we would still practice on weekends.

What Bob brought to the band was that really fluid, musical style. We were smoking pot at that point and taking mushrooms . . . really exploring how to just jam and be creative and really get into the music. And at that point, we'd gotten maybe five or ten songs or so. We'd been playing little gigs, like the YMCA, some house parties, some frat parties. People started to notice. We really gelled when Bob came in the group. We were able to envision ourselves taking the band to New York and trying it out. You only have that time in your life once, where you don't have big responsibilities, and you can just go for it.

2

Our Little Communist Commune

Aaron Maxwell (Guitar, vocals, God Street Wine): I lived in Ridgewood, New Jersey, which was twenty minutes away from the city. I had some friends that were also friends with some people that lived in the city. And they would talk about this guitar player named Kenny Gwyn who was just mind-blowing. People were going down to check him out and stuff. I remember going and my mouth just dropped to the floor. Not only was he a great player, but it was just like this scene that I hadn't seen before. It just felt like these were my people, somehow. We would go every weekend and I usually would be the driver, because I didn't really drink. I would get in my parents' Volvo, fit as many people as I could, and we would drive to the Inner Circle on a Friday or Saturday and go see Kenny play. It was a juxtaposition to the transvestites and the different kinds of things going on, like the Jane West hotel. It was a real sort of education for me.

Steve Eichner (Photographer): The Inner Circle was on the west side, in the Meatpacking District, when it was all prostitutes and dangerous. It was a small room and a little flat stage. And I remember Kenny was a heroin addict.

Billy Cohen (Lyricist, dreamspeak; Staff, Music Unlimited): Kenny played classic rock with these extended jams. It started early, like seven or eight o'clock. He might play through four in the morning. Some nights he would take the money from the door, ride his bike to Alphabet City, score some dope, come back, shoot up in the bathroom, do more sets. It was epic. And all these underage Deadheads would go. [Kenny] was living in an apartment carved out of a basement pool. No windows; it was the weirdest fucking place.

Aaron Maxwell: You would have these white suburban kids from New Jersey and Long Island, mixed with kids who were more savvy, lived in the city, and were Deadheads. One night, I was hanging out, [bassist] Jaco Pastorius was there. He was known to come in, and he borrowed the bass player's bass and started playing the "Star Spangled Banner"; turned everything up to 10. They turned the sound off on him after a while, and he just dropped the bass and walked out. I ended up buying him a sandwich because he had no money on him. It was things like that, for an eighteen-year-old kid . . . it's sort of mind-blowing. It really set me on a course.

Chris Barron: I moved to New York in June of 1988, with a hundred bucks and an acoustic guitar. I was mostly a songwriter and not a very skilled instrumental musician.

Brendan Hill: Our parents were honestly horrified we were all going to move to New York and live together.

David Precheur: We're just in our early twenties . . . man, we were bulletproof.

Jono Manson (Guitar, vocals, Joey Miserable and the Worms): I had many years where I played more than 365 gigs a year without ever leaving Manhattan.

John Popper: What we saw ourselves as was in the tradition of Led Zeppelin or Jimi Hendrix. And those guys were directly connected to the blues because their Jimi Hendrix was Muddy Waters or Little Walter or Charlie Christian. For us, Led Zeppelin was who we idolized and looked up to, and certainly Bobby was a huge Deadhead. I didn't really know much about the Grateful Dead. But when we came to New York, that was kind of the amalgam of, at least in our heads, who we were.

Steve Eichner: We were looking for our own Grateful Dead . . . a younger version of a jam band that we could call our own.

Aaron Comess (Drums, Spin Doctors): We used to call it "The Tour of Manhattan," because both Spin Doctors and Blues Traveler were literally playing five nights a week. We did the exact opposite of what pretty much every other band in New York was doing at the time. Everybody wanted a record deal. So everybody would rehearse all the time, and maybe do a showcase or something. We did the exact opposite, which was that we just played all the time.

Jono Manson: I met Popper before I met the other guys in Blues Traveler. John was a year older than the other guys and so he came over and started poking around, trying to find places where he could sit in and meet people.

Eric Schenkman (Guitar, Spin Doctors): The cabaret law was repealed in '86 or '87. There was a funny thing with the cabaret law where you couldn't have more than a certain number of musicians on the stage at the same time—it was from prohibition. The union was challenging it forever. And they finally beat it and there was actually more clubs suddenly that we were able to play, and they all had a different slant. Some were cover clubs—the Bleecker Street stuff. And some were more original, like maybe the Nightingale, and some were straight blues, like Dan Lynch. We could do it all night long.

Jono Manson: The headliner would play the rest of the night, until four in the morning.

Chris Barron: It kept people drinking and kept people in the room . . . it kept the night kind of moving along.

Eric Schenkman: Everybody got very good.

Rich Vink (Sound Engineer, Blues Traveler): That was a dividing line between all the different types of bands—we were trying to seek out the bands with compelling original stuff.

John Popper: Our parents were all like, "If you want to go to college, we'll pay for it. Otherwise, you have to get a job." And we all said to our parents, "We all want to go to college," and then we would just skip college and play gigs, because our parents were subsidizing us. It was the only option we had, really, because if we had to work jobs, it would have taken so much of our time. This enabled a great period in our lives, where we got to focus on the playing and the songwriting and getting better.

Brendan Hill: Bob and Chan both just took a year off. They moved into an apartment; Bob's mom had recently moved to Brooklyn so they had that safety zone there. He and Bobby got an apartment in a sketchy area of Brooklyn. And John was living at the Stone House, still going to school, and I had my dorm on Union Square. And it was all in. Any money that we made went into the "band fund." People would get a couple of bucks here and there for food, but everything came out of that band fund—strings, drumheads, extra enhancements to our monitors, gas. It really became our little communist commune. But that meant that we were surviving off of the band's money. We got a little bit of money from our parents, but primarily anything to do with the band was money that we'd reinvested from gigs.

Jono Manson: There were two clubs that were both owned by these Italian people. Mondo Cane was on Bleecker Street and Mondo Perso was around the corner. They were both small venues that had stages and PA systems. I don't think they consciously decided this is the kind of music they wanted to have there. But the scene that was happening in the East Village spilled over into these clubs. And unlike other Village clubs like the Bitter End and Kenny's Castaways, which were more like showcase clubs that would have four or five bands a night, the Mondos were more like bar gigs, where if you got hired to play there, the night was yours and you were expected to play four hours of original music. They didn't want cover bands.

Joan Osborne (Singer-songwriter): New York City is a hugely populous place. So you had this opportunity to have all of these different clubs to play in, and you had all these potential audience members. You could play four or five, six nights a week, in different venues around town. New York City has always been a magnet for different artists and different kinds of artists. You had people who came here to study jazz at the New School, you had people like me, who came to study filmmaking at NYU, and you had people who had grown up here . . . just this incredible mix of people who were all interested in doing music. So you had that community you could join. And it was a way to learn a lot in a very short amount of time, because it was all very intense, so much playing, so much going to hear other people play, so much meeting different musicians and different players.

Jono Manson: Joan Osborne said to me, "Hi, my name is Joan and I want to be a singer."

John Popper: When I hear the tapes back then, we were a mess. But you know, we didn't know what the hell we were doing. A lot of things worked themselves out while you're playing.

Joan Osborne: John Popper would show up at these open-mic nights and just mow everyone down and blow right away. So I became friendly with him. And he said, "Well, you should come over and sing a song with us." So I started singing at Nightingale's just sitting in with my friends. I grew up in a small town in Kentucky. So just the notion of being on a stage in New York City, and singing for people, I was like, "Wow, okay. This is a highlight of my life." Had it never gone any farther, I'm sure I'd still be talking about it today.

David Precheur: My plan was to look at the Grateful Dead: They played a different set every night, they played for three-plus hours, and hit five cities in seven days. And so in my head I'm like, we just need to play as much as possible because not only does it expose you out there, but you guys are fucking incredible! If anybody just sees you once, they are going to go home and be like, "Dude, I saw this band last night. Holy shit!" It was a mind-blowing experience. Those guys were assassins, and John's harmonica—there was nothing else like it on Earth. And so people would go and they would have their skulls shaved off! So I knew if we just got out there in front of as many people as possible, as many places as possible, at some point it was gonna catch fire. But in my head, I knew nothing of record companies, pop singles, radio, MTV. To me, none of that was in my business plan. I was tickets and T-shirts.

Jono Manson: The Nightingale Bar started having live music. There was another bar on the same block called Dan Lynch's, which was a blues bar that had started in the late '70s. Bands used to play there.

Cree McCree (Journalist): A lot of times bands played both places.

Jono Manson: One night, the guy who owned the Nightingale, who was a Chinese businessman club owner from Hong Kong, came into Lynch's and was like, "I want to have music in my bar. Can you guys come play there?" We went over and checked it out. There's no stage, no nothing. The place was a dump. And we said yes!

Lo Faber: That became the center of the scene early on. It was a dive bar in the East Village. The owners of it were absentee—they were actually a Vietnamese family who couldn't have cared less about the music in the place. They let Tom [Hosier] book the music; he just worked the door and kept 25 percent for himself and gave 75 percent to the band. Early on, we met up with Blues Traveler, who were playing there every Monday night. And we knew some of them from Princeton because Tomo and I grew up in Princeton. So we had some connections to them. But they were several steps ahead of us. And they were getting their musical thing together by playing not only Monday nights at the Nightingale, but then they would book ten to twenty gigs a month—basically entirely New York City.

David Precheur: We had a rule which was we never took a night off because it would cost us money . . . we would just drink.

Steve Eichner: Any night of the week, you could pop into Nightingale's and that was our social network. You knew you'd see like-minded people, you'd see your friends, you'd find out about other gigs; it was this moving circus in a way. Tom Hosier, he booked it and ran Nightingale's. And he had a great ear for talent. And he loved to cultivate talent. If the Spin Doctors were playing, John Popper might show up, and then they would invite him on stage. You had all of this camaraderie—everybody helping each other, and we're all part of the scene . . . the fans, the bands, the crews of the bands and the promoters and the venues—we were all in it together. The band would get off the stage and we'd smoke a joint together or do shots.

Brendan Hill: Joan Osborne played there, Spin Doctors played, God Street Wine . . .

Cree McCree: There was a pool table in the back. Everybody just set up on the floor.

Rich Vink: It was a sweat box.

Dave Swanson (Sound Engineer, Blues Traveler): When Blues Traveler was there, they used to push the pool table back and cover the exit door so that we'd make more room for people.

Brendan Hill: We would store our equipment at Nightingale's.

Lo Faber: If you live in a fifth-floor walk-up, it's not really that easy to bring your drum kit or bass rig upstairs. Bands would shove their gear in the corner.

Rich Vink: The soundboard wasn't out in front of anything, it was on the side of the stage. You would pop out in front of the speakers to hear how everything was going.

Aaron Comess: We played late after a Grateful Dead show at the Garden. We played at the Limelight and Chris was tripping . . . he came on stage dressed in a bear's costume.

Michael Weiss (Road Crew, God Street Wine): There was this place up in Harlem on 125th Street called the 712 Club, underneath this overpass. And it was a dump. It was a real, real ugly room. They would have bands come in, and then the owners would go and take the door money and go buy beer down the street, and then come back and sell it to the people in the venue. When it would rain, it would rain inside the venue as much as it was raining outside. That was the place that you would go and it was just no-holds-barred until four or five o'clock in the morning. God Street played there a lot, Spin Doctors, Blues Traveler played there.

Billy Cohen: Bar owners said we couldn't play any other gigs, but we played all over town, all the time.

Lo Faber: If you weren't playing one day, you'd probably go out and see one of the other bands that did. Just enjoy the show, or try to pick up girls, or chat with other musicians, whatever. A lot of the time, we'd all be playing different gigs at other bars, but we'd show up at Nightingale's at like three a.m. and have drinks together.

Jono Manson: The Spin Doctors just started playing every Monday night at the Nightingale. Monday night was "the worst night of the week." They turned it into the most happening night. It was packed. If you put 150 people in there, you couldn't move.

David Precheur: Gotta remember the greasy money at Nightingale's, counting it with Tom. It was all in $1 bills—just nasty money.

Jono Manson: If a band packed the place, they would walk away with the lion's share of the money that came through that door.

Chan Kinchla: Chris was in Blues Traveler for a couple of weeks before we realized no way we could have two frontmen, that'd be awful.

Patrick Clifford (Vice President of A&R, A&M Records): Blues Traveler and Spin Doctors played a lot of shows together. They did one show at a club somewhere in Chelsea . . . it was like six or eight hours of nonstop music. Spin Doctors would come on stage, they'd play, and forty-five minutes into it one of the guys from Spin Doctors would leave and Bobby Sheehan would come out and play bass and then Chan would come out and play guitar and then Popper would come in. The next thing it's full-on Blues Traveler.

David Precheur: The cast of characters that were a generation or two older than us—they'd been grinding it out for a decade, decade-and-a-half. And they liked us. So they were like, "Come here, little chickadees, let us teach you the right way to do it." The thing was, it wasn't about doing it the right way to become famous. Maybe John had in his head that we were gonna be huge rock stars, but the rest of us were like how do we do this so we're consistent?

3

For Forty Thousand Dollars, We Could Make a Record and You Can Spend the Money on Hamburgers, Guns, Pot, a Van

As the '80s were ending, record labels started to notice: Something's happening with this scene in downtown New York City and maybe we should sign them. Another, more important figure did too: Bill Graham, rock impresario/promoter best known for his work with the Grateful Dead, as well as owning the Fillmore West in San Francisco and the Fillmore East in New York City.

Billy Cohen: The fall of '86 is when David Graham comes to college. There was a kid who we got into Columbia, one of my buddies from home. His dad was an alum. This kid was brilliant, but he got himself in some trouble with a bong on a debate team trip. Otherwise, he woulda ended up at Harvard or something. But anyhow, my buddy's dad smoked weed. So we got David Melody into Columbia. And Dave [Graham] . . . we met him when he was still in high school. He was this total Deadhead already in high school. One day, I just bumped into him just walking on campus, and he saw we were dressed like hippies so he's like, "Heyyy!" He entered Columbia in the fall of '86 and somehow the fact that Bill Graham's son was in their freshman class—the Deadheads all found this out within like two seconds. And so Melody . . . the way his mind works, he's like, "Bill Graham's son. Is in my class at Columbia. I must find him." So he found him immediately.

The next move for him to make was to make sure I met David Graham. There was a meeting set up. I met David Graham on the roof of Carman dorm, during freshman orientation. I was certainly aware of the Dead and the San Francisco thing. David and I became very, very close. And it was cool, but I wasn't swooning about Bill Graham. It's not like the kids who grew up here in the Bay—you say Bill Graham's name, and they get weak in the knees.

My first experience with Bill Graham was at the Inner Circle, in September of '86. He shows up to see what's happening. We spent the whole night, he and I, standing in the middle of the floor, talking about the scene, what the scene meant, and how the scene could really change the world. And he looks at me and goes, "You know, I haven't heard anybody talk like you in a decade. You have the 'mania.' Welcome to my movie."

David Graham: When my class came in, it was full of Deadheads. In our freshman phone book, it would list your favorite band. So everybody who listed the Dead found everybody right away. I listed the Rolling Stones. But somehow word got out that I was related to Bill Graham.

Steve Eichner: Columbia was basically the primordial slime—keg parties and drug use. Psychedelics. And really smart people. David Graham lived in Delta Phi and was a brother there.

David Graham: When I got there, Delta Phi was a rundown, dilapidated fraternity.

John Popper: David told his dad about us because he was going to get into the business after graduating.

Tom Gruber (Founder, Music Unlimited): Bill wanted to be a legacy for his son.

Chan Kinchla: He came and saw us at Mondo Perso on Bleecker Street.

David Graham: I did not plan on managing bands . . . the real impetus for me, to be quite honest, was so many of my friends at Columbia, and so many people in general in my orbit, loved rock and roll. So, there was a huge amount of people who I could just hook them up and get them started in an industry that they wanted to be in. People were just hungry to be around music.

Patrick Clifford: It must have felt like what people felt in San Francisco in Haight-Ashbury at one point.

Chan Kinchla: We played up at Columbia, opening up for dreamspeak—a pretty popular local jam band of Columbia kids.

Steve Eichner: dreamspeak was the house band. They were the band that everyone got behind.

Brendan Hill: We will let you record our shows, we'll let tapes be traded. That was how we got first introduced to Bill Graham, through his son, David Graham. We played some gig at Columbia University; I think it was November 11. So it was an 11/11 concert. And it was one of these Trip Fests. Sun Ra was playing in one room, we played another, and somebody recorded on a little tape recorder and sent it to Dave Graham. He was in a frat in Columbia, and he sent it to his dad. He's like, "Dad, I think these guys would be kind of cool to manage."

David Graham: That's what turned him on to them. He could see what everybody else saw. And he wanted me to be successful with bands.

Grant Cowell (Road Manager, Blues Traveler): Now be it true, be it not true, I can't say exactly. But apparently Bill had an old Mercedes convertible, and lived on Mount Tamalpais. David gave him a demo tape, he popped it in the cassette player, pulled into a strip mall, and had the music up kinda loud. Some guy walked by, a Deadhead, and was like, "That's Blues Traveler. Those guys are fucking awesome."

Brendan Hill: There's a letter dated August 19, 1989. It was like, "I just heard the tape that David sent me. And I'm really excited about it. I want to tell you, do not sign anything with anybody else until I get out there to meet with you. I'm really interested in signing you. And I plan on being there in September." A couple of weeks from then, we were all sitting in Bob's mom's house. And Dave Precheur brings out this letter that was addressed to him and us. We were all just like, "No. Way. The Fillmore guy? The guy who flies in on airplanes?" We knew that we'd hit the next level of interest.

David Graham: I was actually the one who wrote the letter.

Chan Kinchla: One of our first big gigs was at the Capitol Theatre. Bill, I think at that point, was managing us. We sold it out—we were young, dumb, and cocky, thought we were the shit. Back then, stage diving was a big thing. He yelled at me for kicking some girl's head stage diving—and then he yells at Dave Precheur for disrespecting his son. The problem was, we were so pumped that we were getting screamed at by Bill Graham. We thought it was the coolest thing ever.

Joan Osborne: We were conscious that anybody who comes up to you after a gig and starts talking to you about, "I can do this or that for you, I want to manage you, or I know somebody at a label," you take all that with a grain of salt, because sometimes those people are just full of shit or did too much cocaine.

David Graham: I will claim that I was really the first person to put the seed in John's head. Because John and I would room together in the early days. And boy, that was a shitshow, because he would have all this candy. And I'm really into sugar also. We'd spend nights in front of the TV, just getting all sugared out.

Jono Manson: I remember when the suits used to come around . . . in the late '80s it really started happening.

John Popper: In Blues Traveler's frame of mind, we're like, "Okay, we're the first band in our little scene to get signed. Let's not fuck this up."

Steve Eichner: Even though Bill Graham was behind it, he wasn't there running it. He gave the power to all these college kids.

Chan Kinchla: He gave me some of the best advice: "This band is great. John's great. Your job is, just for a little while, take the attention away from John, so that when it gets back to John, everyone realizes how great he is all over again."

David Graham: Anytime someone did something stupid, or got fucked up, they would call Bill. Okay, for the most part, he wasn't hands on. I was more . . . hands off and trusting of my friends to do work when they didn't really have the experience.

Grant Cowell: One time we went up to his house on Mount Tamalpais to party. There was a special freezer in their house and that was what contained all the Owsley [LSD] and all the good stuff. Very few times that refrigerator had been cracked and we were able to get into the goodies. We all partied—some people more, some people less. Heroin was always taboo.

Chan Kinchla: Bill's like, "It's not a good concert unless the crowd goes home happy, the promoter goes home happy, and the band goes home happy. If any one of those three aren't happy, it's not a good show."

Rich Vink: My partner at the time, Dave Swanson—he and I had in mind finding acts to do spec demo work with. Our place at Greene Street had a lot of label activity going on. It was all mostly signed bands like Public Enemy and Sonic Youth. So we got the idea to find acts that weren't signed and use some of that studio downtime to record demos. The first guy we brought in was Chris Whitley. And the studio owner was crazy about him. So he was like "Anything you guys want to work on, just find them." I went on a vacation to my family place up in Ontario, Canada, and I played the Blues Traveler cassette on the long drive. And the song "Alone" was on there. And something really just rang true. The community coalesced around Blues Traveler, Spin Doctors, and Joan Osborne. So I came back to New York and suggested that they might want to make a better recording. And they were all for it. A friend was building a studio called Loho Studios and we set up to record them—and that was the "Dropping Some NYC" tape. We brought them into Greene Street to try and do even more of a high-end recording. And then our idea of the spec deal would be to try to shop it, which we didn't have a lot of grip on that per se. So I just sort of fell into doing their live sound initially to make sure that their live shows were communicating the stuff we had recorded.

Dave Swanson: They were efficient. They were smoking lots of weed and drinking lots of whiskey and beer and fucking off some too. But it's the pace of eighteen, nineteen, twenty-year olds. They're fast and focused when they want to be.

Warren Haynes (Guitar, vocals, The Allman Brothers Band, Gov't Mule): Stephanie, my wife, was doing A&R for Island Records. Someone sent Stephanie a demo tape that had some of earliest Traveler songs like "But Anyway" and "Dropping Some NYC." She tried to sign Blues Traveler to Island. She was really impressed with that demo. She also tried to sign the Spin Doctors and the Black Crowes and, in each case, the label turned her down. And that's what led to her quitting and starting a management company.

Rich Vink: There was a famous Ukrainian National Home gig that we did with Phish . . . we rented the venue and sold $5,000 worth of keg beer.

John Popper: Bill hired us and hired Dave to be our manager. It was kind of a unique situation, because we had access to Bill like none of the other bands that were being managed by them did. But we also had his son making mistakes on our behalf as well. Because he had a learning curve.

Grant Cowell: Then we were flying out, opening for the Allman Brothers.

David Graham: The idea of bringing in a brotherhood of bands which is something that was very much a Bill thing . . . creating shows, creating packages, the Fillmore—all those discussions, I think, fed John. He had one of those folders, with a map of the United States, and every time they played a new state, he would cross it out.

Chan Kinchla: Man, we were so fucking cocky. You had to be. I mean, we were young enough to be dumb enough to not know better. We got to this place where everywhere we played in New York, it was packed. Now at the same time, the popular music was hair metal and we didn't really fit into that and we didn't fit into mainstream pop. We'd do these showcases and they wouldn't go great, but we just knew it was gonna work out. We got signed by Patrick Clifford. But his record company wasn't that sure.

Patrick Clifford: I was an A&R guy, and when these guys were playing, we're dealing with payphones and quarters and credit cards. I went to Nightingale's on a Monday night at midnight. I came out at four o'clock in the morning. I was like, this is fucking amazing. But it's not like I went to people immediately and said, "Oh, we gotta sign these guys." I started taking people that worked for A&M to shows at Nightingale's. When they started playing Wetlands, at that point, I knew I wanted to sign these guys. I told [my bosses] I want to do this.

John Popper: Bill Graham and A&M Records came at us at the same time.

David Precheur: David was actually, on paper, our manager. And it was me and David running the show. And Bill was just like, "Hey, when you get to nine yards, just hand it to me." We just had this monster of a dad that whatever we wanted, we could have. Bill said, "You're going to fly to LA, you're going to meet all the record companies. You're going to go to your buildings, and you're going to talk to them. And then just tell me which one you like."

Patrick Clifford: The A&M culture was remarkable. It was The Police, it was Janet Jackson. We were trying to do a lot of different things at that point in regards to signing different bands, whether it was Soundgarden or Soul Asylum or the Gin Blossoms and the Neville Brothers and Blues Traveler. The culture was, "Let's get to the greatest artists that we love." Believe me, when I signed Blues Traveler, nobody really got it. It was a slow build, and it was about people seeing the band. I had a meeting with Bill Graham and David Graham, who were managing the group at the time, at the Fuller Building at A&M

headquarters in New York at 57th and Madison. I was convincing Graham that for forty thousand dollars, we could make a record, and you can spend the money on hamburgers, guns, pot, a van, but we had to make a record. When I asked him, "Sir, do you think that's a good deal?" And I thought he was gonna throw me out the window and he said, "That's not a good deal. That's a great deal!"

And then he shook my hand and said, "Good luck."

And I said, "Well, what about good luck to us?"

He looked at me and said, "Good luck."

And we negotiated a deal. And we signed a deal.

John Popper: The deal was okay. My mom being a lawyer helped. We got good counsel. The first thing you do is get a lawyer. So we negotiated a pretty good deal. And I think the best part is that it was all administrative. So it reverted back to us.

Brendan Hill: We didn't get a big budget.

Chan Kinchla: It wasn't some huge deal. We didn't really care. Right before we got signed, Bill Graham became our manager, which for us was a much bigger deal for obvious reasons. What we didn't realize was that Polygram Records bought A&M Records right at that time. There was a big meeting with A&M Records and they're going through each artist they have with Polygram they're dropping or keeping. Squeeze was a favorite band of mine that was on A&M and they dropped Squeeze! It was like smash and trash with the whole company. And I guess because we had such a small record deal, and it was this niche thing, they were like let's give it a shot. We just squeaked by, but we were very close to just getting dropped.

John Popper: At the CMJ showcase, they told us we were on a bill with a whole bunch of bands because every club was doing this thing where you were on a bill with a bunch of bands featured in this seminar, and that was part of what it was. We had forty-five minutes and they told us, "You only have forty-five minutes. You have to do your whole show for them in forty-five minutes." We got a tight forty-five minutes, we worked it all out, got our best stuff planned in. A lot of me blowing harp, up songs, fast songs, different songs, funky songs. The perfect showcase set. And back then, man, you had to learn how to do one of those. It was part of your repertoire; you needed to have a tight set, whatever they wanted. And so we had our forty-five-minute set ready to go. And about a minute before we go on, there's a rumor that Buddy Miles is here. Buddy Miles is here! And then someone runs up and says, "Buddy Miles is here, and he wants to sit in with you guys!" So we're like, "Ohhhhh . . . the tight forty-five!" He comes on and instead of doing one song, he sits on the guitar, then he kicks the guitar player completely off, does all the guitar soloing, then he kicks the bass player off, does a bass solo, kicks the drummer off, does a drum solo! Our set is taking about two and a half hours now. And it's all Buddy. And at one point, it just got so funny because we'd blown our program so far. There was no possible way that we were in a position to tell no to Buddy Miles or honor our forty-five minutes that was tight. The smoke clears and we just figured we'd blown it. And [A&M] signed us because they liked the way we handled ourselves in a crisis.

Jono Manson: They were really worried that they'd blown it. But clearly that didn't happen.

Brendan Hill: They may not have understood exactly what we're trying to do with our music but allowed it to develop.

Patrick Clifford: Marketing plans? They didn't exist, there's no such thing. The marketing plan was me begging people to help pay attention and come to see the band and the marketing plan was for them to go out and play. And the marketing plan was to try to convince the sales team to put records in record stores where they were playing and where they were popular and where they had a little bit of a following and keep playing live.

Chan Kinchla: We didn't get excited. It was just kind of the beginning of a whole new can of worms. It wasn't like some end thing. We were excited to make a record, but we basically just played over our first album. *Blues*

Traveler is just all the shit we had been playing in New York bars for the last couple years.

Jono Manson: They asked me to come to the studio to help them record their stuff . . . you know, tell them where to put the microphones and stuff like that. I can't remember what song they were cutting, but I suggested to them that for the album version, they shouldn't extend solos quite as much as they did live. To draw people in, listeners hadn't yet seen them live, they might want to crystallize the essence of the song in a little bit more of a concise manner.

And they're like, "Nah, nah, nah, we just want to jam it out the way we always do."

"Okay, that's fine."

And I turned to Vink, who was in the control room, and said, "Okay, I'm gonna prove to you that this song is too long. When you hit record, and they start playing, I'm gonna go down the block, I'm going to order some takeout food from the Chinese joint, I'm going to wait for it, get it, and bring it back here. And they'll still be playing the same song."

And I did. I left, went and got chicken fried rice or something and came back.

He's like, "Oh my god, maybe it is too long."

John Popper: Actually, our first producer did the dumbest thing I've ever seen a producer do. He wasn't a bad guy, but he was devoutly anti-pot. And we were all about smoking pot. When we played, that was part of the thing. Especially doing like one- or two-chord vamps. It's really about you getting into it. So before we did "Sweet Talking Hippie," we all snuck a joint.

Brendan Hill: We were used to playing that song baked.

John Popper: And right before we're about to cut it I go, "So and so, we're all stoned." He stops the tape and yells at us for ten minutes! We're sitting in our booth in the ready position. "You've let your families down. What would your parents say? This is your first album!" And then he goes, "Okay, play. Rolling."

David Graham: It was like really? I mean, c'mon.

Brendan Hill: We were all in the room giggling and just like, "Oh shit, he found out. What did we do wrong?"

John Popper: The actual take that wound up getting used is the most chastised, timid "Sweet Talking Hippie" we've ever done in our lives.

Patrick Clifford: The first time they played the A&M picnic, that whole crew . . . Herb Albert and Jerry Moss and Bill Graham and David Anderle—it was in Malibu, which was for all the families of everybody and anybody who worked at A&M Records. And afterwards, Popper goes over and he talks to Stan Getz, who was on Horizon Records at A&M. He starts talking to Stan Getz about [jazz saxophonist and New School jazz program founder] Arnie Lawrence, saying, "Hey, man, we share Arnie Lawrence. You know, he talks about you and he said you're a cheap motherfucker, that you don't tip people in cabs." Stan Getz, who was as big as Popper at that time, got up off a blanket and wanted to duke it out with him!

John Popper: I could see him being a cheapskate when it comes to the cab tipping.

David Precheur: A&M was a very lucky choice at the end of the day. Bryan Adams and a couple other artists had great momentum. And then they were developing Blues Traveler, Soundgarden, and Sheryl Crow. So when one of these bands hits, we'll use all that momentum. To them, that was just dollar signs. If they get three bands to push them through, that's huge.

Jono Manson: A label would continue to support an artist if they didn't sell a bazillion records right out of the gate.

Rich Vink: The whole rush of suddenly working with Bill Graham Presents, the game changer that that was, it seemed to me that it was proceeding at a really down-to-earth level. He put us out with Little Feat, who were a really accommodating crew, and the Neville Brothers and the Allman Brothers.

And then also put us out with Hot Tuna and their crew were complete hard-asses and very hard to work with. So we were getting a good cross-reference.

Patrick Clifford: They were different than the kind of bands that were getting signed, that were coming out of CBGBs and all the hip East Village clubs. Bands from Seattle or bands from Chicago . . . they weren't like Blues Traveler, they weren't like the Spin Doctors. People would be like they didn't get it and I'd say, "If you don't get it, that's fine. Get out of the way, because this train is going to roll and it's going to roll over your feet and it's going to cut off your toes."

After Blues Traveler got signed, Spin Doctors were up next . . .

David Sonenberg (Manager, Spin Doctors): I had my first child in 1989. And we had an au pair, who was going to NYU, and she had been living with us for about three months. She walked in and goes, "Hey, do you ever sign new bands?"

"Yeah, sure."

"There's this band I really like. They're called the Spin Doctors."

I said, "I tell you what, if I sign the band and if they go platinum, I'll buy you a pair of airplane tickets anywhere in the world you want to go and a weekend hotel wherever you're going."

She sent me to a club that I'd never been to: Mondo Cane. I had never been and I'd lived in the Village all my life, and I was in the music business. You go up a little skinny stairwell, and it was like an apartment of some sort, but they turned it into a small club with a bar. I walked in, I sat down, and there was a guy who came over to the mic and he was really good-looking. I went, "Alright, great looking lead singer. That's a good start." But it turned out that he was the road manager, Jason Richardson. He was going one, two, testing, whatever, and he had long hair, cap backwards, and handlebar mustache. Then the band comes out. The guitar player was extraordinary. It was very melodic as it was rhythmic. And then the bass player was totally fucking funky. And the drummer was adding calmness. I figured that good-looking guy was going to come out and front the band, but instead, this geeky looking Chris Barron dude comes out with facial hair, looking like a scarecrow and walking strange and weird. But about forty seconds into the song he won me over. It was really very jammy. Long and jazzy, but combined with rock stuff. Really intricate; a lot of time changes, lots of three quarter times, lots of 5/4 times—they would change effortlessly and seamlessly. And then Chris Barron is singing all these risky kinds of things in a very otherworldly way. And I couldn't pick up all the lyrics, but the lyrics were poetic, and they were smart. There was something Shakespearean about him. And it was romantic. And I was really taken by him.

Aaron Comess: We used to do a thing all the time called "Spinning Traveler," which is where we'd have all our instruments on stage at once. Spin Doctors would play a set, and then one by one, the members of Blues Traveler would come up to where it got to the point where all the members of both bands were playing together. And then one by one, we would walk off and then all of a sudden it would just be Blues Traveler and they'd play a set. We can do four sets where we'd play a set, they'd play a set, we'd play a set, and they'd play a set.

Eric Schenkman: River Phoenix and his sister had a band. They came to New York and they opened for us one night at the Wetlands. River Phoenix was a famous movie star at the time and also a young guy. And I remember thinking, "Wow, this is crazy, this movie-star band is opening for us, there's such a scene now with a line out the door. We've really come a long way." This is before we had a record deal. That scene was really pregnant. So I'm standing at the bar and I was a bit starstruck except for the fact that this guy comes up to me, and he's a guitar player and he starts talking to me about how good he is. I just realized in that moment how hip things had become.

David Sonenberg: I saw them a couple of nights later at Nightingale, which was really just a postage stamp of a place. It was a little bar, but it was jam packed. That blew my mind because they were not only doing this jam stuff, but they had what I think they referred to as the "whitebread" set. Songs like "Two Princes," "Little Miss Can't Be Wrong," "Jimmy Olsen's Blues." Those songs were really pop, really mainstream. But again, the nature of the vibe of it was funky. It wasn't like "pop pop."

Aaron Comess: Everybody wanted to sign us. Everybody wanted to be a manager or producer or record label. We ended up taking a meeting with David Sonenberg, who's a pretty well-known manager—his biggest client at that time was Meatloaf and Jim Steinman. They had the whole *Bat Out of Hell* success. He was already loaded and had massive success. And he wanted to sign us. We went up to this nice office, and I'll never forget, we sat there, and heard his whole sales pitch. And we said no! And he was squirming in his seat because he wasn't used to people saying no. He called us back and asked us to reconsider. He said, "Look, if I can't get you a major label record deal within thirty days, then the deal's up, and we can rip up the contract and the deal's over." We thought about it, and we decided to do it. And that's how we got our deal with Epic.

David Sonenberg: I had done *Bat Out of Hell*, and you know, that's gone on to sell sixty-five million records. At the time, we were selling five hundred thousand albums a week. And then you're playing stadiums, you're playing five nights at Madison Square Garden. It was not easy to get them a record deal. They were a confusing animal. In those days, record companies would listen to this jam stuff, and say, "Hey, this ain't happening. I don't know how to deal with this."

Aaron Comess: We were already bringing nine hundred people to the Wetlands. It was just an undeniable scene that was happening. The hardest sell for the record labels with us was we didn't really have an image. They couldn't tell whether we were the crew or the band. We just walked on stage in our street clothes. This is 1990. You're coming off the 1980s where it was heavy metal, and people were glammed up.

Chris Barron: Our advance was like a quarter of a million dollars. It was no bullshit. What happens is, after everybody gets their cut, I thought, "I'm fucking rich." And then I walked away with like eight thousand bucks. But it was a big advance for the time.

Eric Schenkman: They didn't have any faith in us at all. And the record deal wasn't that big.

Peter Denenberg (Producer, *Pocket Full of Kryptonite*): I made a lot of records with this guy named Frankie LaRocka. Frankie was originally a drummer from Staten Island. He played with the New York Dolls, Bon Jovi's first single, David Johansen, Bryan Adams. He also ended up getting into being an A&R guy. He was originally at Atlantic and then moved over to Epic. The Spin Doctors were recently signed to Epic—they were signed by Don Grierson, the then-president. Frankie got the assignment that we were going to make a live record with them. Back then, the way you broke a band that wasn't a Top 40 pop band is you first promoted to college radio. You would make a live EP, and that would be first taken to college radio, and then that's how they met the band, and that primed the way for when the studio album was released. I met them the night we were making that live record. That was the first time I heard most of those songs. So, my exposure to them was hearing them in their natural environment, the Wetlands, where Chris was walking on the bar. You can hear beer bottles falling over during the quiet parts of songs; it was so present.

Eric Schenkman: Our A&R guy [Frankie LaRocka] was a drummer. When we got in the studio, we worked fast. [The label] left us alone, largely, and LaRocka made some good suggestions. He's the guy to say really slow "Two Princes" down in tempo. So we actually were helped by the record company. They put a lot of pressure on us.

Chris Barron: Once we had a deal with Sony, there was an open question: Would we go after commercial radio? We got into the studio and they were spending a lot of money. And that was our money because it was recoupable to the record company.

Peter Denenberg: Labels, they sign a lot and they see what sticks. Especially then. Grierson, the president, saw them live and probably understood that they were really cool. And Frankie did too, because he's a musician. But my sense was that there weren't necessarily a lot of other people at the label who had any idea or thought it was going to do what it would do. I don't want to say they weren't supportive of it, but they had to make a decision about what they're going to do to promote it.

Chris Barron: Record executives would come in and they would have kooky dumb record executive ideas. And we would laugh them out of the room.

Peter Denenberg: Chris would get a lot of the vocals live. He was nuts. And if you're worried about the part you're gonna play, it's gonna sound like you're worried about the part you're going to play, right? And so here you'd have a take and perhaps it felt great, but it was a little out of tune from the live track, and then you go in to redo that guitar. And if the feeling isn't the same, trying to help someone get back to that place, it's hard. The only solution is time. Nothing else works, right? It's about just working all damn day long, and then throwing that last song on again at two o'clock in the morning and saying, "Hey, take one more pass at this." It's just trying to keep your wits about you, and waiting for that moment, and understanding when that moment arrives—that was the hard moments of that record. There was a two or three week stretch in the middle where we were just trying to get it over the hump, to where the tracks were all happening. People were losing patience with us. And so we just had to tell them: "Wait."

Chris Barron: We had a lot of balls. The president of our label came in and we would laugh at him and then say, "Can you take us out to dinner or what?"

Eric Schenkman: Maybe there was faith in the fact that we were coming out of an actual scene, and in sort of their weird way, they left us alone. Let it percolate a little bit. Jazz ethics were absolutely fine in that jam band space. And so in a way, you know, the industry wasn't really so involved at the beginning. That's why we were allowed to be like that.

Peter Denenberg: The thing about this particular record was that nobody was thinking about it. So nobody was in our face about it. The later ones, there were all these insanely stupid ideas being bandied about. But this one, nobody was bothering us. It was just us trying to make a good record.

Chris Barron: "Two Princes" is a song about unrequited love and "Little Miss Can't Be Wrong" is about being emotionally abused by my stepmother. The lines in there about "nobody at the back door is going to throw my laundry out" . . . my stepmom used to throw my laundry out of the house if I didn't move my laundry fast enough from the washing machine to the dryers. She'd take my wet clothes and throw them out the front door—back door sounded better in the lyric. My brother kept the machete under the bed. My stepmom was kicking my door down at four o'clock in the morning and screaming until the veins were popping out of her neck. Some of these grunge guys, I wonder if they would have lasted ten minutes in my childhood. I'm not shit-canning grunge. I really love Kurt Cobain. Chris Cornell is one of the greatest singers of the twentieth century. Any opportunity I get, I'm like, "Hey, look, we had not just happy-go-lucky songs, but we're a complex band with a lot of different emotional outlets." We always came at this from a song-first stance. Jamming and improvising is great. But you can jam and improvise on anything. The real art is to have great songs and improvising and jamming on those.

Eric Schenkman: When you get really successful, really fast, it's a lot to handle. You can't really make your best judgments.

4

We Had This Vibration Around the Band

At the same time, about three hundred miles north of New York City, a music scene was brewing in Burlington, Vermont—a snow globe of a place where clubs were plentiful, colleges were eclectic, and the legal drinking age was still eighteen.

Trey Anastasio (Guitar, vocals, Phish): Let's set the scene here. Bernie Sanders was our mayor, and he'd come to shows and stuff. This is say, 1983 when we were really starting. Ben and Jerry were actually handing out ice cream—they were starting to blow up a little, but they still had their original ice cream shop that was in a converted gas station downtown. Jake Burton was kind of hanging around and he was trying to convince everybody that you can ski on one ski. It was really a cool time. And there was an overflow from the '70s—the OG hippies leaving the Lower East Side and going up to Vermont.

Steve "The Dude of Life" Pollak (Musician): Trey and I were at boarding school together . . . we were on the same floor. And we became friends very quickly. He was not into the Grateful Dead scene in tenth grade, and neither was I. We had been in a band at boarding school called Space Antelope. Trey had been a drummer before he was a guitarist . . . But he learned really quickly.

Russ Lawton (Drums, Trey Anastasio Band): The first day Trey came up to Vermont to look at colleges, he stopped by Hunts. And Tony [Markellis] was playing and he freaked out. That's Burlington—it's just really freeing.

Trey Anastasio: [Jon] Fishman and I used to play a duet show in Burlington every Sunday. It was a jazz brunch, just me and Fishman. Drums and guitar. And we played the standards, because that's what worked. And this teaches you . . . there's a real learning curve in that.

Steve "The Dude of Life" Pollak: Fish was a character beyond belief. Then Trey put up signs for a bass player. And Mike answered the ad. And at the time, there was a guy named Jeff Holdsworth, who was the guitarist . . . but over time, he was missing a lot of rehearsals and he dropped out.

Page McConnell (Piano, keyboards, vocals, Phish): Phish had already been together for two years. And they came and played at my school and I thought that I should join the band. So I moved to where they were living, and weaseled my way in, much to their chagrin, because it wasn't mostly accepted as a good idea for me to join the band.

Trey Anastasio: I remember playing and looking at the bar and seeing a lot of forty-five- to fifty-five-year-old guys and women after work eating. That was valuable too . . . you have to entertain these people who don't necessarily like you. The thing about playing a house party as a band is you're playing to a very finite cross section of people who love the band.

Steve "The Dude of Life" Pollak: I remember when Trey and I were just hanging out in downtown Burlington, we'd have some lunch, walking along, and then he'd stop into this guitar store. And time would go by and Trey would go into the back . . . and he'd be gone for twenty minutes, thirty minutes, forty minutes. And then finally, after about forty-five minutes he'd come out. Turns out, he was talking to Paul Languedoc, who ran Time Guitars. He was a guitar builder.

Jon Fishman (Drums, vocals, Phish): We had six or seven Dead songs in our repertoire at one point, like our first year, in a college band, playing for parties.

We were always aimed at playing original tunes, those always had the priority; but in the beginning we hardly had any.

Trey Anastasio: Importantly, it was the last state to change the drinking age. And it's crucial to the story, because when I got there as a college freshman, it was '83. College students could go to the bars. It's not about the drinking, it's about the fact that there were more bars per capita in Burlington that needed bands. There were fifty-two bars in Burlington, and they all wanted bands. So the vibe downtown was sort of like Bourbon Street. There was music coming out of every bar. And it was eighteen-year-olds through sixty-year-olds. The quality of the music was great.

Phish quickly found a local restaurant, Nectar's, to start performing regularly at. Their first performance was on December 1, 1984, and they played there forty-seven times through March 1989. As their popularity around town grew and tapes of their shows spread, they needed a bigger place to play . . .

Russ Lawton: It was rock at Nectar's. If you went down to Hunt's, you could do that next level of eclectic. If you're living downtown, you'd start at Nectar's and get a beer, go down to Hunt's and check out a band, and even go up the street to this place Neutral Grounds. There you're doing cover bands that had the PA and the lights and all that kind of stuff—we used to call them "The Fake Famous Bands." They were doing six nights at this place doing Van Halen or whatever.

Anne Rothwell (Founder, Club Metronome): There was this band called "The Other Ones"—that was more on the hippie end. And Phish started playing, and they didn't really fit the mold of Nectar's.

Steve "The Dude of Life" Pollak: Nectar's at first was not packed . . . it was a place where people would get these really good fries with gravy.

Trey Anastasio: Nectar's nights were wild.

Russ Lawton: Nectar [Rorris] was so supportive. He was the man. He's this Greek guy who'd work his ass off—he built that business up. I don't think he was any big music freak or anything like that. He just wanted to get music in there. And he really supported local musicians. Our bass player would call it "I gotta go get a front"—he would play there four nights and you'd get a loan from Nectar for fifty bucks because we got paid on Saturday.

Jon Fishman: We'd get three-night stands, so we didn't even have to move our equipment. Basically, the crowd was our guinea pig. We'd have up to five hours to do whatever the hell we wanted.

Trey Anastasio: We had this vibration around the band . . . I don't know what it was.

Anne Rothwell: The drinking age was also eighteen. When it turned to twenty-one [in 1986], that really had an impact on local music. Suddenly, everybody couldn't get in.

Trey Anastasio: We wanted to gather. Our whole thing at Nectar's and everything was about hanging, gathering. We would all go out and party afterwards. We'd go to the quarry and go swimming. We were interested in the human element, live shows, gathering and friends.

Russ Lawton: You got a couple of colleges right downtown. You get your band together and you get three or four nights a month at Nectar's—that's your rent money. And you get to play a lot of gigs, from like 9:30 to two. So it really puts you in the shape. I think we made $250 a night. We weren't living high off the hog, but we had a shitty place to live and we could rehearse.

Trey Anastasio: There were also so many great bands around . . . there was some competition—healthy. Burlington was a scene. It really was a zeitgeist moment.

Steve "The Dude of Life" Pollak: Over the weeks and months, Phish started gaining a following. More and more people wanted to hear what they were doing. And then as more people were interested, it just kept getting better and better.

Anne Rothwell: Phish was more of a free-for-all. People dancing everywhere. Then they moved to The Front, because The Front was bigger.

Shawn Sweeney (Owner, The Front): In Burlington at the time, there were a lot of great bands—Hollywood Indians and Chin Ho! and Motel Brown. My brother and I bought The Front—we were both out of college and it turned into The Front in late '87. Chico had left Hunt's. Hunt's—that was the real scene. But then he left and Hunt's kind of went downhill and became a really sad dance place called Sha-Na-Na's.

I'd just opened up the club and one of my bartenders was like, "You got to get this band that's playing at Nectar's." So I went up and checked them out one night—and they just finished up a song and then they played "Whipping Post." It blew me away.

It was packed at Nectar's. I was like, "If you guys are interested, it'd be great to have you play down at The Front." The first time they played, it wasn't packed by any stretch of the imagination—I think people were a little put off that they had left Nectar's.

Trey Anastasio: It started getting really crowded at Nectar's. The Front was down the street. And I think we started charging a couple bucks, and people were like, "Oh, that's it. The band is over."

Anne Rothwell: They had that Battle of the Bands where Jon Fishman lowered himself naked in the room.

Shawn Sweeney: Trey came up to me and was like, "Listen, these guys from the South, Widespread Panic—you got to have them." After Phish got there, Widespread Panic came up, Blues Traveler came up, Spin Doctors played there. They were trying to make all ships rise. I would call the band directly. We would have a $300 guarantee. Most of the time, it was an 80/20 split. So out of every dollar [at the door] I made, I gave the bands eighty cents and I took twenty cents.

Gordon Hookailo (Producer, *Junta*): They just booked the studio and came down. We did a four-tune demo. The first thing we did was "Fluffhead," "Golgi Apparatus," "Fee," and "David Bowie." And if you listen to those four tracks, they definitely have a little bit of a different flavor to it as far as the sound goes and the production on it. It leaned in a little bit of a different direction than where we took it for all of the other tracks; all of the other tracks [for *Junta*] were recorded in one very large session, as far as the basics go, and when I say a large session, I mean, I think they came in town and stayed over for a couple of nights or something.

Mike Gordon (Bass, vocals, Phish): The first session we did was in winter of '87.

Trey Anastasio: I think we did it for four thousand bucks.

Gordon Hookailo: It blew my head off, man. They came in, they set up. I usually ask the bands that I'm working with not to play anything that they're going to be recording while we get our soundcheck, while we mic up everything. That's because I want it to be fresh. When I hit record, I want that to be a totally virgin "okay, this is it" kind of a thing. After doing it for so long, I just saw so many bands completely burn out on the tune. Once we got all set up, I said, "Okay, why don't you run through it." And of course, whenever I tell a band, let's run through it, the implication is that I'm not going to record it. So I made sure that I turned the remote control for the two-inch recorder around so they couldn't see it . . . and hit record. I always do that because some bands completely freeze when you hit the recording button, other bands start playing twice as loud. I just wanted it to be natural. So they started playing and my jaw just fell on the floor. I ran out to the office, where a couple of people were, and I said, "You gotta come into the control room and check this out. These guys are unbelievable!" It was literally stunning.

Trey Anastasio: We went down to Boston and we met this guy, Gordon Hookailo, who was the engineer. We kind of self-produced it. There was no Pro Tools or anything. It was recorded on a sixteen-track, two inch, and they sound so good. All the tracks were skinnier and this was the holy grail of analog recording. So when you did a mix, because the songs are so long and complex, like "Divided Sky" and "You Enjoy Myself"—all the reverbs had to change. And all the levels had to change, so all four band members had to rehearse the mix, and you had to do it in real time. So you'd push go, and everybody had their hands all over the board. And one guy's job would be to change the reverb sound for the second verse, because there was only one reverb machine. And, you know, somebody would forget something and it would be like, "Oh, fuck!"

The best one of all was "Esther," and we were all doing the mix together. We had a reverb. We called it the "sleep verb." And you got to listen really closely . . . You know when she dies, when she gets sucked under water at the end and dies? [Sings] "Motionless sleeeeeeep" it goes down a half step, because the chord changes. So the word sleep is a long reverb.

Ben "Junta" Hunter (Manager, Phish): They practiced as a full-time job. They'd practice six, seven, eight hours a day, five days a week.

Shawn Sweeney: Phish took it serious. They didn't party. They had fun, but they kept it together. And they were like clockwork on stage; I would have to beg bands to get back.

Gordon Hookailo: Vocals were absolutely planned out. But they were absolutely into experimenting. We had some really weird instruments laying around the studio, and they were going, "Hey, let's try that!" On "Divided Sky," there's this extremely high kind of percussive sounding instrument that is in tune. And that's a glockenspiel from a marching band that was just sitting around the studio.

Shawn Sweeney: Why did Phish become successful? They were one of the only bands in my bar that would be like, "Hey Shawn, is it okay if we scrimmage on Saturday? Can we rehearse on Saturday and Sunday?" I was like, "Sure, go for it." And I'd be down doing shit in the bar: working on advertising, getting beer and liquor, going up to Church Street, having lunch, and coming back down. They'd be working on songs for five or six hours!

Ben "Junta" Hunter: The idea was always, look, let's just continue to play live because that's where the bread and butter is. If that happens, then a label will come calling and we're not going to be beholden to the label because we already have lights, sound production, truck, a PA, everything that we need to just be self-sufficient and play these gigs.

Trey Anastasio: It was "What are you going to contribute to original music?" That was the whole band ethic. Then we started traveling. And that became our life. It felt there was a certain level of adventure to touring. The country felt really, really huge. We drove in a car. We didn't have GPS. We didn't call home. I wrote letters. You could dial nine out of a hotel, but it was too expensive. So you basically were like, "I'll see you in three and a half months."

5

You Had This Great Art School and Clubs Willing to Try Anything to Sell Beer

Meanwhile, roughly 1,100 miles south of Burlington, in another college town—Athens, Georgia—southern rock started to intertwine with extended jams. The philosophy of Widespread Panic was largely the same as their counterparts up north, except they were immersed in a music scene that already had national breakouts with R.E.M. and the B-52's.

John Bell (Guitar, vocals, Widespread Panic): I got to school [at University of Georgia] in '80 and the Athens scene was really eclectic.

Dave Schools (Bass, vocals, Widespread Panic): The nightclub where I worked, the Uptown Lounge, in Athens—the reggae thing was still strong. That was one form of original music in college towns. The punk scene, of course, and the hardcore scene, and then all the various college indie-rock things that sort of became alternative rock later . . . it was all sort of cooking. You had all these bands like Indecision, New Potato Caboose, and Panic who were doing originals, but also covers.

John Bell: The B-52's had hit. And there were some other bands coming in that were working more with a stage show that was fun and artsy. Musical in a certain way, but a lot of times it was people who had never played instruments before. It was people who were creating live art. You had this great art school, University of Georgia, and clubs willing to try anything to sell beer.

Mikey Houser (Guitar, vocals, Widespread Panic): The only southern rock I'd heard, because I started playing the guitar in Delaware, was Lynyrd Skynyrd. Then I met JB and Dave and I had never listened to the Allman Brothers. I wasn't a Deadhead, I never heard the Dead. As a matter of fact, JB taught me "Fire on the Mountain" and we played that song for a year before I ever actually heard "Fire on the Mountain."

John Bell: R.E.M. was just about to hit it really big—they were definitely on an upswing. A whole lot of bands started following suit of the R.E.M. approach of music. And so there's people wearing a lot of black—not that R.E.M. was like that, but the New Wave uniforms were becoming prevalent. And the songs were becoming more musically friendly to the ear. So the Athens scene—I kind of landed when it was transitioning. There was also a pretty prevalent country-rock scene left over from the '70s. There were enough places to play or some house parties or regular after-hours concert venues that would accommodate anything that was coming out.

John Keane (Producer/Engineer, Widespread Panic): Most of the local upstart bands who played at places like the Uptown Lounge and the 40 Watt were anti-jam. The music was very minimalist, and guitar solos were unheard of.

John Bell: Mikey and I met in college. I'd already been playing around town, troubadour style, for a while. Those were just regular folk songs that people would remember . . . a classic rock kind of thing; you could make out with just a guitar and a guy singing. And so then Mikey and I got together and started playing. We were not trying to do anything except play together and see how that felt. We were basically wandering with each other, as soon as we started playing together. He was learning how to play—I mean, he already knew some stuff, guitar wise. I just knew my regular basic handful of chords. He started discovering his intertwining and the way he plays, which is basically he didn't go rip off a bunch of licks and copy everybody, right? He discovered his own way of playing right down to the volume pedal and all that. And I was over there, just singing. That's how we started out. It was kind of like the way it was with the art-school people. We weren't adhering to any rules, really. We were just playing and seeing how that felt.

Dave Schools: I was a freshman. And I lived in Milledge Hall, part of the Reed dormitory complex, and there was a big quad. A lot of musicians lived in Reed and Milledge. In the quad, there's always frisbee and hacky sack. I had a friend and we were playing hacky sack and this guy just kind of randomly comes up and joins our hacky sack circle.

We start talking, and he's like, "What do you guys do?"

"I'm a journalism student, but I kind of wish I hadn't left my bass at home."

"I've got this friend, John Bell. And he plays up at Abbott's, this bar."

It was him playing solo and he was playing songs we loved, and he was randomly segueing from the chorus of one song into the verse of another—that weave thing the Grateful Dead was famous for. I remember thinking, "This guy is great, but he really needs a band." So my friend Neil brokered a meeting, and JB showed up at my dorm and took me over to 320 King Avenue where we met Mike Houser, and we played. I remember playing "Sleepy Monkey" under a light dose of, or what I thought was light, of magic mushrooms, which grew in the cow fields. Mikey had this little lick he played that had an echo on it and it just sounded unique. The sound, his playing . . . I watched lava pour out of the air conditioning vent onto the floor. I was like, "Whoa." And that was it!

Todd Nance (Drums, Widespread Panic): They'd been together about a year and Dave [Schools] came down from Richmond, which was '84 or '85. So, they had this three-piece, and they didn't quite consider themselves a band yet. They went through different drummers.

Dave Schools: We played parties and once one of our drummers couldn't make it to the biggest gig we had yet, the light bulb went off over Mike Houser's head. He's like, "We should call Todd, my old friend, he's a drummer." And so we called his mom and she said he actually lived in Atlanta, not in Chattanooga anymore. So he drove over and practiced and spent the night and there we go. "Playing drums is better than selling insurance!" He had carpet glued to the insides of his drum heads. I was like, "What's this for?" He's like, "Well, I play with this country band on the weekends . . . they're always telling me I'm too goddamn loud."

Todd Nance: [Mikey] graduated high school in 1980 and he went off to the University of Georgia. I graduated high school in 1981 and moved to Atlanta. He and I didn't actually see each other—I saw him once in '81, and we didn't see each other again until '86. He was at Georgia and he called my mom one night and said they were looking for a drummer. It was February of '86—she gave him my number and he called me up in Atlanta and said, "Hey we got this group—come check it out." So I drove over and said yes.

Dave Schools: We didn't really have a drummer before we got Todd Nance. We had a rotating cast—some banged-on vegetable steamers with spoons and some dude had a hammer dulcimer—you know, whatever sort of percussive element we could find. Todd came in and made the bed, so to speak.

Domingo "Sunny" Ortiz (Percussion, Widespread Panic): I'm originally from Waco, Texas, and I moved to Austin, Texas, in 1975. I was in Austin from '75 till October 5 of 1986. And then I drove into Athens, Georgia, on a Monday, October 6, 1986. And my buddy, Kyle Pilgrim, was the part owner of the Uptown Lounge there on Washington Avenue. I had known Kyle since 1969. He went to a different high school in Waco than I did; he played in bands, I played in different bands. He moved to Athens, Georgia, in 1974, thereabouts. I stayed in Texas and we stayed in contact for all those years via telephone or snail mail. He said he had opened up this club, as an owner of this bar, and he told me I should check out the music scene here. He knew I could play. So I picked up all my belongings and loaded it into my Honda Civic and I drove into Athens that Monday, which happened to be a Monday in which the Panic boys had a regular Monday night gig at the Uptown Lounge.

He said, "Man, there's this hot band that I hire every Monday night. You need to ask them if you can sit in, I think y'all could connect."

I told him, "Man, I just drove fourteen-plus hours to get to Athens, Georgia, and you want me to sit in with these guys? No way."

And he says, "You got to do it, you got to do it."

The next thing I know, we're there at nine o'clock. And he says, "Go ask if you can sit in!" And so I did.

JB, at the time, went to Kyle Pilgrim, said, "Hey man, so this cat says that he's a friend of yours and he wants to know if he can sit in. Can he play?"

Kyle said yes, because he knew I could play. You gotta remember, I'm ten years older than any of these boys. So at the time, they're probably nineteen. And I was twenty-nine.

Mikey Houser: He'd been driving like for three days or something, and he just happened to pull in and we were loading in and we saw his bongos in the back of his car and we said, "Hey, you wanna jam?" So he reluctantly agreed. He didn't know what he was getting into, he thought we were punks, which we were.

Dave Schools: It was like, "Oh, this is a whole new dimension." And it improved the vibe of the rhythm section.

John Bell: I worked at a nursery as a field hand. And Mikey was working at a sandwich shop. And he was also a very, very accomplished pizza delivery man. He was able to look at the orders on the board and see the route in his mind. He would proactively go pick those orders and head on out. There was an efficiency there. He was creating the route that he wanted. His roommate was the manager at Domino's there . . . sitting back having some beers at night, when they'd talk about the pizza business and it's like wow, everything's fascinating if you look at it.

Domingo "Sunny" Ortiz: I was working at Gus Garcia's, the Mexican restaurant in downtown Athens. And I delivered flowers, wholesale. I also worked at the Uptown Lounge—cleaning the club at night.

David Blackmon (Fiddle, Bluegrass Underground): They used to come hear me play all the time in the Normaltown Flyers at Allen's Hamburgers. We just kind of gradually got to know each other.

Dave Schools: In Athens, [the college radio] made fun of us. We were going against the grain of what college radio had become. R.E.M. is the band that's mainly responsible for wrangling college radio. They would go to every town they played in and visit the college radio station, make a friend out of the DJ.

Steve Fleming (Bouncer, Uptown Lounge; Sound engineer, Georgia Theatre): Kyle [Pilgrim] and Duck [Anderson] just opened the Uptown Lounge when it previously had been the Paris Adult Theater—an X-rated peep show movie house. And they were trying to slowly convert it into a music club. Kyle was the musician of the two. He had played in a few bands and knew a few people in the music business and thought it'd be a good idea to open a music club. And yeah, it really was a good idea. I'd always been into music and they started getting busy. One night, he asked me to run the door for him. I was sort of the first employee outside of the immediate family.

Dave Schools: Steve was the man—he ran the door.

Zach Newton (Front-of-House Engineer, Aquarium Rescue Unit): Pretty much all of us worked at the Uptown Lounge. Dave worked the door, Sunny was the bar manager, Mikey and JB would play every Monday night with dollar Rolling Rocks.

Eric Carter (Guitar, vocals, Bloodkin): The Uptown Lounge was like a lot of dive bars. When you went in, you dealt with a doorman and there was a long hallway . . . and when you go in, the room kind of opened up.

David Blackmon: It was longer, more than wide.

Steve Fleming: The Uptown Lounge had a forty- to fifty-foot-long hallway that came up dark. We had the cover charge and an ID check at the end of the hallway and it opened up. You did a U-turn as you came into the door, and the stage was backed up against the sidewall. There were a couple glass swinging doors that was the load-in and load-out for the stage. There was a little small courtyard with a tree growing up in the middle of it—oftentimes we would catch people climbing over the roof, trying to climb down the tree to sneak in.

Mikey Houser: We were the black sheep. We were playing jam rock when everyone else was playing jangle rock.

John Keane: Nobody played covers—that was not considered hip at all. Any band who did so was looked down upon. I was in a cover band called Strawberry Flats at the time, so I have firsthand experience in this area. We played '60s and '70s psychedelic covers along with a few originals and were pretty much ignored by the local music rag *Flagpole* and the local hipsters. But the UGA students came out in droves and packed the Uptown Lounge when we played there. They of course had plenty of money and drank heavily, so the management were happy to book us in there on a regular basis. I recall hearing some of the trendies grousing about it. How dare we play covers in Athens, Georgia, the mecca of hip? And how dare we hog the Uptown Lounge for an entire weekend? I remember being onstage and dodging a Michelob bottle that was hurled at me by a disgruntled musician at one point.

Mikey Houser: People had . . . called me "Panic" for a while because I used to get those anxiety attacks, so that kind of became my nickname. I was thinking about that word "panic," and all of a sudden a sign for the "Widespread"—it seems like it was either the "Widespread Depression Orchestra" or "Widespread Blues Orchestra" or something like that—came into my vision and I thought, wow, "widespread" and "panic" really go together great. And that was just it. For a while we didn't know what to do, whether to be "John Bell and Widespread Panic" or just to be "Widespread Panic." But we ended up just being Widespread Panic for no apparent reason. The only reason we don't talk about it much is 'cause, you know, that was kind of a sensitive spot for me, having had those attacks or whatever, but I was cured when I met my wife.

John Bell: Everybody's trying to get that weekend slot. We got a couple of gigs with Kyle and we're looking at the calendar and stuff and it became obvious nobody ever wanted Monday night. It was always open.

We were like, "We'll do a regular Monday night gig if you want us to, sir."

Domingo "Sunny" Ortiz: My buddy remodeled the Uptown Lounge and he moved his refrigerator outside and built a deck. And we would always go back there before the shows, hanging out, and there would be pigeons on the roof. And that's where [the song] "Pigeons" came about.

John Keane: I have to admit I didn't get it at first. I never really listened to the Dead growing up. I was more of an Allman Brothers guy. Panic had songs that were more like suites with very disparate movements. They sped up, they slowed down, used wacky time signatures and very complicated song structures. Their lead guitar player sat in a chair and stared at the floor for God's sakes! Hipsters we were not. But do you know what was even *less* cool than what we were doing at that time? The most uncool thing anybody could possibly do? Play Grateful Dead covers! Hippies and tie dye were a relic of the past, weren't they? Nobody in the area was doing anything even close to that. Enter Widespread Panic.

John Bell: Kyle knew we were selling some beer. It always comes back to that. We were actually doing three hours of music in the night. There's no goofing around. There's no going to the bathroom. There's no stopping to tell a joke or have a beer. You just play. It's a big difference when you're playing in front of people than if you're just sitting at home playing in front of the TV.

John Keane: They had difficulty getting a show at the Uptown Lounge at first for obvious reasons. They had *songs* that were twenty minutes long. Even the UGA students wouldn't show up for that. Not yet, anyway.

John Bell: We'd get free beer and it was a buck a head coming in and we'd get the door. They were telling us we should really go to two bucks after we were kind of established. It seemed so greedy. We said, "Okay, we'll do a buck fifty, okay?"

Domingo "Sunny" Ortiz: Our bar tab would be more than what we made.

Steve Fleming: Dave Schools was one of my doormen for a while. Dave's such a jovial, nice guy. His main job was to make sure people didn't slip around behind the people that were paying and getting their IDs checked. I said, "Dave, you're gonna sit here, cross your arms across your chest, put a frown on your face. People will try to run you over. Being Mr. Goody-Goody doesn't work in this business." He was coming on just to get a little extra money when they were still struggling. But shortly after he was working for us, they really started taking off. So that stint at the door probably only lasted four months.

Dave Schools: I was the cash guy. And I would back up Linda, who was the ID girl, if someone gave her a hard time. But frankly, Linda could take care of herself.

Todd Nance: They tried to hire me to enforce underage drinkers and I said, "I ain't that guy."

Domingo "Sunny" Ortiz: There were lots of nights where Kyle Pilgrim just ate the bar tab, because we wouldn't have made any money, and our manager would have gotten a little bit upset. He'd have to pay $200 to $250 worth of a bar tab and we definitely made like 110 bucks.

John Keane: When the band finally did stop [playing], they would pack up their stuff and go to the house on King Avenue they all shared. Conveniently, it was about three blocks from my house. No need for me to worry about driving home. There they would sometimes set up and continue to play until the sun came up. You can imagine how thrilled the neighbors were to be living next to the new Haight-Ashbury.

John Bell: We'd done some recording and, you know, we'd been on the road, we kind of had our thing going. We just got with our first and longtime manager, Sam Lanier. And next thing was like, "Hey, we want to make a record."

6

It Was Fun, but Kind of Demented

Back up in New York City, the scene was thriving. Blues Traveler and Spin Doctors had label deals, while another band with roots in studying jazz and playing rock music started to emerge from the Nightingale's scene: God Street Wine.

Lo Faber: I spent a year working for the family business, Eberhard-Faber, a pencil company. Half the year, I was in our factory out in Pennsylvania, and then the second half of the year, with our sales force in New York City. I started wearing a suit and tie and going to work in the city. Everybody said I looked like Alex Keaton from *Family Ties.* I was selling art products to grizzled old commercial artists. I had the boss's name, I was the boss's son, and that was obvious to everybody. It was a hard position to be in, so I quickly decided to go to college and play music instead. God Street Wine formed in the fall of 1988. We were all but one going to college in New York City and three of us were studying jazz.

Aaron Maxwell: I went to Manhattan School of Music and I met, very early on, Lo and Dan, who's the bass player for God Street Wine. We were in classes together; they had transferred up from NYU. We got friendly and just started hanging out. And Lo is doing a lot of songwriting at the time on his little TASCAM cassette four-track. He had all these little tapes, meticulously labeled.

He was like, "Oh, I need somebody to sing some of them."

"Well, I'll give it a shot."

So we started doing that. Jon Bevo, who was the keyboard player and was also going to NYU, was friends with Dan. Tomo, the drummer, was a longtime friend of Lo's growing up in Princeton. So we just started jamming. And we would rehearse in Midtown at this little rehearsal studio until we got kicked out because this jazz piano player, Michel Camilo—his drummer said our drummer hit too hard. So we got kicked out of the studio. We got a gig from Tom Hosier at Nightingale Bar. That was our first official gig. That gave us some validation.

Lo Faber: My ex-girlfriend, who was our manager for the first year, got us our first gig in December of '88 at the Nightingale Bar. We had no knowledge whatsoever of the music business, of forming a band, of what we would have to do, or anything at all like that.

Jon Bevo (Keyboards, vocals, God Street Wine): Lo was the main guy. At this point, he was the driving force of everything. He wanted a keyboard player who could guide or control a bit. That's how my relationship with the band started—as the underling.

Aaron Maxwell: Lo was influenced by the Talking Heads and the New Wave thing. But also bluegrass. His mom was in a bluegrass band, and my dad played Dixieland jazz. There were a lot of different cross-sections of stuff that we could draw from.

Tom "Tomo" Osander (Drums, God Street Wine): I got a call from Lo in late summer of '88 saying, "You should move to New York, we should start another band." I had been working in a Volkswagen dealership and it was a really cool job where they would give me time off to go and see the Grateful Dead. So I was doing that, but getting frustrated—I wanted to be playing music as opposed to seeing music.

Aaron Maxwell: I'm sure the first shows, we played pretty late and I probably got shocks from the microphone. The crowd was just our friends, assorted girlfriends, and parents, probably. We loaded all our stuff in a station wagon . . . we had a paid gig, right? You don't think about the limitations. We were in music school and dabbling with jazz harmonies, and that led into the improvisational thing. That's what we were studying.

Lo Faber: Blues Traveler were several steps ahead of us. They had started playing the Nightingale a few months before—they were playing every Monday night, which was a great move, because nobody else played on Monday night. So they were starting to get all these kids coming to see them on Monday. Another band that was doing that was Billy Cohen's band dreamspeak. They were a Columbia University band, and they started playing in Columbia fraternities, but then they started playing downtown too. Blues Traveler used to publish a little postcard—an actual physical postcard every month that was just a calendar grid. It was called "gigs at a glance." We just tried to copy Blues Traveler. Again, we had no idea how to do this! So we were like, "Okay, well, they seem to be doing all right, let's just do everything they do." So we started publishing our own postcard mailing list—getting people to sign up at the gig and playing our own twenty gigs a month. Once in a while, we'd pick up a gig out of town, like at a college or a frat, or some bar, up in the Hudson Valley or in New Jersey. We played to many, many empty rooms. Gradually, we started getting kids driving in from New Jersey, coming over the George Washington Bridge, wearing tie-dyes, Grateful Dead fans, looking very out of place in the East Village. But this was the scene. This was the fan base.

Tomo: When I moved in, I got a job at Tower Records up at 66th and Broadway, the Lincoln Center store. I would work there during the day, then we would rehearse at night. That was my schedule.

Jon Bevo: I was just happy to be there. The music was challenging, it was intimidating. There's two guitar players and back then we had a lot of energy and tried to play as many notes as possible. So having me, who couldn't play that fast, was not necessarily a bad thing.

Tomo: We certainly weren't making any money. It was get on, play your set, get off kind of stuff. Playing the Bitter End was like that—six bands on a bill, those kinds of things. Same with the Continental, down at St. Mark's. It took a while to feel like we were settling into what we were doing. Eventually Nightingale's would have given us a "headline" gig where we had enough time to play a whole proper set. At least a year into it, we filled the Nightingale Bar—if you put ninety people in there it was sardines. It was really small and sweaty and loud but terribly exciting. One night there was a queue out the door and people were jammed in there. We finished this epic jam out of this song called "Electrocute" . . . when it came back down from this really high level and dropped down to the gentle groove, there was a roar. A proper Dead at the Garden kind of roar in my mind. Chills. It was the first time that had happened, where they got it, we got it.

Aaron Maxwell: Our manager was this guy Scott, also known as bullethead. We went through this book of managers, because we wanted to find a manager. And he managed Mojo Nixon, who we liked. We were sending little press kits to everybody and we sent one to him. We were playing a gig at the Nightingale Bar and there was a line down the street, wrapping Second Avenue. And he happened to be walking by, and he was like, "What the hell? What band is playing in there?" And it happened to be us. And he happened to have just gotten that kit from us that week. So he ended up becoming our manager.

Scott "bullethead" Reilly (Manager, God Street Wine): I lived a few blocks from Nightingale's. I would walk by, heading home on Mondays, and there was always this giant line of young people trying to go to the club. And it caught my attention.

Michael Weiss: We had stolen a bunch of *Pollstar* magazines from Wetlands one night when we were down there playing. And I started just cold-calling music managers, entertainment managers, because we were looking for full-time representation.

Scott "bullethead" Reilly: Bullethead Management comes early in the alphabet. Mike Weiss called me and I was like, "Yeah, I know God Street Wine," which floored him right then and there.

Michael Weiss: Everybody was making a hundred dollars a week.

Dan Pifer (Bass, God Street Wine): The summer of 1990, somewhere in there, we played something like seventeen gigs in the month of August, all in New York City. We hit this point of declining audience. There was McGovern's Bar, we'd play there once a week, Nightingale, we'd play there once a week. You'd have all these weekly gigs and it was just way too much to play in the same area. You couldn't expect people to come out every night even though a lot of them did come out night after night. We realized we really just had to start getting out of the city and expanding places that we played.

Scott "bullethead" Reilly: In the early days, it was all about touring. How do we make this more efficient? How do we widen the range?

Lo Faber: One of the first early gigs out of town was at the Rhinecliff Hotel. And that ended up being a home base—a couple hours to the north [of New York City]. And the Rhinecliff wasn't really a hotel—it was just a bar. And it was very ramshackle, right on the edge of the Hudson River. And it was run by this old guy Ed Tybus—he was a veteran of the Battle of the Bulge. He and his wife Ruth had run it forever. And he started having bands and knew nothing about having a venue; they just started letting bands basically play in the living room of this joint. You brought someone to work the door yourself, you collected the money that you made. Ed would give you two beers per band member. Eventually we were just packing the place . . . hundreds of people would be there, and the place was so small that hundreds would be outside in the parking lot. And even then, Ed would just give us two beers per band member.

Tomo: We stayed in New York for a year or two before we decided we really wanted to do this. And then we decided the way to do it was to get a house together, get out of the city, in a place where we could afford. That's when we moved up to Westchester.

Lo Faber: Eventually we got ourselves a band house up in Ossining, Westchester County. Everybody either finished college or quit their jobs or both, and we all moved in together. Because eventually we were making enough money to just barely support ourselves.

Jon Bevo: It was dirty. We were out in the woods, but near a bunch of highways. So we could travel upstate and down to the city very easily, so it was a good center point. We had rented a big grand piano and we had some recording equipment.

Michael Weiss: Every Friday night, when we would get paid, we would have a poker game. Every Friday night, early Saturday morning, there were people who ended up with no money left for the week to eat. It was fun, but kind of demented.

Dan Pifer: The deal was if you lost all your money, people had to take care of you.

Lo Faber: I taught them all how to play.

Scott "bullethead" Reilly: They were just figuring it out on their own. And I had a lot of experience with bands on the road. They were like, "Well, we're interested. Can you come up to our house and play poker with us?" It was sort of made clear that that was going to determine whether or not they asked me to be their manager. Lo had been playing poker since he was a little kid and Tomo was bolder than any of the guys in the band and would just aggressively bully them out of lots of hands. So the two of them usually dominated the game, which I learned.

Lo Faber: Not as many people played. You can take advantage of that.

Scott "bullethead" Reilly: I've been playing poker since I was eight years old. But I was broke, and it's hard to play poker broke because the money means too much and you don't play well. But they were broker. And I went up to that house. To me, it looked like, "Wow, okay, these guys are serious. They got this house, they all live here. They're invested in this thing. This makes sense." And, you know, I was the only winner at the poker table that night. And it was really because I got more aggressive than Tomo.

Dan Pifer: He acted like he had played a few times but wasn't very good. And he crushed us. It spoke volumes to us of a manager's ability. He didn't come in and kiss our ass; he played cards and played to win.

Aaron Maxwell: We wanted to be successful, and be able to have radio play, and that kind of thing, but also through the music that we wanted to do.

Lo Faber: The only template for a rock band to have a career was getting a record deal. So we got a record deal.

7

It Was Almost Like a Vow to Poverty

One of the most eclectic acts to emerge from this time period was based out of Atlanta, founded by the avant-garde musician Col. Bruce Hampton, who had made inroads in the rock scene in the late '60s and early '70s with his band the Hampton Grease Band. Aquarium Rescue Unit was Col. Bruce and a handful of younger musicians in the Atlanta scene.

Oteil Burbridge (Bass, Aquarium Rescue Unit): What we were doing, we thought for sure, there was absolutely zero audience for it. And in retrospect, there was zero.

Zach Newton: None of us were getting rich. None of us were in it to get rich.

Jeff Sipe (Drums, Aquarium Rescue Unit): I came from Boston and moved to Atlanta in '83 and started working in the Top 40 scene around town. At that time, it was really vibrant. There were lots of clubs to play, and the music scene was bustling. And musicians were actually making decent money. There was no shortage of work for most of us, down there in Atlanta. It was a growing city—two million people at the time. And the music scene was really vibrant, including some art music and some non-commercial oriented music. I met Bruce Hampton the following year in '84, through Dan Wall, an amazing jazz pianist. He and his wife Carol and Ricky Keller were part of a scene down there that would occasionally play some jazz stuff. But they would really be very experimental, especially with Bruce's group, the Late Bronze Age. They were just trying to break all the walls down.

Oteil Burbridge: Col. Bruce always had these really great musicians in Atlanta. The best guys in Atlanta always played with him.

Jimmy Herring (Guitar, Aquarium Rescue Unit): I met Jeff Sipe right after I moved to the Atlanta area. This was late 1986. And I heard him play at a performance and was just stupefied how great he was. I was new in town. And I just approached him: "I'm new in town . . . I loved hearing you play, I would love to play with you." The first thing he says is, "What are you doing tomorrow?"

Jeff Sipe: Bruce was a magnet for a lot of us, in that he would attract players who were frustrated on some level with the local scene, playing Top 40 music or playing other people's music or not really getting as deep as they wanted to get into music. There's a lot of players down there that are very accomplished musicians who can play jazz and classical and R&B and a lot of different genres on a very high level. Those musicians were looking for more expression, more full expression of their own artistic abilities and sensibilities. So Bruce was a magnet for those types of musicians. My first gig with him was at a place called the Harvest Moon in Atlanta, a tiny little club. He had hired me and I'd showed up to the gig not really knowing what to expect. He had fifteen musicians on stage and it was all improv. There was nothing there, except what you made on the spot, in the moment. No charts. No discussion. No "Let's play in this key." It was just wide open. Somebody would start something and everybody would fold into it. About the third song—and I use that term loosely—I realized there was so much freedom in Bruce's approach to music and expression, that it really transcended music on some levels. It went into more emotions that music kind of pushed. It was more than music. It was a big spirit going on. The love and the tolerance and the acceptance and the encouragement was all wrapped up into this one really fun, thrilling, musical experience that night. And I remember after the third song I looked over at Randy Honea, a brilliant guitar player down there in Atlanta, and I told him, "I think I found my calling." And he immediately responded, "Yes, I think you have too." I started working much less in the local Top 40 scene and started working in Bruce's various configurations. Now, this was also an agreement to work for a lot less. It was a vow of poverty. It was a chance to practice and play and go deep, deep into the art of music and drumming. I found a deep well in Bruce, let's say.

Matt Mundy (Mandolin, Aquarium Rescue Unit): There was a band before I was in the Aquarium Rescue Unit. I think before Jimmy was in it, too. As I understand it, it was Bruce, Oteil, Jeff, a banjo player named Jeff Mosier, and a very great guitar player still to this day, Charlie Williams. And Count M'Butu. It was much a revolving thing for a lot of the first year, with any number of players on stage. And a lot of people were on stage and didn't even play! They just read a poem or something like that.

Oteil Burbridge: Col. Bruce was just such an anomaly, such an alien, you know? He's like, part professional wrestler, part Zappa, and an old, old Black blues guy trapped in this white guy from Georgia's body.

Jeff Sipe: He didn't know chords, scales, key signatures, time signatures. He just played his emotions, random notes, wherever he was on the instrument, that's the note he played.

Derek Trucks (Guitar, Derek Trucks Band, The Allman Brothers Band): He just saw the absurdity of a lot of the stuff. He completely despised the music of the late '70s and '80s. He was an antidote to that.

Matt Mundy: Jeff invited us to come and open up for the Aquarium Rescue Unit one night at a place called the Point in Atlanta. And so we did. And things just kind of took off from there. Jeff invited me to come sit in with him and Oteil and some bluegrass people. Bruce was always hanging around Jeff [Mosier]'s house. And so as it turned out, Bruce just kind of asked me three or four times to come sit in. Finally I did.

Jimmy Herring: It wasn't even two weeks later and Jeff calls me up and says, "Man, these guys just moved in. You got to get over here. These guys are unbelievable." And it was Kofi and Oteil Burbridge. We started playing together, but we never played a show. We were trying to write music together and we were trying to get enough music where we could play our own shows with all original music. We were into music that wasn't happening that much anymore like Weather Report. I was really into the Dixie Dregs and Mahavishnu Orchestra. With all their influences, we were trying to write our own music. Not too long after, Sipe started playing with this guy that I'd heard about but never had seen or heard. And it was Bruce Hampton. We would show up for rehearsals, and he'd be like, "Man, you guys got to hear this Bruce Hampton guy, man. I mean, it's so liberating." The only music we'd ever played together at that point was the music we were trying to write together. We weren't playing any covers, and they didn't know I love playing blues. And I didn't know that they like playing two-beat music—bluegrass type stuff or country or, you know, folk music or any of that. None of us had ever seen that side of each other because we were trying to do all this fusion stuff and write our own music. So Sipe started doing that and then Oteil started doing it with him. And, you know, these guys are like the Michael Jordans of their era. And then they started playing with groups. And I figured Bruce must be just a virtuoso, you know. Which, of course, he was in his own twisted way. They joined his band so I show up to hear them play. And I swear to God, I was absolutely frozen. It wasn't about musical virtuosity, it was just this free thing that was almost bordering on performance art, you know? Eventually, they invited me to come sit in, and so I showed up. I had a guitar. Small amp. And I came in to watch the show. They did three sets. And I was so blown away after the first set, I was just like, "Oh my god, I wanna play with these guys so bad." So I just hung out with them during the set break after the first set. Then they did the second set. And the second set, it just absolutely killed me. I mean, I was blown away. I was just like, "Man, what do I got to do to play with these guys?" But I wasn't going to invite myself. After the second set, Bruce goes, "You got a guitar with you?" And I said, "Well, yes sir. It's in the car." He said, "Go get it." I couldn't get to the car fast enough. And I played the third set with him and it was an epiphany.

Oteil Burbridge: We had few people watching. It would be mostly improv. And whoever was left, was really hardcore. And Bruce knew they really got it. The best guys in Atlanta, he always played with them. All of our favorite players really loved him. But we didn't really know why yet.

Jimmy Herring: It started out as a Monday night, only one time a week. We would play this place called the Little Five Points. It was just a little tiny pub in Atlanta.

Oteil Burbridge: That's where all the crystal shops were, the New Age stuff, actors, people that were doing plays. You had performance art, visual artists of every medium, musicians of every stripe, especially the kind of counterculture ones . . . it was the crazy part of town where it was all going on.

Jimmy Herring: Bruce had a longstanding relationship with all the people in Atlanta. Getting gigs in Atlanta wasn't hard, but it was never about trying to build a following.

David Blackmon: The Atlanta music scene was already extremely well-organized, unionized . . . I was working that scene, too. Athens was more freelance, more underground. And it's always been that way.

Oteil Burbridge: [Aquarium Rescue Unit] became popular in Atlanta, to where we were playing and selling out the Little Five Points to the point we moved up to the Cotton Club. And then we started going out and touring around other places like the Georgia Theatre, where we did our first record. We made a small circle. We were adopted by the hippies. It was definitely that way in Atlanta on a micro level. We had all the freaks: We had hippies, we had a lot of artists, musicians, wiccans, witches. You know, a lot of the witches came out to see us. It was all there in Little Five Points, in Atlanta.

Michael Rothschild (Founder, Landslide Records): It was kind of funky. Dirty. We're not talking about fancy counters and tables. I guess it would hold a hundred and fifty to two hundred people. It was on two levels. There was a ground floor where the stage was and then there was a balcony as well. It was right there, in the middle of Little Five Points.

Jimmy Herring: It wasn't about the money. It wasn't about making a living. It was literally like one night a week, and there was no money involved at all. You would work all week, doing whatever you could, just so you could have Monday night to go out and really play your heart out. You took whatever kind of jobs you could get during the week.

Jeff Sipe: You remember the movie *Animal House*? It was all of that, all over the place. You know, a gig is a gig sometimes, and we had to do those things. I remember in Athens one time, a giant food fight that broke out. Food started ending up on us and our equipment and we had to barricade ourselves behind some tables and a door to avoid the mess. But we didn't mind. Any place we got to play, it was that joyful.

Matt Mundy: We played a place in Huntsville, Alabama, that was called the Tip Top Cafe. It was a place out of the chitlin circuit in the '20s. It was a thirty-seat place and nobody there. We didn't know how to get there. Jimmy decided he's gonna show us and he's looking at the map and said, "There's a road right there, it'll get us there real quick. It just cuts off everything." We went there and it was the state line. And that was his nickname: State Line.

Jimmy Herring: That's correct. It was mostly about self preservation. And I get it. I love driving. Nothing will freak me out more than a bad driver. I can't handle a bad driver, I can't handle a driver who's not paying attention behind the wheel. You know, steering the band with their leg while they roll a joint—I'm not gonna tolerate that. And I'm like, "You can either let me get out or get the fuck out of the driver's seat . . ." That's kind of where it became like that. And not to say that I have anything against rolling a joint! I'm just saying, I don't think you should be doing it while you're driving with eight people in the vehicle.

Matt Mundy: Washington, DC . . . we played a place called the Bayou. So we're going from there to New York City and somebody knows somebody that's gonna put us up because we didn't have any money. We were making nothing. We go to her house and she says, "The lounge chairs are on the roof." And so we slept on the roof.

Jeff Sipe: We started going out a little bit further, extending the radius from Atlanta . . . going out to Colorado, up and down the eastern seaboard down to Florida. The scene was kind of experimental. The audience was largely people who loved the energy we were bringing, even if they weren't familiar with what we were doing. They liked *how* we were doing it.

Oteil Burbridge: One time we were playing the Point and we emptied the place out. We went to three in the morning or something like that—really late. And there were only two people left in the club. And we had long run out of our songs and so at the end of the night I was like, "Who are these two people that like stuck it out?" It was G.E. Smith and Laraine Newman from *Saturday Night Live.* And they were like, "That's the greatest thing we've ever seen." And they tried to get us on *Saturday Night Live,* but they couldn't because we didn't have a record out.

8

Hit the Record Button and Get Out of the Way

By 1987–1988, Widespread Panic had started to branch out of the Uptown Lounge and Athens, playing gigs all throughout the South—focusing on bars that would have them and colleges looking to fill musical voids for the students.

Michael Rothschild: The first place I saw them was in Atlanta at a place called the Harvest Moon Saloon, which was a relatively small bar. I looked at the crowd and I was thinking, this is slick, reminds me of the Fillmore East from 1970, the way kids were dressed and dancing. They did some really cool cover versions of things from the Grateful Dead, for example. It was pretty refreshing to me, even though it was retro.

John Keane: One day their manager Sam Lanier called me up and said they wanted to come into my studio and make an album, so I booked them for a week or so. Their gear man Garrie Vereen brought their stuff over in his battered Dodge pickup. My studio was basically a couple of bedrooms in my house and was very rudimentary at the time. They were all crammed into a fourteen-by-fourteen bedroom and I was in the next bedroom with a mixer, some speakers, and a sixteen-track tape machine. I had one good mic and a bunch of not so good ones. The windows were covered with plywood, and there was a window unit stuck in one of them to keep the room cool. On quieter songs, I would have to go in and turn it off because it made a racket. There was a closet in the bedroom where I put the guitar amps.

David Blackmon: The studio was on Hillcrest Avenue at the time, right behind the hospital. It was just a house that he had slowly remodeled and converted into a recording studio. I was living just three houses down from the hospital.

Mikey Houser: It was just a two-minute walk from the "band house."

John Keane: We recorded *Space Wrangler* very quickly. I don't remember exactly, but I doubt they spent more than a couple grand on the whole thing. They gave me production credit, but I can't say I ever told them what to do.

Dave Schools: We didn't have enough money to make the whole record at once. So we would go in and record basic tracks for a couple of songs and weren't doing many overdubs. And then we'd have to hit the road and make some more money. We finished some rough mixes of three or four of the songs and left for a long drive that we were going to do overnight. And listening to those, it was so exciting as we left town to go play more gigs.

John Bell: We recorded the bulk of the record and it wasn't shortly after that that we started talking to Landslide Records.

Michael Rothschild: Landslide Records started off doing stuff with Col. Bruce Hampton and his band, the Late Bronze Age. And we did a little jazz stuff. We really wanted to concentrate on acts from the Atlanta area and from that region around Atlanta. We started doing stuff with Tinsley Ellis and his band the Art Fixers, which was straight up blues. Panic really appreciated the people that I was working with. They loved Bruce. And they just fit right in that way.

Todd Nance: He started to come and see us and he saw something in it and he offered us a deal, on one condition, and that was that we stop playing "Nights in White Satin."

Dave Schools: He put our record out, we grabbed a lawyer, we inked a very simple deal.

John Bell: It was an independent label that had all the inner workings that you needed to get a record out without schlepping it yourself.

Michael Rothschild: It evolved over a few weeks. There was a period of being in touch with them and getting to know their manager, Sam. I probably had generic contracts that were easy to make up and fill in the blanks with names and dates. And I think I just filled it out, and they were happy with it.

John Bell: Since all our tunes are kinda quirky, he suggested putting in a cover that was a little less quirky. And that's how [J.J. Cale's] "Travelin' Light" came about.

David Blackmon: They paid me with a bottle of tequila.

John Keane: I voiced an opinion once in a while, but the best thing to do with these guys is hit the record button and get out of the way. Make sure the guitars are in tune. They would play each song a few times and we would pick the best take and record over the outtakes with the next song to save tape. It was recorded mostly live, then we went back and overdubbed vocals and extra instruments like David Blackmon's fiddle.

Michael Rothschild: We had an office on 14th Street in Atlanta. And we had a pretty good distribution network of indie distributors around the country—there were just a handful of us who were actually central to moving the label forward. I think we started with maybe three thousand copies, and some of those would have been promotional.

John Bell: One of the big things was, it was right at the time where shelves in the stores were changing—going to CDs. Watching the percentage of sales was incredible . . . you'd just read *Billboard* magazine and see the whole shift was going to CDs. We were one of the first bands to put out a CD at that time, it was just the timing of it. Obviously, it became the norm. But for us, that was a big deal.

David Blackmon: They paid me later on, when they started making money that way, but I didn't hold their feet to the fire. All of a sudden, I had a check in the mail one day.

9

The Bus Broke Down and I Got Off

John Bell: We had a full bus. I forget how many rows, but we had all the seats taken out, except for the driver's seat and I think the seat behind it and the one on the passenger side. It was a friend of ours, one of our first fans and supporters, Tom Gunther. His aunt and uncle had a place on Tybee Island that they were renting and somebody couldn't come up with their rent and they took that school bus in trade and offered it to us for four hundred bucks. So that's how we got our school bus.

John Keane: They purchased a school bus with most of the seats removed, which they would park across the street from the Uptown when they played there. It happened to be right next to the police station, but that didn't stop them from using it as a mobile smoking lounge.

Domingo "Sunny" Ortiz: It was late one night, we had played Atlanta, and then our next gig was in Birmingham. And nobody could drive the bus. So I said, "Well, hell, I'll drive the bus, it's no different than a pickup truck. I can maneuver a stick pretty good." JB was saying, "Now, it's kind of quirky . . . the clutch is kind of quirky, a little loosey-goosey." We were going down the highway and I shifted gears and then all of a sudden it would not go. So here we are busted on the side of the road, in a school bus, pretty close to a state penitentiary on our way to Birmingham, Alabama.

Dave Schools: And you know, it wasn't too long of a trip, but once you've broken down, it's a really long trip.

Domingo "Sunny" Ortiz: A con had escaped.

Dave Schools: No generator and a historically cold night . . . desolate interstate, near the penitentiary.

Domingo "Sunny" Ortiz: We spent the night on the bus and in the morning we had a tow truck tow the bus to a garage that was close. And he rigged up the school bus so that we could make it to our show.

Dave Schools: The next day, once we got everything fixed up, and got to our destination, it was on the news that . . . and this could be me embellishing, but I'm gonna say the Black Widow murderer had escaped and was loose in the woods where we were broken down.

Domingo "Sunny" Ortiz: We rented a U-Haul to get us back to Athens. JB had the bus fixed. And the bus lived on for a few more miles.

10

This Was Our Hangout. You Could Rip Lines in There! You Could Smoke a Bong!

Dave Schools: The epicenter of the northeastern scene was the Wetlands.

Lo Faber: It was about four times, maybe five times, the size of Nightingale.

Jono Manson: It had a PA and big lights . . . it was more of a legit venue.

Eric Schenkman: It became a hub of the scene. If you ever played at Columbia University, if you ever knew who John Popper was, if you were in any way associated with anything to do with Bill Graham Productions.

Pete Shapiro (Owner, Wetlands): Larry Bloch, who started Wetlands, believed that if you played Wetlands, you gotta separate sets to allow people to interact with each other.

Dean Budnick (Founder, Jambands.com): Larry Bloch was first and foremost a Deadhead. He ultimately nurtured that scene right and brought in the next generation: Phish, Traveler, Spin Docs, Dave Matthews Band, ARU.

Pete Shapiro: Larry Bloch said, "I picked a spot in New York I thought no one would ever want to live . . . that's why I put it near the Holland Tunnel."

Billy Cohen: Larry opens up Wetlands and he's got this fully conceived notion of what Wetlands is: a community center and a nightclub.

Russ "In the Bus" Weis (Environmental Director, Wetlands; Office Manager, Strangefolk): I became quite close to him. He was not easily categorized. People would think he's an ultra-progressive liberal guy—sure, he was quite progressive in his social issues in a personal freedom area, and yet he was not your classic liberal by any means.

Tomo: When we started playing the Wetlands . . . that was the target.

Pete Shapiro: I grew up in New York City. I graduated high school in '91. And I was never at Wetlands, '89, '90, '91. I always meet people who are like, "I was at Wetlands for Blues Traveler in '89 and I was sixteen. I took acid for the first time!" I was not actually one of those kids.

Derek Trucks: There were certain clubs like the Georgia Theatre, and then you get up to New York City, and there's the Wetlands and you're like, "Oh, this is the northern version of that."

Marc Brownstein (Bass, vocals, The Disco Biscuits): I lived in Greenwich Village, 6th Avenue and West 12th Street. Most of the bands that I was going to see in the Wetlands scene were funk bands: The Authority, Milo Z, Mexican Mud Band, Shockra.

Billy Cohen: I'll always remember this party before the opening of the Wetlands. There was a downstairs lounge and this big round cocktail table. It was sort of like a seating area. And it had this massive amount of weed on it. And Steve Eichner, he and I are sitting on the floor where there's this giant mound and the whole club is decorated like the fantasy of one of our dorm rooms.

Aaron Maxwell: It was the coolest clubhouse. They would have anything from punk shows, rap, reggae, to jam bands. It had a good sound system—it was the first time we mic'd all our instruments.

Jono Manson: If you look at printouts of the calendar of any given week at the height of their activity, the range stylistically of bands that played there was extremely eclectic. Everyone didn't have access to everything all the time, and people were hungry for new things.

Andy Bernstein (Author, *The Pharmer's Almanac*; Co-founder HeadCount.org): You had multiple scenes coming through. The Wetlands in a lot of ways predates what I think of as the jam band scene. The way to find out who was playing at the Wetlands was the *Village Voice.* The *Village Voice* at the time was *the voice* of culture.

Warren Haynes: The whole Wetlands thing—that became my musical home. I went to Wetlands every opportunity I had and to see as much music as I could.

Dean Budnick: Early on, you'd see the Traveler guys, particularly Bobby Sheehan, just sitting at the bar.

Chan Kinchla: Where I was at the Wetlands was down at the corner of the bar, upstairs. There's this little nook and that's where we would hold court and just party all the time.

Russ "In the Bus" Weis: It got this reputation of being a hippie haven.

Oteil Burbridge: People would go downstairs and smoke weed. People coming up nowadays can't imagine when we were so criminalized for marijuana, you know? And I just couldn't believe it.

Russ "In the Bus" Weis: There were tapestries—it was like your hippie living room.

Dean Budnick: It reminded me of my parents' panel basement, where you go to have a sesh.

Russ "In the Bus" Weis: People smoked a lot of pot down there.

Andy Bernstein: The very first time I went to the Wetlands, we went down into the basement and somebody with dreadlocks came down and said, "Hey, if you're going to smoke weed, just please burn incense."

Dave Swanson: Nobody gave a shit and nobody got arrested.

Andy Bernstein: There were pillows on the floor and little alcoves that you could hang out in.

John Popper: We went downstairs and there's these pillows on the floor. That's where we liked to hang out—the Pillow Room. It was a series of couches and pillows, and I'd look around, and there's all these really cute girls hanging around, looking at me. And it was kinda cool! We felt like we'd arrived. This was our hangout. You could rip lines in there! You could smoke a bong! You could set up shop and nobody would bug you there. If you're coming up, you need a place like that. I think I've had sex in several rooms in the Wetlands.

Eric Schenkman: I was more involved with playing the guitar and being really tired afterwards and probably pretty hungry. And I don't really drink so I'd be pretty high on weed.

Cheryl Liguori (Manager, Wetlands; Co-founder, Fox Theatre): The sight lines weren't great. So the stage was opposite a hard surface wall that had those murals on them. And there wasn't an easy way to do the stage anyway.

Dave Swanson: They had a decent sound system, which is what I cared about.

Cree McCree: There was a VW Bus and all kinds of literature about various things you can get involved in . . . progressive causes.

Steve Eichner: They had this whole other aspect where during the day they would plan protests, they would plan marches, they would plan different kinds of environmental initiatives. And they had petitions you could sign in the club while the bands were playing. So the idea was not just music, but it was also the environment and public policy.

Russ "In the Bus" Weis: I started as the assistant environmental director, and then about a year or so later I became the environmental director. And that's when I was referred to as "Russ in the Bus" because we had the psychedelic-painted '66 split-windshield Volkswagen inside the club that Larry's wife's dad had found in a field in New Hampshire. My office was inside and so I became "Russ in the Bus." I would set up all of the environmental pamphlets and there was a big calendar of events where we would take magic markers and write every day what was going on around the city and around the world. We got the most petitions signed on certain causes in the state of New York, because that many people would pass through.

Cheryl Liguori: Originally it was going to be just a place to hang and dance to recorded music. New Potato Caboose played the first Saturday night. And it was balls to the walls. It was pretty clear people were hungry.

Trey Anastasio: Everyone was interested in only what your original song sounded like. That was it. So, if we went into Wetlands, there were a lot of bands there. For instance, the Roots used to play at Wetlands. I'm talking about a lot of bands . . . maybe two, three bands at night.

Russ "In the Bus" Weis: Larry didn't want there to be any separation, in status or in physicality, between the acts and the audience.

Cheryl Liguori: I tended to work the Mondays (reggae), Tuesdays (Dead Center), Fridays, which were more funky. In order to get two days off in a row, you had to at least one day a week, pull a double shift.

Aaron Maxwell: I happen to have suffered from panic attacks and severe stage fright. I wish that I could have relaxed a lot more. One of our early gigs at the Wetlands, we were opening for Blues Traveler, and I was freaking out. I'm like, "I don't think I can do this, man. I don't think I can do it." Every time I did, it would get a bit easier. Chan said, "Man, Aaron looked like he was playing for his life tonight!" Little did he know!

Cheryl Liguori: We would go through fifty cases of Budweiser on Blues Traveler nights.

Karl Denson (Saxophone, vocals, The Greyboy Allstars, Karl Denson's Tiny Universe): It was sweaty. It was dirty. It was always packed.

Andy Bernstein: It was hot as fuck.

Russ "In the Bus" Weis: John Popper nicknamed the place "Sweatglands."

Joan Osborne: Everybody in the place would just be dancing their asses off, and so the temperature inside the club would rise and rise and rise, and you end up coming off the stage and just being soaked.

Jeff Sipe: People elbow to elbow.

Al Schnier (Guitar, vocals, moe.): We wanted to play the Wetlands in New York . . . we knew that was ground zero for this scene we were becoming a part of. But you couldn't just go play the Wetlands; you had to earn that and play your way up to the Wetlands, which meant playing all of these other places. That started with Tuesday nights at Nightingale's, because that's what everybody else did. Blues Traveler did it. Spin Doctors did it. That was the way you got to ultimately play a weeknight at Wetlands.

Russ "In the Bus" Weis: By the end of a Blues Traveler night or Spin Doctors night, the place would be a wreck—stuff hanging off the walls, the calendar would be melted, and everybody would be just like in this big, sweaty, happy mass of people.

Cheryl Liguori: I would spend an hour counting all the bars, all the ticket sales, all the merchandise from the bus, food sales, everything. The manager that night would go downstairs and count every penny and everybody waited with the two heads of security . . . we would walk across to Canal Street and do a night drop.

Andy Bernstein: Wetlands was where bands were selling six or seven hundred tickets and getting them to a point where they could tour nationally.

Dean Budnick: You'd be in there late-night with Traveler, they'd stop selling alcohol because they had to—and you'd go till dawn. There's nothing like it in New York City . . . you walk out at dawn, the city's coming alive. It's pretty amazing. The idea of being in that club, in fellowship with the band, and your fellow fan, was something really extraordinary.

11

Everybody Had Just Done a Marathon and My Guys Were Up There Swilling Jack, Smoking Cigarettes

While the Wetlands was planting the seeds for a broader jam band scene, Blues Traveler, the Spin Doctors, and God Street Wine knew they had to start branching out from the city. And they quickly learned how to do it, using each other's contacts as well as booking gigs outside the bar scene.

John Popper: The Wetlands was courting us.

David Precheur: We absolutely were shoehorning people into Wetlands and playing it once a week. We did Saturdays, we did Thursdays, we did Wednesdays. And we would just leave a line outside. And every square foot would be fucking jammed. We *were* the fucking Wetlands. That's all there is to it.

Chan Kinchla: The Wetlands opened, it was a great next step, but we were already well on our way. Wetlands kind of came towards the end of our New York experience.

John Popper: They were trying to pay us shitty. We had to negotiate our way up, and do more gigs to do better.

David Precheur: All of a sudden, fraternity houses and community boards had a little bit of a budget. They could throw us like twelve hundred bucks to come up to Cornell. It was enormous money. So all of a sudden, it was like, "Wait a minute, we can go outside the city." And the band is just in Olympic shape. Not only can they fucking play for four or five hours, they don't need any sleep. We had a gig one day—they said play this backyard. It was like at six o'clock and nobody was there. They were like "Just wait, just wait, everybody's taking a shower." And it was the lung cancer benefit for the Red Cross. And everybody had just done a marathon and my guys were up there swilling Jack, smoking cigarettes. We were mismatched, but we got paid like two grand. That's when we realized the road was where it was at.

John Popper: You smell a lot of vomit and Jagermeister for a while.

Grant Cowell: We let everybody tape, so your tapes are getting passed around. And that was where the Dead thing comes in . . . people are playing your tapes or handing them around and that's how you're building your audience. And by touring constantly, your circle just kept getting a little bit wider, a little bit wider, a little bit wider.

Aaron Maxwell: Colleges paid incredibly well. They would all have budgets, and if they didn't use that money this year, they were gonna lose it for next year. So they would hire bands and there was a market for it.

Lo Faber: Even early on, we got five to ten thousand dollars to do college gigs—come play in a quad or a field or a gymnasium. And those paid our bills, and they also built our following. For some reason, the kids who did the college radio stations were often in another culture, but the kids who had the money were totally our people.

Grant Cowell: I think we were getting 10K a pop back then.

Aaron Maxwell: You usually got everything on your rider that you ever wanted plus you were set free on college campuses. People would start taping us and we became known for putting on really good live shows that were not the same every night.

Jono Manson: If you play that much, for a concentrated period of time in your hometown, and then you graduate, that's great. On the other hand, if you keep playing that much in your own hometown for years and years and years, it can also work against you.

Grant Cowell: You're living in guy heaven. You had women, drugs, rock and roll. I was the guy that had the black book for drugs.

Al Marks (Executive Director, Artist Development, A&M Records): Patrick Clifford called me. I lived in DC at the time and we had a radio station there called WHFS, which was freeform progressive. They played whatever they wanted to play, like, Little Feat would go into Pharoah Sanders and Pharoah Sanders would go into John Coltrane and John Coltrane would go into Bonnie Raitt. Depending on the radio guy's tastes, you could hear anything on that radio station, except what you would hear on a Top 40 station. A&M had bands like Marti Jones and Don Dixon, Suzanne Vega, Squeeze . . . a lot of bands from the New York area. A lot of the bands that we had were "minor bands." So we would have to spend a lot of time developing them, and we'd have to find ways to do that. And Patrick called me up one day and he says, "Hey, I got this band I just signed . . . they played Wetlands here and they're down in your area, George Washington University." It wasn't Lisner Auditorium, but their gym. And he says, "I want you to get down there and meet 'em." So I drove down and they were loading themselves—they didn't have roadies or anything. And I was really intrigued by what their soundcheck sounded like. I introduced myself as the A&M guy, and instantaneously, John Popper and I got along. He's going, "You're a record company guy?" I was wearing a Hawaiian shirt and jeans with long hair. I didn't look like a New York record company guy. I stuck around for the show and they played to college kids. That was the amazing thing. I don't think anybody over twenty-three was there. And it was sold out. And I said, "How do you do a sold-out show in my marketplace? I've been here for twenty years." Chan turned to me and said, "We do a lot of colleges." And that's where I learned that that whole jam band scene was all colleges. Frat parties and Wetlands were the spawning ground. And these guys would play NYU frat parties, Fordham, they'd go to Philadelphia and play Temple. And we hadn't even released a record yet.

Aaron Comess: One of the first places where we developed a nice following was up in Ithaca, New York. It had that sort of a hippie college town vibe.

Chris Barron: Blues Traveler recommended this room called the Haunt.

Aaron Comess: Blues Traveler was doing well up there.

Chris Barron: It was a great, dark, funky bar. And there were a lot of college kids there from Cornell and Ithaca College and a lot of hippies, too, that were hanging out. And there was always great weed up there. Back then, we used to make a hang out of it. We'd go skinny dipping after the shows with a bunch of people, and sometimes you'd end up sleeping in a house with a bunch of hippies . . . everything was much more catch-can, barefoot, and silly.

John Popper: All of our friends were going to colleges all around the country. We started realizing that a lot of our friends are now at this point where they can hire us. So we were already jumping in Bob's mom's Peugeot station wagon and driving to Miami, Ohio, or up to Maine.

Chan Kinchla: The college circuit was what got us on the road.

Chris Barron: From Ithaca, we started branching out to other towns. I don't think we were always playing the right room, either. Our booking agent booked a lot of heavy metal bands and metal was still just trailing off then—Poison, RATT, Mötley Crüe were still plugging it out as grunge was on the rise. But those clubs were still going strong. So we're playing these rooms like Hammerjacks in Baltimore and Harpos in Detroit.

Eric Schenkman: We played in between a wet T-shirt contest.

Chris Barron: We didn't always have the reception we might have hoped for, but there was always a couple of people in the room that recognized the caliber of our playing.

Joan Osborne: I had this manager who was really a friend. He was looking at my schedule of playing shows in New York City—and I was literally playing six nights a week in New York, and he said, "You should start to think about going to some other towns." We started expanding to places like Burlington, Vermont, which had a lot of people who wanted to hear music up there, places like Rochester and Buffalo and Boston and DC and Philadelphia. Whenever we would do a show in these towns, people would come up afterwards and say, "Oh, I want to buy your album, I want to buy your cassette," because it was cassettes back then. And I was like, "Well, I don't really have one for you to buy." I thought, "Well, I really have to get on this and figure this out." Thankfully, there was this DIY tradition, mostly coming from punk bands in the '70s and places like the DC scene . . . they had this real DIY aesthetic. So there was information out there, but you'd have to go to the library or bookstore to find it. So I found that information and got some money from a club owner out on Long Island who believed in us. That was the genesis of Womanly Hip Records.

Dave Frey (Manager, Blues Traveler): There was a famous meeting where Bill Graham came up to the Capitol Theatre in Port Chester, where Phish were opening for Blues Traveler. He came out to tell them, "You've got to straighten out your act and get a real crew." There were things that would happen, like they would carry two front-of-house soundboards, and two monitor desks.

"Why are you carrying two?"

"In case one goes down, we've got a backup."

"Why don't you tell the sound company who you're renting this from, if their shit breaks, they've got to fix it, they're liable, like everybody else does."

Bill just had no patience for that, you know? So he told them to clean house or else, and John stood up to him and said no real quick. And Bill backed down.

Brendan Hill: We'd be playing gig after gig after gig. We were with Bill Graham and he put us on a bill with the Neville Brothers at the Palladium, and a Housing Now benefit at the Mall in DC. It was in front of five thousand people, sandwiched between Tracy Chapman and Jefferson Starship.

Chris Bowman (Talent Booker, Trax): I learned about Blues Traveler when I got a promotional packet from Tom Gruber and David Graham. I listened to this little cassette with a pink label on it and was like, "These guys are fucking awesome. But there's no way UVA would let me book this band that not a whole lot of people heard of yet." I approached Coran [Capshaw] and was like, "Hey, this band reached out to me at UVA and I don't think UVA will let me put on a band that no one has heard of." And he was like, "Yeah, I've heard about Blues Traveler. I'll co-produce Blues Traveler with you." We did a hundred and forty people and I walked out with seventy-five bucks and ended up hanging out with Chan and Bobby late. I thought I'd hung the fucking moon.

Al Marks: We got airplay on all the college radio stations. And we started to sell records. We didn't have a lot of money to spend and we had virtually nothing because we weren't generating a lot of money. So we basically had to count on our relationships with the promoters—we would tie into retailers as the band came through the marketplace. John would bring his harmonica and they'd play acoustic in-stores.

Patrick Clifford: We'd play shows in Colorado, every ski resort for two or three days in a row, and then go to the next one. And the next one, the next one. And it was the word of mouth of all these kids that were on spring break, that would go back to their respective homes or their colleges and tell each other about Blues Traveler. We would ski with kids all day long. We would give records out, we'd give stickers out. We'd have the music playing on the ski lifts. And then they would play at nighttime.

Grant Cowell: In the springtime, we'd all take our golf clubs. You'd roll up to the golf course in a tour bus. They're like, "What the fuck is this?" "Hey, we're opening up for the Allman Brothers tonight. You want some backstage passes? How many you need?"

Joan Osborne: We did some college gigs. I was seen as a blues artist, especially back in that time. We would do some colleges, but also blues clubs, things like that. Our thing was less of a dance-oriented thing than say, for example, the Spin Doctors, where they were literally about keeping people dancing all night long.

David Graham: There was always a little tension between me and Dave Precheur because I was like quote-unquote the "big-time manager type" because of my background. But he was the band's guy. He and their crew, some of them really had a good work ethic. But did we all have good work ethics? Who knows. As a band member? John Popper. John Popper had a hell of a work ethic. He knew his limits—if he was gonna party, he knew when to cut it off, whereas maybe some of the other guys in the band wouldn't. John also was dictatorial. He's very much a dictator. And that's why Bobby Sheehan was really important, because when John goes off on something and gets lost in his mental leadership, it was Bobby who could bring him down to earth. They had a work ethic to pile into a fifteen-passenger van, and drive to Florida, and open for the Allman Brothers and smell each other. But then there was the time where the band decided to buy their own sound system. Take it on the road so that we could have the buyers rent the sound, basically. So they cobbled up eighty thousand dollars, got a big truck for it, played one gig, put the gear in the truck, came back out, and the truck was empty. Very first night, the stuff that they wanted as their sort of side business, was stolen. I had to call Jim Garneau at A&M and say, "Listen, Jim, oh, by the way, we need eighty thousand dollars." I think we did get it back. I called Bill and said, "Look, the guys lost eighty thousand dollars' worth of equipment. We're going to help them out."

Dave Frey: I was in New York, working as a promoter doing shows. I'd noticed that [Blues Traveler] were doing things that you'd like to see a band do. My experience in the business was primarily on the show side, selling tickets. The situation at the time was probably hard to imagine compared to how things are now. I grew up in Chicago. Bands would start out and if they were pretty good, they could probably work all the time. The drinking age was eighteen, there was nothing to do. The only thing they do is go out and see bands. And everything was cheap. Ticket prices were three bucks, beers were fifty cents. You could go to four shows a week and people would. There were local bands around Chicago, because you could play your two-hundred, three-hundred-mile radius, everybody could quit their job. Everybody could make maybe three to five hundred dollars a week in the band, live like kings, drink free beer, get laid. Because there's all this work, because the circuit was so strong, you could play a thousand shows in three years. And if you play a thousand shows even if you're just kind of okay, you're gonna get good, because you're gonna learn. What would happen is when you played your thousand shows in those three years, you probably end up with a hundred original songs. Blues Traveler went into A&M and had a hundred songs.

Grant Cowell: We started off in one black van. Then we went to Dodge minivans and we were pulling a trailer behind us. We were going somewhere in Colorado, and we didn't have chains on the tires and the trailer started to weave behind us and basically threw us off the road. We went down an embankment, almost down a cliff. A rock stopped the van from going any further. Thank God, you know, nobody got hurt.

John Popper: Once we got management, and we got signed to a label, Bill put us in front of the Allman Brothers. So we had access to real bands and real venues.

12

We Were an Alternative to the Alternatives

Just like their counterparts up north, Widespread Panic were cultivating the South. Space Wrangler *had done well, and as the '80s closed they were logging hundreds of gigs a year. Labels started to take notice.*

Dave Schools: We were talking to a couple of major labels. Michael knew that he probably wasn't gonna get a second record out of us. But finding the bigger horse to hitch the wagon to was really difficult.

Michael Rothschild: The band wanted to try to do bigger things. And I offered to help them in that regard. We thought the best way to do that was to schedule a trip up north and have them play. We invited several major label people to come see them; a lot of Panic fans came up from Georgia to be at that gig. Dan Aykroyd was there, I don't know how he heard about them. New Wave was the thing at that time, rap was coming in. They knew a band like Panic was not going to sell millions. And that's what they were looking for.

John Bell: We'd already been doing our thing for five years by that point. And we were pretty determined to stick with what was familiar to us. And we thought variety was better, you know?

Dave Schools: At the same time, we're out there doing 180–230 shows a year. And we were just constantly writing . . . a lot of the canon material, we came up with during that era. And we had no way to release it, because we were talking and talking and talking and looking at these giant potential record deals.

Eric Carter: We used to live at this place on North Avenue that was like our second band house that we had here. We got [Panic] to play a party . . . we were having a backyard party. And they were kind of starting to happen there. Their management at the time got kind of pissed off that they were playing somebody's house party: "You can't be playing at somebody's house, you know, we got gigs, we got real gigs!"

John Bell: We had a good buzz going, we were filling up some clubs. And that's when folks took notice, and SBK Records had just formed. They didn't get the music at all. They just knew there was something happening that was selling tickets. They wanted to rope us in a contract. But they really didn't get us. They were just entrenched in the old school. They were gonna sign as many bands as they could and one out of ten might prove themselves and then get all their resources. They immediately started talking about putting us with other songwriters. Folks we've never met. They even talked about some of the band members being left behind, shit like that. And we weren't budging. They couldn't believe we wouldn't do it. So they kept sending people out, going to a concert, having a great time. And then they'd come back with a contract with some terms. And we were like, "We can't work like this." With dollar signs I think they thought we would cave. It definitely wasn't meant to be. And Capricorn, on the other end, was still an old-school record company, but a little more maverick.

Derek Trucks: It was obviously a flavor that was different, because it was in the South. The Allman Brothers and Capricorn . . . those influences were still felt.

Dave Schools: We were being managed at one point by Phil Walden Jr., whose father was Phil Walden, who started Capricorn Records. He put a peanut farmer in the White House and a record company out of business, as he was fond of saying. But he was reassembling Capricorn. And there was no nepotism there; he came to see us in Nashville at Elliston Place. I think there were maybe eight people at the show, including the bartenders and Phil Walden Sr. He sat us down and said, "Boys, it's a big country." We understood to get out there and tour and work on your craft.

Jeff Cook (Senior Vice President of Promotion and Marketing, Capricorn Records): I was head of rock promotion at Elektra Records in New York City when I got the call from Phil Walden about coming back south to restart Capricorn. Elektra was one of the great success stories in the music business at that time because they had hired Bob Krasnow as the new president and he was charged with moving the label forward from the Eagles, Jackson Browne, Linda Ronstadt, and he quickly set about signing new, cutting-edge artists like Metallica, The Cure, The Pixies, Mötley Crüe, The Sugarcubes, 10,000 Maniacs, and so many more. I was blissfully happy to be a part of breaking these artists at radio but I just couldn't resist the lure of returning to Atlanta and the chance to work with Phil. He had a reputation as a wild man and a crazy genius.

Buck Williams (Manager, Widespread Panic): Phil Sr. was a world-famous rock guy.

Jeff Cook: There were no meetings with financial departments, no begging some giant corp head for permission to do anything. It was just us leading with our hearts and doing our best.

Dave Schools: He heard us playing at a fraternity . . . there were two or three in Athens that encouraged original music. So Phil Walden Jr. was a Phi Delt. We played outdoors on the lawn and wound up playing three sets and having to play some songs twice because we ran out of material. Phil Jr. showed up and he's like, "You know, my daddy used to run Capricorn Records and he's putting it back together," and we're like, "Yeah, sure, kid, whatever." And it turned out to be true.

Domingo "Sunny" Ortiz: We had met an agent in DC that really liked us. He said, "I can get y'all work but y'all gotta want to work. It's a lot of driving."

This was before we signed with Capricorn, before we had buses. We would ride in a mini-truck with our equipment. We converted a small section of that truck as a sleeper. Sometimes Mikey and I would sleep in that compartment or Mikey and somebody else—but we had two qualified drivers that we would trust. One driver would drive the truck with our equipment and another driver would drive a six-passenger van that we had bought from the money that we had saved up.

Dave Schools: That was the dream back then. The world hadn't been dashed. If you got a record deal, you could get tour support if you needed it, get merchandising, get publicity, get decent photos. We had it all. Phish got signed to Elektra. Blues Traveler signed to A&M. Capricorn signed Aquarium Rescue Unit. We were all getting the benefits of national distribution—Rolodexes that all the record company people had for art and photographers and publicists. It was cooking concurrently, while the alternative Lollapalooza thing was exploding. College indie rock suddenly became the alternative. We were an alternative to the alternatives.

Jeff Cook: They weren't writing three-minute hooky songs like Van Halen, The Cars, or Aerosmith and I knew radio wasn't going to lead the way on this. At Capricorn, we collectively agreed that we would support the band on the road, much as the Allmans or Grateful Dead had done with relentless touring, so they could build a reputation as a great live band, while I did my very best to convince the more daring stations at radio to begin to embrace them.

> *The band signed with Capricorn in 1991, and went into the studio with famed record producer Johnny Sandlin, who notably mixed the Allman Brothers'* At Fillmore East *and* Eat a Peach, *as well as produced* Brothers and Sisters.

John Bell: We were doing pretty well. But this was an obvious step up with some stability. So that was a bigger game than we'd been playing before. The record company had turned us on to Johnny Sandlin. We'd done all our recording previously with John Keane . . . and we wanted to appease the record company, and we didn't really know any better. Rejuvenated Capricorn Records had all their backing and money from Warner Brothers . . . we were going to be the first release on the new label. Phil and Johnny had us going to Emerald Studios in Nashville and we also spent an afternoon in Sun Studios cutting a few tracks.

Jim Bickerstaff (Assistant Engineer, *Widespread Panic*): John Keane had really set them up for success. They knew how to get stuff done in the studio when they walked in the door.

Dave Schools: Johnny wanted us to go to Memphis because he knew that we'd like Memphis and there was a studio up there called Kiva where Stevie Ray Vaughan had recorded his last record. And so we went up there, and we were trying to record some stuff, but we just continually had these technical difficulties.

Jim Bickerstaff: Johnny didn't really try to influence the sound, he let that come from the band and the natural organic musicmaking. He was a master at providing an emotional safe space where people could create, no judgment, and no specific direction, just an occasional suggestion.

Dave Schools: There was a whole lot of downtime, which leads to either a fucked-up band or a bored band, either of which is probably not going to record great music. So Johnny's solution was to call up a buddy over at Sun Studios, where they run tours through and you can look at Jerry Lee Lewis and Elvis pictures and the gear and think about all the great stuff that was recorded there. He's like, "Well, you know, it's still a functioning studio." We went in there at night, after all the tours were done, and plugged up those original instruments and cut a few covers. Even though we didn't use any of them on the record, we did go back and re-record the Van Morrison song "Send Your Mind" at Emerald Studios in Nashville.

John Bell: All I remember is doing "That's All Right, Mama."

Todd Nance: I remember sitting in the studio on the couch playing the same guitar Scott Boyer played on "Midnight Rider" for Gregg Allman.

Jim Bickerstaff: I brought a bunch of my Fender amps in and would occasionally tweak guitar tones. We blew a couple of them up, I remember the white smoke. I don't remember the song, but one of Mikey's solos made it to the record with the sound of a burning Showman [amp] as it died. It sounded cool, so we kept it.

At the same time, the band knew they had to expand their live reach beyond the South.

Dave Schools: We needed to form alliances and we needed to continue to push the envelope. And that's the way it worked: organic. A highway of venues that you could play starting up in Burlington with Club Toast or Nectar's, and then the Wetlands, and then Ziggy's in Winston-Salem. Of course, the Uptown Lounge and Georgia Theatre in Athens, the Cotton Club in Atlanta, and other little dots and dashes in between. That was a good circuit, especially if you could fill it in with college gigs.

Domingo "Sunny" Ortiz: Phish could not get gigs in the South. And we couldn't get gigs in the Northeast. So we swapped: "We'll open for you guys if you come down to the South and open up for us."

Todd Nance: We played the frat houses during the week to make money and buy equipment and then play the clubs and lose the money on the weekends. It takes a few years to build it up to where you can really start traveling and going on tour. A really cool radio station up in Chicago started playing *Space Wrangler* from the get-go and they'd call and say, "When are you guys coming up here?" And we were like, "We can't get past Richmond yet . . ." But it took several years before we really toured. We'd leave on Wednesday and come home on Sunday.

John Bell: At that point, we're working with first-level promoters, not just with the club owners. So they would have a familiarity of what bands might go well together. It wasn't unusual to have two or even three bands on stage one night. That's how we met Jerry Joseph and Little Women. That's how we met Blues Traveler and then Phish. We went up into their territory and opened for them and then it was like, "Okay, we can reciprocate. Come on down and you'll get exposed to this market. We love you, they're gonna love you. And we'll have fun together." We'd do these shows in Vermont or Maine or wherever and after the show, we might go to somebody's house and there'd be Shockra playing. It was the same kind of headspace of being friendly and not being competitive.

Domingo "Sunny" Ortiz: Our first show together [with Phish] was at Myskyns in Charleston, South Carolina, where they opened up for us. For the underground music scene that we were involved with, for club owners to take a chance on bands who they didn't know . . . they weren't going to risk that. You gotta remember there were a lot of—and this is not derogatory—there were a lot of hair bands that did the hair songs. They did commercial songs that people would recognize and get up and dance. Club owners, I mean, they're businessmen. They have to pay rent, pay for their liquor, pay for licenses.

Trey Anastasio: We went down to the Georgia Theatre and drank a lot of Jagermeister.

John Bell: It wasn't unusual to hook up with other bands in an opening situation. By this point, we're really turning into original bands with covers instead of a cover band.

13

They're Playing Songs That Were Not of the Time

In September 1990, Phish released their second studio album, Lawn Boy, *on the indie label Absolute A Go Go Records. They were playing up and down the East Coast as much as possible, as well as extended runs in Colorado. Sue Drew, a young A&R representative who had signed They Might Be Giants, decided to check them out at the (now defunct) Marquee in New York City as the year was about to close.*

I used to see Phish's name in the *Village Voice.* They were playing at Wetlands and I was always curious. Then one day, the *CMJ,* which was the *College Music Journal* . . . I had a subscription at my office and the *CMJ* arrived. Their album, I think it was *Junta,* was on the cover . . . it was that or *Lawn Boy.* I thought, "Hmm, this is interesting. This is that band I keep seeing. Let me go pick up this album." So I went down to Tower Records, and I put it on and it was the strangest thing I had ever heard. Every few days, I might play it again and go, "This is really interesting." So I made it my business to check them out when they played live next, and I kept looking for a date at the Wetlands, but the next time they were playing was at a club called the Marquee on the west side of Manhattan. I went down there this particular night and as I approached, I just saw all these kids on the sidewalk, just loitering, hanging around. It was just unusual. And they were all a certain kind of kid: college, kind of hippie, some kind of preppie. I walked into the club, and I couldn't believe what I was seeing and hearing—it was just a scene that I had never seen before or experienced. The band comes on and starts playing. And the musicianship was outstanding. And I just thought, "Wow, there is definitely something here with these guys." They've got this scene. They've got these musical chops, and they're playing songs that were not of the time. Nirvana, indie-rock, was really big. And these guys were not that at all. And I'm always attracted to things that aren't like anything else. And so I watched the set, and I was just knocked out by how into it everyone in the crowd was. They were just fanatical.

After the show ended, I thought, "I've got to go find these people and tell them I'm here and I really loved the show and all this stuff." I went and found them and I had a nice little chat. I'm sure I gave them my card. And I'm sure they were like, "Yeah, this isn't at all what we're interested in right now . . . a major record label." So it was all very pleasant and I was very much impressed and I went home.

I started trying to find out where they were playing on tour. They were playing the Chance up in Poughkeepsie and I went up to Poughkeepsie. By this time, I think I had been in touch with John Paluska, who was managing them at the time. He said, "Well, why don't you come up to Vermont and see the guys?" I don't know if they were doing a gig or if I just went up there to take them to dinner. But regardless, I did go to the house. And I did sort of see them practice. And they told me their routine—how they got together every single day and had these musical games they would play and practice. We went to dinner . . . and we had a lovely dinner . . . the four of them, and me and John. And I said to them, "I really would be interested in signing you to Elektra."

My philosophy was always the fewer the A&R people were there, the more worthwhile the artist was. A&R people tended to flock together for these things that got hyped up, and eventually a bidding war, and then really nothing would ever happen. That's generally what happened. So I always avoided that.

But nobody else was interested. And I said to the guys, "Listen, when you're in New York next, come to the office. And let's just have you come see Elektra Records." They graciously did that. And Elektra Records had a secret weapon: our CD cabinet. Because we had a ton of promo CDs from artists past all the way to the present day. And it was really an exquisite roster of talent, right from the very inception of Elektra up until that point. Whenever you wanted to sign an artist, one thing you would do is say, "Oh, come to the CD cabinet and choose some CDs, whatever you'd like. And so we started negotiating a deal . . . and that was in '91.

The fact is this: Every artist is unique. Every artist will come with their unique needs and wants. And you never want to have a quota. At Elektra, at that time, we signed very few things. But everything we signed, we expected would have a certain trajectory and success. There were other labels, even in the Warner system, who had a different philosophy: It was sign anything and everything and let's see what sticks. The goal [at Elektra was] discriminate; sign only the best in every genre; and let's work it. The head of the company used to call them "million dollar bullets" because regardless of what the signing advance was, it costs a million dollars to market and promote an artist. So no, there was never any expectation. If a super talented artist came along, and I wanted to sign it, and I could convince my boss that this was a good thing to do, it got signed.

The trajectory generally was: The first album was an introductory album, it sort of introduced the artist to the world. The second album, you started to make inroads into better press, maybe some radio, getting a toehold into the culture. And by the third album, you were hoping that you'd have something on the radio. There was never any pressure, initially, it was just find something great and let's get it out there and see how it goes.

The head of A&R was this amazingly talented guy, Howard Thompson. He was British. And he had been in America for quite some time . . . but Phish would have never been an artist he would have been interested in signing, not in a million years. But he could see that I was enthusiastic, and I was a believer, and that the band was already on their own trajectory. They had already put out two independent records, which we were then going to release on Elektra. And then put the third one out, which was *A Picture of Nectar.* So he got the path the band was on, even though musically speaking, it really wasn't his thing.

You don't want an A&R staff that has similar tastes, right? And so it was convincing him, that "You may not like this music at all, and that's okay. But

I love it. And a lot of other people love it and more do every single day. So I think this is something we should do."

When the company finally saw the band at Roseland Ballroom, Howard came up to me and he's like, "I have a new favorite drummer. Jon Fishman is my favorite drummer." They got it. When you see them live, you get the musicality, and you get the uniqueness of this artist. The chairman of Elektra, Bob Krasnow, just had a grin on his face the whole concert. And when the band played "Take the A Train" . . . I mean, he just loved it. Shortly thereafter, he promoted me to vice president. Was I worthy of being a vice president at age thirty? I don't know. But he promoted me and I'm sure it was that Roseland concert that helped that happen.

It just went gangbusters from there. I introduced them to their agent, Chip Hooper, who really got it. Chip really understood what the potential was. And by the way, this was a band who absolutely did not want to do anything traditional in the record company marketing sphere. They didn't care about radio, they didn't really care about television, they didn't want to be on the cover of magazines, they just wanted to do their own thing, and grow this thing the way they did.

14

We All Had Bands and This Punk Sort of "Fuck You" Attitude

With Phish starting to take off in the Northeast by word of mouth and live tapes circulating constantly—more acts started up and were looking at Phish as the model of how to do things. At the same time, both Nirvana and Pearl Jam were about to break grunge into the mainstream, setting off an "alternative" counterculture that took over MTV and the radio, and kept flannel shirt makers in business for the foreseeable future. We now truck up to Buffalo, where moe. was starting to take shape.

Rob Derhak (Bass, vocals, moe.): Chuck and I met in the dorms at the University of Buffalo. And after about a year of becoming friends and playing around together, we found a drummer, who had ended up being the first drummer for moe. He had another friend who was a guitar player, and then we became Five Guys Named Moe. We were playing some parties—playing covers and some originals.

Ray Schwartz (Drums, moe.): We did a bunch of covers. We definitely played Elvis Costello, Joe Jackson, Steely Dan, R.E.M.

Al Schnier: There were Americana bands, world beat bands, ska bands, and everything in between . . . and bands that played a variety of those things. And everybody played with each other. There was a thriving music scene, with live music seven nights a week. Buffalo was a regular stop for most touring bands of all levels, whether they were at the club level, or at the stadium level. We're very close to the Canadian border, so there's this whole other influence of music that's coming in from Toronto at the time. I can't tell you how many times I saw the Barenaked Ladies before they had a song on the radio—they'd routinely play clubs in Buffalo.

Jon Topper (Manager, moe.): I was pretty active on campus and then slowly around Buffalo, promoting shows. I didn't mean to go into the music business . . . I actually wanted to go to school to get my library science degree, but I didn't get into the program. What I would do is I would open up the *Village Voice* and whoever was playing Wetlands, I would be like, "Alright, I gotta bring them to Buffalo." The very first band I ever promoted was Zen Tricksters. Then I did God Street Wine and Shockra.

Rob Derhak: We had a culture of bands around . . . it was sort of a punk attitude, but we're all friends and we hung out together. And we all had bands and this punk sort of "fuck you" attitude. But everybody had slightly different musical tastes. So we were playing gigs with a band influenced by The Replacements heavily and another by R.E.M. and then another one by Cream. We're all using our influences to rub off on each other. A lot of the jam bands were coming out of the New England area, and the New York area at the time, and they weren't even jam bands yet. They definitely had a feel that was a lot closer to something like '70s Grateful Dead, Allman Brothers, that kind of stuff. We sort of had that influence, but we were also a victim of being around these punks all the time. We just had this "What if it was more of a Chili Peppers thing where we jammed out, or The Minutemen."

Chuck Garvey (Guitar, vocals, moe.): We also liked Zappa and Steely Dan.

Rob Derhak: We could play better than the other guys.

Chuck Garvey: Really?

Rob Derhak: We could pull off a Zappa tune.

Alan Evans (Drums, Moon Boot Lover, Soulive): Funk, hardcore, metal, every style of blues. There were so many places to play in Buffalo.

Ray Schwartz: People thought Buffalo could be the next Seattle, in the sense that there might be some successful acts to come out of this primordial soup that was the music scene. You had people who were kind of punk, people who were into jazz, people who were alternative . . . it was a pretty eclectic mix.

Alan Evans: I used to go see the Goo Goo Dolls—back in the day, the Goo Goo Dolls were a hardcore band. Neal [Evans] and I went to this gig one time in a church . . . the rec room of a church—straight mosh pit. Cats were going crazy.

Rob Derhak: Al moved to Buffalo and I became friends with him because he was the boyfriend of a girl who was good friends with both Chuck and I. Al soon joined the band and we had a three-guitar army for a couple shows and then the other guy just sort of phased out. And we became moe. after that. We dropped the "Five Guys Named" and that's just what happened.

Ray Schwartz: I had a friend who was having a Halloween party. He probably just asked do we want to play the party. Dave [original guitarist] didn't want to do it. We had already been rehearsing and practicing, but still hadn't played anywhere. So it was just Rob, Chuck, and I playing this party.

Al Schnier: They started playing together the previous Halloween, and I actually heard a demo tape that they made. I remember hearing it and thinking, "I would love to be in a band like this someday." It was just funny and fun, and had all these other influences. And I thought, "This is great. I want to do something like this." And it was original and that was part of it, too. I don't think I was in Buffalo for two weeks before we started playing music together. It was fantastic. They had a house party coming up, because that was about the extent of the gigs they did at that point. Their other guitarist couldn't make the gig and they knew that I played music and we talked about jamming at some point and they were like, "Hey, do you want to do this house party with us?" They gave me a list of songs and a couple of cassettes. This was maybe on a Tuesday. And by Friday, I learned all ten songs, which I think really impressed them. I don't think we played four songs before the police came and shut down the party.

Rob Derhak: Jamming—all we wanted to do was play together and write songs and go up in an attic, drink as much beer, and smoke as much weed as we could.

Chuck Garvey: Piels.

Rob Derhak: Yeah, drink Piels and get sick eating old wings. I didn't get much joy from doing anything else besides looking forward to every day when we were just going to get together and jam. Like, I didn't give a shit about anything else.

Chuck Garvey: When we started writing a lot of songs with Al it was more like we put our heads down.

Rob Derhak: We got a few months under our belt of just jamming. And then we realized we might have something pretty good. All we wanted to do was keep writing music and play music and book more gigs. At first, we were booking, hustling, making our own posters, going into Kinko's and getting copies made, and people were taping them to the lampposts at every place we could. Eventually we got our friend Jon Topper, who was booking shows around at school, who had a lot of connections . . . he started to book our band.

Jon Topper: I split the booking duties with Al and then took it all over.

Al Schnier: Everything we all did had that very DIY attitude to it. And every band we were friends with certainly had the same thing. We're all making our own flyers. We're all promoting our own shows. We're all putting out our own recordings. We're all collaborating.

Rob Derhak: Part of the jams came from us just searching for our sound, honestly. Some of the angular stuff is kind of my fault, because of the lack of musical training I had. I'm like, "Why don't we just go do this? And this!" And a normal musician would just be like, "No, that doesn't make any fucking sense. You can't do that." We would just figure out how it worked.

Alan Evans: People were making a living playing music in Buffalo. You could go to Rochester, Syracuse, kind of cruise out.

Ray Schwartz: We played the Essex Street Pub a whole bunch. Broadway Joe's was another one—that was right by the college, one of the UB campuses. There were other ones like the Continental, Nietzsche's was another one, the Ellen Terry Theater was kind of an art thing. Not only was it a music scene, but it was an art scene.

Al Schnier: The Essex Street Pub comfortably could hold about seventy-five people. So on a good night, if we had a hundred or more people in there, we played our asses off, and played a four-hour show . . . those nights just felt so good. You could almost be—standing in the corner of the barroom, you could almost reach the bar and get a pitcher of beer. That's how small the room was.

Rob Derhak: Everything was fair game. We stretched a lot of our songs, because we wanted to have longer shows. We were trying to play in bars all over the state and beyond. We were fortunate enough to go to a state school and some of us had aid, some didn't, and we didn't have any "walking around money," but we had an attic or a basement where we could just do this shit.

Chuck Garvey: And we had a lot of time. We didn't sound like other bands. We would listen to music but not while we had our instruments. We didn't want to sound like anything else except ourselves.

Jon Topper: Later on, when Chip Hooper became our agent, I'd be like, "Can we just fill a college gig and get some money?" and he would be like, "Dude, you guys aren't cool enough for the colleges."

Ray Schwartz: We played a show in Oneonta because there's a SUNY. We slept on someone's floor, you know, played some party. One of the marketing terms that we would evoke would be "everything but the kitchen sink music." We felt like we could just pull anything from anywhere. You just had to like it, and it didn't matter. And the thing was it wasn't just across songs. It was within songs.

Alan Evans: Managers would always tell us to just leave the Northeast. But you didn't have to. You could literally be a working band and just play in the Northeast and build that with the help of the tapers because people were always traveling. Word starts to spread.

Jon Topper: The one thing that guys would always say is college gigs used to suck. If you played in a dorm setting or something, the kids would come down, listen to you for two minutes, and then leave. You only had a couple fans there.

Al Schnier: We were always scheming on how to expand our audience. So you're always modeling what you do after the bands that are already doing it. That might have been our immediate peers, like the Ominous Seapods, or Moon Boot Lover, or the bands who came before us and were really successful, like God Street Wine, Phish, or the Spin Doctors. Bands who were now touring and playing to rooms of five or six hundred people. We would look at that stuff all the time. We would look at their mailers, look at their tour dates, look at all of those things and see if there was a way that we could follow in their footsteps.

Over in Burlington around the same time, the Phish scene was certainly palpable; two guys met at the University of Vermont and formed what would become Strangefolk, a more roots-oriented rock act with pop tinges.

Reid Genauer (Rhythm guitar, vocals, Strangefolk): We started as a duo—two words: Strange Folk. To be fair, we sorta sucked when we started.

Jon Trafton (Guitar, vocals, Strangefolk): I went to UVM and I was already into Phish by the time I decided that's where I wanted to go. And they were part of the reason why I even wanted to go there. I had friends that were there, and tapes. And they're this kind of underground bar band that was just mindblowing.

Reid Genauer: More or less, I went to college to start a band. We drove into Burlington and before my mom could even find a spot, I jumped out of the car because there was a reggae band playing on Church Street. Burlington had an unusual density given its isolation. That probably had to do with Phish, but I didn't know who Phish was. I just knew there was a music scene. I didn't know the difference between Phish and Fishbone.

Jon Trafton: Burlington's scene was more of the popular times—what was on the radio like Nirvana, Pearl Jam. Grunge was definitely the big rock sound. I don't recall there being any like grungy bands in Burlington at the time, especially in 1990. But there was definitely a punky, indie vibe. A lot of bands that fit the vibe of the Velvet Underground. There was a hippie element, but also kind of an alt element. But it wasn't necessarily one thing. There was an edge to it.

Luke Smith (Drums, Strangefolk): There were so many bands in Burlington and around Burlington, so many local bands playing all the time. And of course, Phish was always in the air and in the consciousness of any musician in Burlington, whether they wanted to admit it or not.

Reid Genauer: There were a bunch of us in the quad at the University of Vermont, in circles. I locked on to Jon immediately . . . he was just literally the most aligned aesthetically. We got a gig at a place called the Middle Earth, which was in Winooski. It's just over the hill. And it was every Wednesday and I was putting vocals and guitar through my Roland amp. Each Wednesday, more people started coming. It was free beer, which at the time felt like you'd won the lottery. I mean, it's called Middle Earth. There were guys that were just slightly older than us, early twenties, that just graduated.

By the end of the summer, it was a thing. And then school started. And we got a gig opening for Acoustic Junction. We played a gig at a place called City Market. You could get any sandwich with sprouts on it—that kind of place. He had acoustic music, as a background thing. I went down to the owner and was like, "Hey, would it be cool if me and my buddy played?" He had no idea what he's getting into. We promoted around school. The place probably fit maybe a hundred people . . . probably more like seventy-five. And it was wall-to-wall. We drank every beer in that little cooler. All the smoothies were still there. It went from there and then we decided we wanted to be a band.

Our drummer Luke Smith was in a fraternity and I knew a bunch of the guys because I'd go play pool on a Sunday afternoon or something. But it was just never my trip to be in a fraternity . . . I don't do cliques very well. But they let us play and I think it was right before school started, in the parking lot there. We played and we got the reaction and the sound man recorded it on a cassette. And I'll never forget getting into the car with Luke Smith—he had a little red Volkswagen Rabbit that you could see the ground move because there were holes in it. He popped it in his tape deck, and it was like, "Holy shit. We're a band!" It was the first moment it coalesced.

Luke Smith: I met Reid the first week of school, freshman year. We were living in the freshman dorms on the main campus at UVM. I had some congas with me in my room and he was playing guitar outside one day. And that's how I met him. We did some playing in the dorms and outside of the dorms our freshman year. I was trying to play lacrosse at UVM. And I was pretty well engaged with that a lot of the time. I'd grown up playing drums and playing music. So I had that foundation of music. Reid passed me a tape; I was like, "Oh my god. I don't know who this guy is on guitar, but this is what I want to do now for sure." I hung up lacrosse pursuits and really turned my attention to playing drums seriously. I played a little bit in high school, but most of my music experience was centered around going to see the Grateful Dead.

Jon Trafton: We did a lot of cold-calling, and I gotta credit Reid with that.

Luke Smith: Reid was absolutely the guy making those calls. He was the business guy.

Jon Trafton: There was a musician's guide, I think through the *Boston Phoenix*—a list of venues and the number to call for booking and where to send your stuff. We'd just start local, and we go over to New Hampshire, down to Connecticut. An early first goal of ours was to play college towns, figuring that's where our people are gonna be.

Luke Smith: Basically, I just badgered Reid. "Come on, man. I want to play with you guys. I want to play with you guys!" And I every time I'd see him around campus, I'd say, "Let's do it. Let's set it up."

Reid Genauer: Pretty quickly, we realized that we had an audience that would see us wherever we went. So I walked into the Metronome first; Anne Rothwell owned it. And she was skeptical. And I was like, "Believe me, it's gonna work." And I do think it was something like two bucks or five bucks. Jon actually drew the posters. I Xeroxed them and put them up around school and town. And we sold it out. It was wall-to-wall; she couldn't believe it. We started getting gigs around town. And I wasn't doing it for the money. I was doing it for the love of it.

Luke Smith: I had been taking a percussion ensemble class and so I had a connection there. I was able to gain access to the main ballroom upstairs in the Southwick Music Building at UVM. You could access the drum set, which was downstairs—so I had to go back and forth on the far end of this ballroom to get the drum set up in pieces. I was doing this twenty or thirty minutes before I was supposed to meet with Jon and Reid. I had never met Jon in person; I just knew him through what I had heard on the tape. While I was on one of these trips down to get another piece of the drum set—I came up and could see there was some commotion going on in the far end. It turns out, these two kids were breaking in and stealing the stereo out of this big, locked cabinet on the far end of this ballroom that was UVM property. My adrenaline just totally kicked in because I was like, "This is my responsibility. This room is my responsibility." So, you know, all the stuff that's in here at this time is my responsibility and I can't believe these guys are doing this on my watch.

I dropped everything and was like, "Hey!" They went out the big doors at the top of Southwick and they were carrying components from this stereo. They're going out the front door and then they split. One guy goes to the left, the other guy goes to the right. He dropped whatever components he was carrying, and I was like, "Oh, I'm definitely getting you because you just broke whatever it is that I'm responsible for." So I chase this guy down, tackle him, and basically citizens arrested this guy. Made him come back, pick up the stereo parts, hook everything back up, make sure it all works. And while he was doing that, Jon and Reid arrived. So I was managing this near theft/apprehension situation while I was first playing with Jon and Reid. The kid comes over and he's like, "Okay, it's all wired in, and I think it works."

"Okay, well, you gotta go get the other guy."

"I don't know where he went."

"Well, you gotta go get him and make sure we get everything back in here. Give me your shoes." So he gives me shoes. This is in between songs. And I think Jon was totally oblivious still. And I didn't want to interrupt what was happening. I was trying to get the gig!

Jon Trafton: I think Reid and I met up and walked over together and when we entered the ballroom, there was Luke with the culprits, who looked very scared and remorseful.

Luke Smith: He comes back with the other dude and they hook everything back up while we're playing. We were playing "Alaska" and we took it out on a big ride—like a twenty-minute ride. And these two would-be thieves pulled up chairs. And they're listening and enjoying the first show that I played with Strangefolk.

Jon Trafton: He was cool to the kids and let them go but not before giving them a serious grilling.

Brett Fairbrother (Manager, Strangefolk): I was going to college in southern Maine, at the University of New England. The original Strangefolk was at my college. I brought them to the Hang. And they played as the duo. Packed room. That also planted the seeds for the early fan base.

Reid Genauer: The conviction had a lot to do with it. We played shitty coffeehouses—school-sponsored coffeehouses at Slade Hall, where Phish actually played one of their first gigs in the basement. I saw God Street Wine play in the basement of Slade Hall. It was just dawning on me that music of that caliber could be played at any scale.

15

The Gossip on This Band Was Like Wildfire

Down in Charlottesville, Virginia, the scene was percolating with a five-piece, all from different musical backgrounds. The Dave Matthews Band did something revolutionary out of the gate: With a fierce live show, they upped the ante by including a violinist and saxophonist into their repertoire from day one. The resulting effort became hard to define . . . and quickly gripped the mid-Atlantic.

Chris Bowman: The music scene in Charlottesville pre–Dave Matthews was more of a hotshot blues scene. The Charlottesville music scene was based around Trax. Before Trax, there was the Mineshaft Cellar. Bands like Blue Sparks From Hell, or New Grass Revival, they would come in and play the C & O. New Potato Caboose and Indecision would play The Mineshaft. Trax, at that point, was more like a metal bar. Coran [Capshaw] took Trax over in '88, '89. It was very exciting because it was a bigger room—it had larger production potential.

Dave Matthews (Guitar, vocals, Dave Matthews Band): When I moved there in the mid-'80s, it felt like such an enlightened space. There was so much great art being made there, and so many different kinds of people all getting along—students and musicians. I was completely seduced by Charlottesville.

Chris Bowman: Coran was the person who took the greatest advantage of it—he saw the big picture. He recognized the fact that the first place they were going to make real money was going to be in fraternities. And if they were good, they could crush it at the club.

Dave Matthews: The first gig we had, that we ever played, was on Earth Day. We kept getting pushed forward, 'cause nobody knew who we were, and they kept pushing us. And we ended up being the last band and there was only two hundred people there, compared to at the beginning of the day when there was a thousand . . . which is a hell of a lot to have on the downtown mall of Charlottesville, Virginia. But when we played, everybody danced. Of the two hundred people that were left, every single one of them was dancing and they'd never heard us before. By the end of it, they were all dancing. That's sort of the, that's one of the biggest moments, even though it was so early on. That was really surprising to all of us, 'cause none of us expected that to happen. None of us expected people to get up and start dancing and start celebrating around what we were doing.

John Alagía (Producer, *Remember Two Things*): I'd never seen that combination of a fiddle and a saxophone and Dave—his crazy guitar. There's almost a King Crimson guitar, but it was African. It was a whole new thing. I think I was really intimidated by how unique they were.

Dave Matthews: We all come from different musical backgrounds . . . the result is a big stew.

Chris Bowman: The Charlottesville music scene was based around Trax. Bigger bands would come in and play that room. There was a little bit of a jam band scene. The music scene was fraternity based as well. That's where the guaranteed money was.

Bruce Flohr (Senior Vice President of A&R, RCA Records): As I got into my career, in 1991, I moved into a marketing job, where my job was to market bands and also find new talent. An intern walked into my office, and he had two cassette tapes. One was Big Head Todd and the Monsters, and one was Dave Matthews. And I listened to both and I immediately gravitated to Dave Matthews. I fly to Charlottesville . . . this is in 1992. I walk into the club thinking I'm going to see a guy on a stool on a guitar and I see four hundred college kids losing their fucking mind to a band that was part Rush meets Return to Forever and I didn't know what the fuck to make of it.

Jane Tower (Operations Manager, Dave Matthews Band): Trax was absolutely the place to be. It'd be packed every single Tuesday.

Doug Derryberry (Engineer, *Recently* EP; Mixer, *Live at Red Rocks*): Every Tuesday, they would have six or seven hundred people in Trax. Every Wednesday, they would have five hundred, six hundred, seven hundred people in Flood Zone (in Richmond). And the weekend, they would be playing frat parties or clubs in other towns because the gossip on this band was just like wildfire. It was out of control. Everywhere you went, college kids and prep school kids had their Dave Matthews bootleg tapes.

Jane Tower: I worked with Coran my last year and I remember riding shotgun from Charlottesville to Richmond, because Dave Matthews would play every Tuesday night at Trax and Wednesday night at the Flood Zone. I'd be doing my homework in the front seat.

Chris Bowman: Summer '92, Dave Matthews was starting to blow up. Coran and I were friends with the Blues Traveler guys—and Rich Vink, their sound guy, would come and stay with us, and he loved the Dave Matthews Band. I remember giving Rich the tape from May 6, '92, at Trax and have him play that recording [during set break]. We stood back and watched the crowd—you could see the crowd rushing over to their friends, pointing to the speakers, and saying, "Yeah, this is the guy Dave Matthews I've been telling you all about."

John Alagía: The very first moment I was at the Bayou, looking at that band, I felt like, "How can I record it?"

Jane Tower: Every Tuesday, the band would come and have a team meeting before the shows.

Doug Derryberry: Carter and the band used that "Ants Marching" beginning drum schtick for years. They would start their show before they were a known entity with that backbeat. Nobody knew it was a backbeat. People usually thought it was like a line check. It sounds like a line check, they're checking the snare, and then all of a sudden, the band comes in. And then as you know, over the years, it became a three-, four-, five-minute noodlefest before they even got to the song. Everywhere they went, where they weren't known, they could pull that stick out and use it to great effect. You're like "What the fuck is this?"

Warren Haynes: There was a small festival on the side of this mountain in Virginia. And it was the Freddy Jones Band and my band and Dave Matthews Band and Widespread Panic. Widespread Panic was headlining and I remember I knew *of* the Dave Matthews Band but at that time, they hadn't really ventured out of Virginia that much . . . but were apparently already really big in Virginia. The rest of the world didn't realize to what extent. And so I was thinking, "Well, why am I going on before the Dave Matthews Band?" And my manager said, "Oh, they're really big in Virginia." So Freddy Jones Band played, and there were a handful of people. And then my band played, and there were a few more people, but still a fairly small crowd. And then as soon as my band finished, the mountainside was just covered with people.

> *For the band's debut album,* Remember Two Things, *they took an unconventional approach: They just mixed live tracks with two studio cuts and released it on their own Bama Rags Records. It was also notable at the time for incorporating a "3-D art" cover—if you stared at the image long enough, you should've been able to see a new image emerge.*

Doug Derryberry: They would come to our studio and often spend the night. We'd have meals together and get a chance to hang a little bit. The one who came the most was Dave, but also Boyd came a couple of times, Carter came a couple of times, Leroi came a couple of times—just to patch up stuff that really wasn't going to fly on the record.

John Alagía: Dave was always coming to my house, my little recording studio. It's called Rutabaga Studios. We just started sketching out ideas—he'd come up and you just start playing in front of a microphone. We carried on doing that in Arlington, Virginia, at my house, and his house in Charlottesville for years. June of '93, I was down at Trax with Dave and Coran, his manager. They took me out to the parking lot and said, "Hey, we want you to go on the road with us and make a live record." We packed up in my little Bronco or Blazer and just started driving around the country recording shows on multitrack. We did some shows at Trax, some at the Flood Zone, Nantucket, New York City. I think Providence. It was a slew of shows. And then I came home and just started going through all the recordings.

Doug Derryberry: We were unofficially discouraged from sharing our recordings. [Soundman Jeff] Bagby was very generous about patching into the mixing desk. And maybe a time or two somebody at the studio on the sly may have duplicated something. But it was not our habit or our practice. It was understood between Coran and Dave and John that John was trying to get them to do a record with him. And, you know, there were quite a few people that would have liked to have done a record with them.

John Alagía: I was so shy and nervous . . . all I wanted to do is just try to capture the band live. Dave was, I think, a little reluctant to have his band recorded at such an early time. But it was just remarkable. Jeff Bagby was always recording the band from the soundboard and house board mixes could have been released.

Dave Matthews: There was not a lot of saxophone and violin and acoustic guitar happening in rock and roll at the time—or now. But this was pre–Hootie and the Blowfish even. We didn't fit in at all with what record companies might be looking for.

Bruce Flohr: It just started baking into my soul that this was special. I spent seven months with my coworker Pete Robinson, traveling up and down the eastern seaboard, sometimes in the band's red van that they traveled in, trying to get them to sign to RCA Records, which they had no interest in signing with. They could give two shits. One of the reasons why I think they ended up at RCA is I think they simply felt sorry for us. We couldn't break a plate at the time. We had come off the *Dirty Dancing* soundtrack, we were in leadership upheaval, we just didn't have any credibility in the rock space at all. And Epic Records, I know, was looking at them at the time. I remember hearing that Epic didn't want to sign them because they didn't like the way the band dressed. If you go back and look at the early photos of the band, there is a slew of wardrobe on that stage, from checkered pants and striped shirts to leather jackets with tassels. You gotta remember during this time that we're pursuing the Dave Matthews Band, the radio has Nirvana, Pearl Jam, Smashing Pumpkins, Soundgarden, Alice in Chains. And here we are signing a band that is led by an acoustic guitar that has a violin and a saxophone as some of the main components.

Dave Matthews: We just played . . . that's all we did. We had a sideways plan to get signed, but we never really focused on it.

16

But Do You Really Want to Be a Rock and Roll Hotel?

Chan Kinchla: Bill Graham, Dave Graham, and his friend Tom Gruber thought it would be fun to start this summer ranch where they could throw concerts [in the summer of '91]. And it was just run by a bunch of partying twenty-year-olds with some of Bill Graham's money.

John Popper: David Graham went to this upstate place with some friends and it was a ranch, but all the horses looked very abused. I think they were left and abandoned on the ranch when the guy bought it. He was in the process of restoring the horses and some weird thing was in the ground because a bunch of trees—you could punch through 'em and they were dust. They were fake trees almost, chalk trees. Dave's vision was: "We build a stage, people will come, we build a resort, people will come." It's upstate New York. The perfect getaway. And you know, to his credit, he did it. They did some shows there. But these are young kids not knowing what they're doing. But I always was convinced there was some sort of poisoning in the sediment because all the trees were dead.

David Graham: It was a thing that had to happen. It created the authenticity of the jam band scene.

Ken "Ranch Man" Hoff (Owner, Arrowhead Ranch): It was a little force to be reckoned with. I was twenty, my wife was nineteen. We had the same stage that they used for Paul Simon in Central Park. We had a bar there even before Bill Graham, although we didn't sell any alcohol. So we never had any police come in—there was always a private party. You'd have all these musicians come up from New York, in between all these other gigs they'd have at Wetlands and other bigger shows. And they'd come to Arrowhead to come down from everything. Chill out in the Catskills, eat some good food, and smoke some good weed.

Steve Eichner: Arrowhead was the next step—a growing-up step. We were all working towards the same goal, which was the music, and our scene and our art and our craft. So Tom and Dave Graham and Billy Cohen, they were all into being into the music business end of it. And I was into the photography part of it. And the bands were into the music part of it. And Kenny, he was into the building the venue part of it. But we were all wearing many hats. I was doing the overnights on the stage with security. And I was parking cars. And I was doing photography and moving equipment and helping the band set up. We were the new Merry Pranksters in a way—we read about the '60s and we all wished we lived there. So we transformed it to the '90s. And it was still so innocent—it was still before the internet and before cell phones and before email.

Ken "Ranch Man" Hoff: Michael Ahern worked with Bill Graham at the Fillmore. He was Bill Graham's right-hand man—like in the embassy of BGP [Bill Graham Presents], Michael was one of the main lieutenant generals. So he and Bill fly out in the helicopter and land in the middle of my horse field. Now I knew he was coming. And I had done a little homework, and I'm like, I'm a nice Jewish kid. This is a nice Jewish elder man coming to see me. I'm getting bagels. So we went down to New York City in our ranch van, our horse hay van, to Zabar's to get bagels and nova, whitefish, different salmon, everything. And we put out a huge spread for Bill's coming! And Bill comes and we show him the whole ranch and he's just smiling. And he is looking at me and my wife the whole time. He's not saying much. I'm trying not to get too excited, but I'm like creaming in my jeans at this point—this is a big deal for me. And I'm showing him my house and my home and my property and my business and my life. I'm showing him everything. And Bill is like, "I love this place. You guys, you and your wife remind me of me and Bonnie, when we bought the ice-skating room," meaning the Fillmore. And he says, "So you got this little hotel and you've got this little good ranch. And this is really kitschy. But do you really want to be a rock and roll hotel?" I hadn't really got to that point—I just wanted to do some concerts. I wasn't thinking about changing the whole dynamic of the Arrowhead Ranch business.

I go, "Well, yeah."

"Do you know what that entails?"

I said, "I kind of think I get the gist of it."

"Alright, get your crew together. Meet me out on the front lawn. We're playing touch football."

And Bill Graham takes off his T-shirt and he shows me his scars. He just had an operation for gallbladder removal.

"I want to do this with you. What do you want to do?"

I said, "What do I want to do? I want to put on shows! I want to do concerts! Let's do big shows here. Why not? We have the space."

He's like, "Oh, no, we just built Shoreline Amphitheatre a few years back—that was on a garbage dump. This is going to be great."

The whole thing is just like a dream sequence.

Tom Gruber: Bill Graham's first job was being the person that clears the tables at a Jewish resort only about fifteen minutes away from [Arrowhead Ranch]. The proposal for Arrowhead had the cost of building the venue amortized over thirty years. I'm not sure if you've heard that term before, but it means paying it out or booking it over thirty years. So if it costs $200,000 or $300,000 to build, there'd be a $10,000 cost for thirty years. He wouldn't look like he was losing money in the first year.

Ken "Ranch Man" Hoff: He grew up in Hell's Kitchen in New York and would come to the Catskills and be a busboy at the hotel that was ten minutes down the street from my house. And he took me and my wife to the hotel and brought us into the kitchen. When you walked into the kitchen, the old guys, who were still alive, who still worked at this place, were like, "Billy! What are you doing here? It's nice to see you!"

Tom Gruber: I came to Bill with the proposal for the first-ever environmentally sound concert series. And I said, "Bill, the venue will partner." I partnered with the New York Public Interest Research Group, and they committed thirty volunteers for every festival to handle recycling. And I announced that there would be no trash, but before it happened, Bill Graham came to me. He took a red-eye and showed up at my door where I lived. And he said, holding the Arrowhead proposal, which says we'll have glass, paper, and plastic recycling centers. And Bill said to me, and I swear on my grandmother's soul—Bill said to me that he had a credible threat from the New Jersey and New York City based mafia against my life.

"I have received credible threats from the mob that they will take you out before they let me start doing trash-free events."

That would take away the mob's roots. Bill Graham would say things like, "You know, you live in Harlem. Somebody could crush your skull with a baseball bat and just walk away and they wouldn't even investigate it."

Steve Eichner: Even though Bill Graham was behind it, he wasn't there running it. He gave the power to all these college kids.

Ken "Ranch Man" Hoff: It was unorganized to a certain extent . . . it was like the Manson Family farm, without the violence.

Billy Cohen: We didn't have the budget to have a massive amount of security.

John Popper: I remember a huge table full of cash and luckily I wasn't responsible for it. I just walked through that room, but that was the thing—I walked through that room. Why am I in the accounting room? Just walking through there, you know, trying to get a joint with my samurai sword. You don't need me walking through the count room with just buckets of cash on the table. I'll bet you a few dollars went missing.

Chan Kinchla: I just walked by and was like, I have a feeling that if you're trying to pay people or something, you don't leave mountains of cash around. The thing about Arrowhead Ranch was it was an unmitigated disaster.

David Graham: The inmates were running the asylum.

Billy Cohen: The overnights, I ran. I mean, I was head of production, but I had to run the overnights because we had no staff. And the only way I could do it all was I tripped the entire time and I dosed friends of mine to stay up all night.

Ken "Ranch Man" Hoffman: Kids could bring kegs, they could bring bottles of liquid acid, pounds of mushrooms. I didn't care.

Chris Barron: I think I took a lot of mushrooms. And I think I was tripping on stage.

David Graham: You could just walk in really. Any Deadhead of their worth would be like, "Huh. Buy a ticket or just walk in over there . . ."

Tom Gruber: Every Phishhead started having Arrowhead soundboards, because we just released them.

Steve Eichner: I was on the radio, doing the overnight, and I was talking about weed. And somebody said to me, "You know, the state police are monitoring these channels. Don't talk about all this stuff on the radio."

Ken "Ranch Man" Hoff: The hotel was divided up into four buildings. And on the side of the street where that big stage was—behind the stage was a bunk house. Fifteen hotel rooms in it, five downstairs, ten upstairs. So that way it became a backstage hotel. One of the only things that we were down on there was nitrous. We hated it. So David hired the security company—their guys who did Jones Beach. Total goon security from the city would come up every weekend, the same security detail. And they'd confiscate the tanks from the campers, but they'd bring them to the production office where they'd duct tape the windows with plastic bags and seal the cracks under the doors. And they'd have parties there where they'd open all the tanks at once and everyone would just sit in that room and hot box. Constantly they were doing this. So people were passing out in the hallways. It was like a rite of passage.

Chris Barron: They had a beaver problem at Arrowhead Ranch.

Rich Vink: I ended up in the basement of the main house and there was a little jam session going on. And I ended up picking up a guitar and playing "Let Love Rule" with Lenny Kravitz for, I don't know, thirty minutes or something.

Steve Eichner: Lenny Kravitz came and he played bongos. He and Chan were dating the same girl, Serena. And she came up with Chan in the tour bus and wound up leaving with Lenny in a limo while Blues Traveler was on stage.

Cree McCree: I saw Serena, who was Chan's girlfriend, get in the car with him and drive off. I was like, "Oh shit man, that's harsh."

Chan Kinchla: Here's the funny thing: I had cheated on her. It was New York, we were all touring. She was traveling, modeling, whatever. Young twenty-one-year-old bullshit. But we kind of got back together. I think she got back together with me just so she could fuck me over. [*Laughs.*]

David Graham: As an experience, it was not terrific because it was a struggle financially. And it was a struggle logistically. I had to apologize to Phish because I couldn't even give them their guarantee.

Tom Gruber: We lost a small amount of money. And Bill was not used to losing money.

Billy Cohen: You could see what it could be. A lot of what has happened in the festival world is really connected. What happened with Arrowhead and what happened with H.O.R.D.E.—both of those things really came out of

Gruber/Graham getting them in motion. And that really came out of what we did on campus at Columbia.

Tom Gruber: We met with Ben and Jerry for breakfast and they said they wanted to underwrite the whole second season.

Ken "Ranch Man" Hoffman: My staff had to do all the cleanup and all the bull-shit and deal with everything. And it was just getting really bad. So I pick up the phone, I call Uncle Bill, and I say, "Bill, listen, I don't mean to complain. We're having a great time here. This is awesome. But we have an issue. We can't keep working with David and Tom. I mean, these guys are just like, blah, blah, blah. And I gave him a few instances of what was going on.

He said, "Kenny, let me stop you right there. Listen, you think that I spent this kind of money at your place, and I don't have people from my office watching what's going on there? They might be guests. They might be just coming to the concert. You don't even know who they are. I know what's going on up there. I know. I know what David's doing. And listen, rest assured you're not gonna have a problem with David. If he can't behave, I'll take him out of there so fast. You know what I got planned for next season?"

I said, "No, we haven't even got through the first season yet. What are you thinking?"

He says, "Maybe Santana, maybe the Allman Brothers. How about a Weir-Wasserman, maybe get Jerry Band."

I'm like, "Oh, yes, boss. Sure, whatever, Bill." He says he's going to talk to David and everything will be okay, because Bill's gonna wave his magic wand and everything will be fine. And I've accepted that. Bill flew out after that conversation again, and just sat with me and my wife in the horse field. Just us and him. And he was like, "Look, I'm so sorry that my son's behaving this way all over the board. I want you guys to know that you're part of my family. You're under my umbrella. And there's no way I'm going to let this thing just fall by the wayside because these kids can't behave." And I was in tears, my wife's crying in his arms, and it was really fucking sad and touching and beautiful.

David Graham: I would never have done it again, just because it was a massive loss. And then of course, my dad died the following October. So that was the end of my East Coast, the end of Music Unlimited. I was living their lifestyle. And that can't work. So, you know, we parted ways.

John Popper: Certainly he had his times of youthful excess. But we all kind of did. I think for him, it got to be a particular problem.

Kenny "Ranch Man" Hoff: Five days later I get a phone call. We were sponsoring the *Grateful Dead Hour* on WNEW FM in New York City.

"Brought to you by your friends at the Arrowhead Ranch. Don't forget, call 1–800–36 RANCH for all your ranching needs!"

And Mario Martinez, the DJ, he would call us at the beginning of the show and we'd always be like, "Yeah Marty, this weekend we have Solar Circus and *Relix* Records is doing a party," and we'd promote on the radio with Marty. Five days after this whole shit went down with Bill and this whole conversation with him and my wife and the crying and all that, Mario Martinez calls me out live on the air and says, "We got Kenny Hoff from Arrowhead Ranch on the phone. Kenny, do you have anything to say about today's announcement about the tragic death of Bill Graham over San Francisco?" I'm like, "What, are we on the air? Are we live? I got to hang up." And I hang up and I call out to the West Coast and all the numbers are fucking busy. I have every number that you can have for BGP at this point, including Bill's personal number. Everything's busy. There's no answer anywhere. It's just nothing. So that was the end for Bill. The next day, I got a phone call from David. And he was on a plane on his way to San Francisco to the funeral to deal with his dad and he said, "I can't believe you fucking ratted me out to my dad. And you told my dad that I was a junkie? Fuck you, fuck your ranch, fuck your wife. Fuck all your shit. I want to have nothing to do with you, man. You're a fucking asshole," and hung up the phone.

David Graham: That did not happen. The last person I would call after my father died is Ken Hoff. I mean, my dad just died. I think I'd have bigger fish to fry.

17

We Were All Destroyed

Dave Frey: Bill died on the 25th of October, 1991.

David Graham: I was in his bed, in his apartment, on 64th and Madison. The then president of the company called and said, "Well, I'll be honest with you. Dad's plane is missing, and we found a bunch of wreckage, and it looks like the plane."

So I said, "He's dead, right?"

And he goes, "Yeah."

Dean Budnick: The sad truth of Arrowhead is they have that one amazing summer and then he dies in the helicopter crash and his business sort of falls apart.

John Popper: Bill was the force that was getting us access. A record label didn't really listen to us about what we thought should be the single. But when Bill told them what the single was, they'd be like, "Oh, of course." So we had somebody who was protecting us from all the stuff we didn't know because we were young. And we didn't even know how to give our input. It always sounded like a question with us, but he knew how to make a statement out of something and say, "No, this should be the single."

Chan Kinchla: We were playing a gig at Colby College. We were on the tour bus, just waking up and I remember John coming up and saying, "Bill's dead."

Billy Cohen: I was working for David Graham in New York at the time. I was supposed to be going to a wedding and I had been at the bachelor party the night before.

John Popper: We were all destroyed. Dave, more than the rest of us. It was so sudden, and he didn't want to stop yet. We were just starting out with him . . . we'd gone through our growing pains.

Rich Vink: When he died, he was the first death that we all processed together.

Cree McCree: I saw all the band (except Brendan) the night before Halloween, in the Wetlands family corner. Bobby was hit really hard, 'cause he, too, lost his dad and he wanted deeply to communicate to David Graham the signposts of grief he himself followed.

Billy Cohen: We got out in San Francisco for the funeral, which was a traditional Jewish funeral within three days.

Dean Budnick: After the fall of '91, people would still come in occasionally and do some shows at Arrowhead . . . but the promise of '91 sort of fell by the wayside as a result of that relationship.

Billy Cohen: When he died, basically everything changed in a whole lot of settings.

18

An Oasis for All These Artists to Come and Have a Family

By early 1992, Phish, Widespread Panic, God Street Wine, and Blues Traveler had played all over Colorado for years, building up a fan base through the various ski towns and their bars, and graduating to college campuses. It only made sense for Boulder to open its own version of what was happening back east with the Wetlands, Trax, the Georgia Theatre, and Metronome.

Jon O'Leary (Co-founder, Fox Theatre; Front-of-House Engineer, The String Cheese Incident): I met Don Strasburg at a friend's house in Boulder, and that was probably somewhere around '90. We were talking about how much interest we had in music and stuff in the area, and we were like, "Well, we should put a thing together . . . grab some coolers full of beer and make a little place." We were thinking about doing a little warehouse outside, with nothing in it, basically. That started our journey towards the Fox Theatre . . . we wanted to do something, we hadn't figured out how to do it yet.

Don Strasburg (Co-founder, Fox Theatre): I came to that place because I was a Deadhead, as were most of my friends . . . all of us came of age, more or less, between '82 and '86.

Jon O'Leary: He came from Colorado College, where he was a student promoter.

Don Strasburg: There was this subculture that was really evolving. And now we're all getting a little older, going to college, and I'm in Colorado, but there's a diaspora of these people who were in high school across the country . . . and now these colleges are breeding grounds for this community. So Phish comes to Colorado, right? At this point, Colorado was known as a pretty hip place. It wasn't known as a hippie place . . . and suddenly there's this community in Boulder that starts becoming really strong and vibrant.

Jon O' Leary: Eventually, we met up with Dickie Sidman—he was the production manager for the Boulder Theater and had just left. We started talking about doing this band thing . . . with his years of experience, he was a good person to get together with and talk about how we can make this happen. And so we started looking at several different places; we looked at places in malls, and other venues. Don, he ended up walking into the Hill in Boulder and we were actually ready to have this place sign with us. And at the very last second, our ability to get that place fell through. So then we ended up going to the old Fox Theatre, which was a movie theater at that point, and asked the guy if we could talk to them about taking over when they were done. So then we started pushing on that, and then we had to get the money . . . so we started asking a bunch of people that we knew to see if we could come up with some money.

Cheryl Liguori: Cash flow is always a challenge. It was expensive to build. And there was debt service. But it was really getting agents to sell really great acts and getting in that rotation: This is *the* place you have to play when you come through Colorado.

Jon O'Leary: To go from making a place where you start with beers in a cooler, to actually having to rip out a theater and make bars and build the whole place . . . that became the intensity. I did all that. I was the guy who got the general manager and the architect and made the plans for the whole inside venue, the stage and all that stuff. My idea was to come up with a plan to make the venue into a place where you can see from every point . . . kind of like an amphitheater type of vibe.

Tye North (Bass, Leftover Salmon 1993–2000): Around the time I moved to Boulder, there was a sampler CD of the twelve major bands in Boulder. Half of them toured a bunch and at least half of them could sum up the Fox.

Cheryl Liguori: The Boulder Theater, at that time, wasn't as fan-friendly. The Fox was built as a place for the fans.

Jamie Janover (Musician): There's a complex web of people and organizations surrounding the evolution of the management of the Fox and the Boulder Theater. There was competition at that time and pretty wide separation, I would say, between those venues. Sometimes they were competing for the same thing . . . Boulder Theater, still, is known for doing world music, jazz, wedding conventions, corporate parties, whereas the Fox was designed from the ground up to be a super-intimate music venue.

Keller Williams (Musician): The Fox was probably the best sounding room in the country for that capacity.

Don Strasburg: We had our own temple. And we could start bringing bands to the temple.

Dave Watts (Co-founder, Shockra; Drums, The Motet): He had a vision for the Fox Theatre, and what kind of music it could support and grow.

Jon O'Leary: March 6 of '92 was the actual day that we started—with The Meters.

Don Strasburg: The Fox became this island in the middle of the country where it was an oasis for all these artists to come and have a family. Suddenly this entire ecosystem could route [a tour].

Dave Watts: We were the second touring act to play the Fox . . . probably four or five days after they opened. And we did a free show there; it was our first time through Colorado. Just getting to the venue and having the sound guys jump out the back door and be like, "Hey, can we help you with your stuff? Welcome to the Fox!" They were so chipper and happy. And we were confused . . . we were so used to that East Coast "everybody hates their job" kinda vibe.

Jon O'Leary: We got to know Phish pretty good. They had a big show in Boulder, at Balch Fieldhouse. During the set break we talked the band into taking their day off and coming to the Fox Theatre and they were like, "Oh my god, it's not really us, it's the crew." So we had to talk them into doing it. They did that show on the next day. I think they'd just done like three or four thousand people at Balch Fieldhouse. So they were way too big at that point in Colorado.

Cheryl Liguori: I didn't move to Colorado to specifically work at the Fox, but I got sucked in. I started a couple months before they opened just to do some marketing and PR for them. And then I left for a few months. And then Don asked me if I would come back as general manager.

Jon O'Leary: I put a whole shitload of emphasis on making it sound good by putting up acoustic spray everywhere, which costs a whole bunch of money, and then we put curtains everywhere. And we just deadened the sound because it really needed it.

Cheryl Liguori: With a business in its infancy, there's a lot that you have to pay attention to all the time. The money was the biggest thing: How do you spend what you have wisely so that the lights are on, the taxes are paid, and payroll is paid . . . all those things that can get your business into trouble. When the Fox first started, it was a 21+ club. The push [to make it 18+] really started coming from the bands—it was about maximizing their fans and getting their fans in to see them.

Don Strasburg: We were selling a lot of fucking tickets. It was a fucking party. We didn't really know how fucking good it was . . . but we knew goddamn well it was the fucking best.

19

If I Can Drink More Tequila Shots than You, We're Going to Push the Spin Doctors

The Spin Doctors released their debut album Pocket Full of Kryptonite *on August 20, 1991. Within less than two months from that day, grunge and "alternative" would take hold of the country: Pearl Jam released their debut* Ten, *Nirvana released* Nevermind, *the Red Hot Chili Peppers released* Blood Sugar Sex Magik, *and Soundgarden released* Badmotorfinger. *Jams, these were not. The Spin Doctors soldiered on, and almost went unnoticed.*

Eric Schenkman: It seems like when you hear "Two Princes" . . . it's a big song. It seems like we just blew up. But actually we didn't blow up. There was a lot to get there.

Chris Barron: There was not a lot of marketing. We were labelmates with Pearl Jam. Back then, there were these little local papers, these local rags. And there'd be a full-page ad for Pearl Jam's record and a full-page ad for their gig. And nothing for Spin Doctors. They really just sat on us.

Eric Schenkman: They were confused by us. We were kind of a side door.

David Sonenberg: As far as the record company was concerned, they didn't fit the mold of what was happening.

Aaron Comess: We were traveling around the country, in our van. And everywhere we went, we saw these huge Pearl Jam posters in the record store and hundreds of their records sitting there. We couldn't even find our record.

Chris Barron: We went out and just did a lot of hard touring. And they wanted us to come back and make another record. We're like, "No, we're gonna stay out here. And we believe in this record."

Aaron Comess: They just didn't really give a shit. About a year in, Epic Records wanted us to make a new record. They were like, this record's dead. We were in there, the band, our management, and we said, "Hey, we're out on the road, without any help. We're self-sufficient. We're paying our rent. We're not taking tour support, packing clubs around the country, and we've sold sixty thousand records," which at the time was pretty good, considering it was totally grassroots. And we said, "Why don't you put out 'Jimmy Olsen's Blues' or 'Two Princes' . . . fans really love these songs." And they were like "Nah, nah, nah, those aren't hits." It was really at the advice of our manager David Sonenberg . . . he saw similar things happen with Meatloaf years before. He was like, "You guys are doing really well. I think we just gotta go back on the road. I really believe that if you just go back out there and keep doing this, something's gonna give somewhere."

Peter Denenberg: And there was sort of a perfect storm.

Chris Barron: There was a guy named Jim McGuinn, who was a program director at a station in Vermont called WEQX. And he wrote some passionate letter to the label and was like, "You know, we did an in-store promotion for *Achtung Baby* and more people bought *Pocket Full of Kryptonite* during it. And there was a gig at this place in Albany, Bogie's, and it was twenty below and there were people around the block. He was like, "What the fuck are you guys doing?"

Aaron Comess: Jim McGuinn started playing "Little Miss Can't Be Wrong" and it went to number one on his radio.

David Sonenberg: Radio was important. So there was a formula for stuff to get on the radio.

Jim McGuinn (Program Director, WEQX, Manchester, Vermont): I was the program director and one of the DJs at WEQX, a funky radio station broadcasting from an old Victorian a block off the main drag in Manchester, Vermont, a small ski town about an hour's drive from Albany. We'd had a bit of success playing songs from Blues Traveler, and heard rumblings about this band from Burlington called Phish, but most of our playlist consisted of a combination of alt-rock like The Replacements and classic rock like the Stones. So Spin Doctors were kind of in that sweet spot. We were running commercials for their gig, and the music hook used in the spot was from "Big Fat Funky Booty," from the EP. Soon enough, we started getting calls and requests for the song in the middle of a commercial. That does *not* happen normally.

Chris Barron: One of the radio promo people [at Epic] challenged the president of promotions and the VP of the label to a tequila shot contest.

"If I can drink more tequila shots than you, we're going to push the Spin Doctors."

She drank like seventeen shots of tequila, and just drank these other two executives—superiors—under the table. If the wrong people don't give a shit, they toss you into the loss column, and let you wither on a vine. But if you've got a champion willing to drink a bottle of tequila for you, I guess you do okay.

Peter Denenberg: The head of promotion at Epic, his college-age son had a friend home from school. And he was trying to impress his son's friend by giving him free CDs of all the people they had on the current roster. And the kid was like, "Yeah, you know, I'm not really into any of these. But do you have any Spin Doctors?"

And the guy was like, "Well, who the hell are they?"

"They're on your label!"

So he went back to the office that Monday after that experience and it was popping on commercial radio. And they pushed the button to give the real push. You literally could sense a switch was flipped.

Jim McGuinn: Fast forward a couple months, and Epic is putting out the album, and knowing that about the song in the commercial, we decided, let's put this in rotation! Pretty sure we started with "Little Miss Can't Be Wrong," although by the end of the cycle we'd played five singles—"Two Princes," "Jimmy Olsen's Blues," "What Time Is It?" "How Could You Want Him," maybe even "More Than She Knows." The audience reaction was immediate. Requests, and maybe most interesting—local sales. The SoundScan system had only been around for a year or two, but I developed all these formulas to try to "index" or translate an artist's local sales compared to the national numbers to help us get a read on whether our audience was going out and buying a CD and if our airplay could be "proven" to be important to an artist's development. Our station was one of those left-of-center (despite being at 102.7 FM) outlets that played a lot of new music and had a smaller, but more passionate audience than the Top 40 or Classic Rock competition. So anytime we proved our value to labels and managers was great.

I think Epic expected them to tour and build a following slowly, and didn't see much potential in putting in the effort to try to "break" the band. This can be a smart strategy at times—nothing puts you more in debt to your record label than a failed radio or video campaign. At the same time, as an artist, one of the main reasons you sign with a label in the first place is to get the leverage of their relationships and (at that time) ability to penetrate retails, which was nearly impossible for indie artists back in the early '90s.

So I wrote a letter to Epic, to the then-label president. I had two people that worked on their promo team already onboard and starting to realize that pouring gas on the record might be a good idea. In the letter I explained the local sales success, the radio reaction, how they were clearly reaching an audience bigger than the "jam band" scene, and I projected something like, "If Epic does this right, you might sell three or four hundred thousand copies." What did it sell? Seven million?

After that letter went to them, decisions were made to "work" a song to alt and rock radio. And there was a phone call to us, which was really kind, to take our input—which song should be the single? I think we argued for "Little Miss," but the label decided to start with "Two Princes"—although in time both would do quite well at alt, rock, and Top 40 radio—which was an outcome I had not even considered.

Peter Denenberg: You go from second guessing all the work that you've done and feeling like well, you did the best you could, to oh, maybe we're geniuses.

20

The Colonel

Zach Newton: There's so many Col. Bruce stories I'm almost hesitant to tell Bruce stories just because the myth exists and I want to leave it there. All the stories you hear, I will confirm are true, even the ones that couldn't possibly be true.

Michael Rothschild: Bruce was always the one telling the stories.

Oteil Burbridge: You were just laughing your head off . . . at the same time that you were totally amazed.

Matt Mundy: We didn't have any idea of his age. He was very secretive.

Jeff Sipe: Bruce would pay serious attention to everybody.

Oteil Burbridge: Bruce never did drugs. But he came up in the time of LSD.

Michael Rothschild: Bruce had a way of saying so-and-so was the "number one crazy person" he knew.

David Blackmon: He'd rather talk to the janitors at the end of the night than any of the road crew.

Jeff Sipe: He always loved baseball. As a kid, he would collect these baseball cards and he would memorize everybody's stats, from the earliest players to all the way up to the current times. You could ask him about anybody and he would know their batting averages and their errors and runs and their birthdays. He started noticing that certain astrological signs would present themselves in certain baseball positions. For example, he noticed that a lot of pitchers were Sagittarius. When you think about the arrow being shot to the target as Sagittarius, it's the same thing as the pitcher throwing the baseball to the glove to the catcher. So he started piecing all these things together.

Zach Newton: Bruce told me after I joined the band, he had known me since I was four years old.

I was like "What do you mean?"

"You're that kid that hung out in Tarmon's basement!"

My best friend in kindergarten, first grade, was Tarmon Kelling, who was Harold Kelling's son. And Harold was the guitar player for Hampton Grease Band and they always rehearsed at Harold's house.

"You're the kid with a big head that always hung out with Tarmon!"

Jimmy Herring: Bruce never liked to sit in one place too long.

Jeff Sipe: There's two kinds of musicians: those who have played with Bruce and those who haven't.

Michael Rothschild: Bruce was not a great musician himself. But he recognized them. The Hampton Grease Band was famous for being signed to Columbia Records. What people have said was they released the second-worst selling album in Columbia's history.

Steve Fleming: He could pull some great musicians around him . . . he himself wasn't necessarily a stellar musician. I mean, he was quite accomplished, but it was more that he had the capability of pulling together some great musicians.

Michael Barbiero (Producer, Blues Traveler's *Four,* Gov't Mule's *Gov't Mule*): Bruce used to do this thing where he would let people solo until he dropped his shoe.

Steve Fleming: I remember his Late Bronze Age era before Aquarium Rescue Unit. They used to play the Uptown Lounge pretty regularly. Just oddball instruments—trash cans and tubas . . . stuff you wouldn't expect in a rock show.

David Blackmon: He was extremely good at putting incredible bands together and recognizing raw talent. And whip them into shape, as far as the things you do on stage and things you don't. In other words, you don't sit there and annoy the audience by tuning up with 110 decibels through your amp and all that kind of crap.

Jeff Sipe: Often we would be playing and the group would be sounding really, really tight, and really good, very dynamic. And we thought of ourselves as providing a silver platter for Bruce. The band would present Bruce up on this silver platter, and then he would tear it all down and destroy it. And we would all laugh. And then we would do it again, building back up again. And he would destroy it. But that was part of his sage magic. I think he was trying to bring us to a place that was very real. It wasn't about commercial success or impressing anybody on a serious level. It was the joy of expression and how magic that could be.

Matt Mundy: A lot of those songs on our album, *Mirrors of Embarrassment,* we didn't hear the lyrics or know what they were going to be. It was done at Bobby Brown's studio called Brown Sounds, a huge, very commercial studio. And we were a non-commercial band. Bruce would come in at midnight and work from midnight to the music that we had laid down. We'd come in the next day and there was a song. I think a lot of it was poetry that Bruce had in his back pocket for years.

Derek Trucks: All these other bands came through him and then blew up. But Colonel would always say, "I'm a minor league baseball coach, just getting people ready." He took a lot of raw musicians, and some really talented musicians, and stripped away the ego part of it and a lot of the bullshit out the other end. Not everyone—there's some people that came through the Colonel who kept their bullshit and mediocrity. But a lot became superheroes when they came through Colonel's schools.

Michael Rothschild: I was invited to a party and the head of Arista Records at that time was Clive Davis. Clive had been the president of Columbia Records when Bruce and his band had signed with them. And I told him that I had started a label and said, "In fact, we're working with one of the acts you used to work with—Bruce Hampton." He said, "You know, the music's sort of wild," and he walked away. The rest of the night he just glared at me and never came back.

Oteil Burbridge: When I heard Col. Bruce's first record, *Music to Eat* . . . that's the Colonel's greatest record, by far. I think it should be in the Smithsonian.

Zach Newton: It was the "van game."

"Bruce, how do you get from Atlanta to Detroit?"

And he would just reel out the mileage on the roads off the top of his head. Anywhere in the country.

Derek Trucks: [I met him at] the Cat's Cradle. I remember playing a show, opening for the ARU . . . I remember meeting Colonel and him either guessing my birthday or getting really close. One of the things I remembered was on the back of his T-shirt, he had a bunch of Colonel phrases and Virgil Trucks, who was my great-uncle, who pitched in the majors . . . his name was on the back of his T-shirt. That was the strangest and coolest thing.

Zach Newton: Usually Bruce was driving the van. Bruce would be driving and we'd pull up into Tuscaloosa and be at a stoplight and he'd roll down the window and holler at somebody on the sidewalk, "Hey, you know where a band might be playing?"

Jimmy Herring: He could guess people's birthday. He would usually start out by guessing their astrological sign. If he was correct, he would then move on to guessing their birthday. And I saw him do it. He nailed people to the wall sometimes, it would freak them out.

David Blackmon: He immediately guessed my birthday.

Jeff Sipe: We were playing at the Little Five Points Pub in Atlanta and finished the first set. We were over by the bar, getting a soda. And Bruce and I were talking to two ladies who said, "Hey, we enjoyed the show and blah, blah, blah," and then he immediately pegged one of the ladies' birthdays and started talking about her relationship with her brother and her dad . . . they were not getting along, but that she would be the one to heal the relationship in Knoxville in the very near future. She started crying. He started crying. He said, "I'm sorry. I'll stop. I'll stop." She said, "No, please continue. This makes perfect sense."

Michael Rothschild: Bruce was heavily into mushrooms. He cultivated mushrooms in his house, you know, boxes of spores. But he was also a health nut. And so there was a period where he did not eat—he went on an all-liquid diet for forty days. When he decided to break his fast, the first thing he ate were some of those mushrooms. And then he said, upon being a little bit sick, that a martian had come down from the sky and lifted the roof of his house and told him to come outside. And he swore to me that was exactly what happened.

Matt Mundy: Oteil told me a story one time: Bruce charged ninety-nine cents to get in because he insisted on giving everybody a penny back. He didn't feel like his show was worth a dollar.

Jeff Sipe: We were in Knoxville, Tennessee, '89 or '90 . . . the very beginning of the band. And we're at a place called the Planet Earth in Old Town, Knoxville. We were up in the penthouse of the building and just before the show, we were all sitting around the kitchen and there was a knock on the door. A young lady walks in, sits down, and says, "What's happening fellas, excited for the show?" And he said, "You're a Pisces, born on March 3." She freaked out and ran out of the room. And then she cracked the door, peeked her head back in, and she said, "How the hell did you do that?" He invited her to sit down and continued to talk about how her father was in jail in Texas, that he wore wireframe glasses and had a tattoo, and he was in for cocaine smuggling. And it was true.

Jim Bickerstaff: We were cutting tracks for *Mirrors of Embarrassment,* and Bruce came in at two a.m. one morning and pretty much cut all the vocals, mostly in one take. I asked him at one point if he wanted to punch in on a particular vocal track. He said, "No, they were going to hate it no matter what." I think he was speaking of the Capricorn staff at the time. I know there was a conflict with the label, but I don't know the details. If you listen to "Memory Is a Gimmick" on that record, he is speaking to Phil [Walden]. Lines like, "the bookkeeper . . . had an eraser." Or, "I'm on a plane, I'm on a plane to Hall County." I know the label was looking for a gimmick to help market the band. If you listen carefully to the last line of Jimmy's talk box solo on that song, you may discover what they thought about a gimmick.

Derek Trucks: Colonel was the one that just tied all of it together. And I think everyone kind of came through him at least—at least the Widespreads and Phish and all of that. They were all disciples of the Colonel in some way.

Jeff Sipe: What he imparted on all was the power of intention in music. He would constantly ask us: "Why are you here?" Well, it wasn't the money, that's for sure. Sometimes we'd make thirteen dollars on a gig. What was our motivation? What were our reasons for being on stage and playing with him? And we would always ask ourselves those questions, you know, because there's a million reasons why anybody would play music.

21

An Emaciated Third-World Exodus, Run by a Few Homeless People and Coyotes

Chan Kinchla: It was summer and we wanted to play outdoors.

John Popper: We were looking for an acronym and I was thinking, "Horizons of Rock Developing East Coast" because I thought that was what was connecting us. But we made it "Developing Everywhere" because the next year, we got bands from Colorado . . . and we could include other bands from other areas. We really wanted to get into an outside room, in the suburbs.

Rich Vink: The only way for you to play sheds in the summertime was to open for the Allman Brothers. They were the only ones that were hip to younger jam bands.

Grant Cowell: By that point, too, we had been opening up for bigger acts like Jerry Garcia Band and the Allman Brothers.

Chan Kinchla: None of us were big enough to do it on our own.

Grant Cowell: Combined together, we could get pretty close.

John Popper: Being clients of Bill Graham management and Bill Graham Presents, we got a lot of insights into what they did for Lollapalooza. So . . . I started talking to him and Dave Frey, who was working with him, and we were talking about H.O.R.D.E.—this was an idea a bunch of us had. "What if all these club bands . . ."

Dave Schools: H.O.R.D.E. was a miracle of utopian socialism.

Steve Eichner: It was an amalgamation of all these bands, but it was also a validation.

Chan Kinchla: We had Bill Graham shepherd some of this concept because we were twenty-year-old kids. We got all the people involved—some people from Widespread, some people from Phish, Spin Doctors. We all met up at Bill Graham's and put together an eight-day tour where Phish could only be in the north, so we got Béla Fleck in the south. Aquarium Rescue Unit were our idols.

Béla Fleck (Banjo, Béla Fleck & the Flecktones): The sheer musicianship turned us on.

Jeff Sipe: The first H.O.R.D.E. tour was really just eight dates—four in the north and four in the south.

Page McConnell: In a lot of ways Popper was driving the boat in terms of arranging the meeting, putting it together, and even the name H.O.R.D.E. Mike [Gordon] came up with a slew of hilarious names and he read out some of them at the meeting. He's got a knack for funny names and I can remember a couple off the top of my head: Rock Donkey Dunkle and East Coast Rock-a-Sooey.

Dave Schools: Five elected band members and their management showed up and went into a conference room in New York City. And then the managers were functionally dismissed from the room and the band guys came up with a way to make the tour work.

John Popper: We had done more traveling than all these other bands. Phish, at the time, was really focused on the Northeast, but they were starting to head down south. Widespread Panic was the Southeast.

Matt Mundy: Bruce goes to New York for a meeting. He didn't really tell us what it was.

Eric Schenkman: It was decided that whoever had the most eyeballs was at the top of the bill. So at the time, I guess it was either Traveler or Phish.

Dave Schools: The whole vibe of the H.O.R.D.E. was joining forces to conquer those who don't know.

Chan Kinchla: Aquarium Rescue Unit was the jam bands' jam band. We all aspired to what they were doing, even though they were probably the least well known.

John Popper: ARU was from the south like Widespread, but they were looked up to by all the bands. Musically, they were the guys. We'd all watch their sets, even though they were the smallest [act]. [Col. Bruce Hampton] was the driving artistic vision for all the bands that first year. He served as an example of the best kind of musician you can be. It wasn't the richest one, or the biggest audience. It was the "openest ears."

Béla Fleck: We had the closest ties to Aquarium Rescue Unit, who might have been even weirder than us.

Jimmy Herring: Sometimes we'd go on at 12:30 in the afternoon and play to one, and then our show was over. Our band was a band that goes on at midnight, that plays for three hours. So I remember struggling with that.

Matt Mundy: I had never heard of the Spin Doctors before the H.O.R.D.E. tour. Blues Traveler, Widespread, Phish—we had traveled extensively with the previous two years. They wanted us and Widespread to rotate first position on the tour. We would end our set with a song and they would come out and blend our songs, so by the end of the song, it was Widespread Panic. I was a twenty-two-year-old traveling at a hundred miles an hour.

Chan Kinchla: The time we were putting together H.O.R.D.E., we were touring Germany opening up for Lynyrd Skynyrd. We were trying to get calls to organize H.O.R.D.E. in the dressing room.

John Popper: H.O.R.D.E. was an emaciated third-world exodus, run by a few homeless people and coyotes. A lot of those first ones looked really empty.

Derek Trucks: A lot of bands then were either just hitting or they'd gone from clubs to filling amphitheaters and people who were not famous are all of a sudden famous. It was fun to kind of watch the way certain people handle those things.

Dave Schools: Popper's a total weapons aficionado. We did a lot of shows with Blues Traveler. We had a day off in Phoenix, Arizona. And I didn't go with him. But some of the guys went to a shooting range and Popper was so excited because it was the first time he could shoot a machine gun. Popper is popping off, you know, hundreds of rounds per minute.

Trey Anastasio: John almost shot me in the head. He had this fountain pen that he kept in his pocket. And I pulled it out and opened it up, and I was aiming at my head and he's like, "Watch out!" He said it's a .22 in there.

Eric Schenkman: Every band got a "H.O.R.D.E. sword." A real fucking sword.

Dave Schools: The H.O.R.D.E. sword—we didn't know what was happening. But they arrived on the last show with the first H.O.R.D.E. tour, at Merriweather Post Pavilion. It's a huge broadsword, fit for a Viking. And it's got the logo of every band that participated in the tour etched into the steel blade.

Dirk Stalnecker (Production Assistant, Blues Traveler; Tour Manager, Widespread Panic): I had to go and meet the sword maker because one got fucked up.

Matt Mundy: Bruce got the sword. But I'll guarantee you that his wife, if he didn't put it in a pawn shop for a gambling debt, probably has it.

Jimmy Herring: All the other bands had a day off, but our management would book a gig in some town and we'd go on at midnight.

Dave Frey: Between when the tour was booked and when I locked up the bands and the show actually played, Spin Doctors pretty much went platinum. Heavy rotation on MTV, heavy rotation on rock radio. Cover of *Rolling Stone*. *SNL*. And as that was happening, we saw ticket sales for H.O.R.D.E. blowing up.

John Popper: The Spin Doctors album went huge.

Aaron Comess: When the H.O.R.D.E. tour was happening, "Little Miss" came out. When we booked the H.O.R.D.E tour, nobody was really on the radio—it was this whole grassroots thing going on. By the time the H.O.R.D.E. came around, "Little Miss" was a hit. It was on MTV, it was on the radio—and our record started to climb up the charts. We were this one band on this jam band tour, all of a sudden charting with a record.

Billy Cohen: Now they're renegotiating deals like their time spots and their pay.

Dave Frey: So Spin Doctors are calling, saying move us up the bill. So I had to wear the black hat. I called Widespread Panic and they're saying, "We're not moving down the bill. We're not giving them any of our money." They were playing like, first or second, and selling more than half the tickets, right? We had a really, really successful year. And it was on them. The whole time they were saying, "We're a lot more than just a jam band! We're a rock band!" And they were. At the time, they were competing with Pearl Jam. Pearl Jam were on Lollapalooza and had the same problem . . . they played at two in the afternoon and were the biggest band on the tour. And the promoters loved it, because everybody showed up early.

Jimmy Herring: We didn't have a bus. Every other band on H.O.R.D.E. had a bus.

Dave Frey: When we were at Jones Beach, the fourth night of H.O.R.D.E., the promoter, Ron, comes up to me, and we'd sold out, right? And he's like, "What's your tune right now? Let's book next year! Let's go, let's go, let's go!" Working me really hard. I go out back to clear my head, by the oyster bay. And Page is out there with John Paluska. I said, "Ron just blew me up about doing this next year." Page was like, "We're never doing this again, ever." And I was like, "Oh, well was it the catering? What's wrong?" And Paluska cut him off and said, "We're looking at ourselves. Like we're a very nice restaurant, and we're the main course, and we don't like appetizers. It's all about Phish from now on." I don't think they ever had any preconceptions that they were going to be a hit on the radio or anything like the Spin Doctors. Two bands who took two very different paths at the same time.

Zach Newton: H.O.R.D.E. brought the jam band out of the underground, put it on promoters' radar, and suddenly it was a money-making opportunity.

Al Marks: It was like a Grateful Dead show, where you would have all these booths.

Oteil Burbridge: That was the first time I felt what the Grateful Dead and Allman Brothers scene would feel like.

Al Marks: People were hanging out and selling things. At a certain point, we started to sell product because initially, we didn't—there was no way for SoundScan to capture the sales. Right around '95, '96, we would have a retailer like Tower Records come and set up a booth. And all the sales would go through each marketplace and go through SoundScan, so we could get chart movement.

Rich Vink: Getting really entrenched in the whole festival, traveling circus vibe, it changed our perspective and gave us a lot more chops in other areas.

Al Marks: I was on the road with every H.O.R.D.E. tour. We would arrange radio interviews and set up backstage meet-and-greets by spots in the marketplace. One of the best H.O.R.D.E. festivals was in Cleveland. The night before, I worked it out so that Sheryl Crow, Blues Traveler, the Allman Brothers, and Screamin' Cheetah Wheelies would do a free show for the radio station that was sponsoring the H.O.R.D.E. tour. The show wasn't really selling well. We rented a club on the flats in Cleveland, and Sheryl Crow played a set, Blues Traveler played a set, the Allman Brothers played for two hours. And then all the bands got together and played with each other. The radio station was broadcasting and the next day the show sold out.

Page McConnell: I don't know if the term jam band was really thrown around much before then but it did somehow solidify the genre in people's minds—if not in my mind, then at least in people's minds. And in my mind it was recognizing that yes, there's something going on out there that's bigger than us.

Oteil Burbridge: That was the first time I was exposed to that scene and a lot of hippies.

Steve Eichner: It was like giving birth to your baby and then sending them off to college.

John Popper: We didn't feel like we were championing a scene. But it became known as "jam band stuff" for a second or third generation. And I'm all for that.

22

This Is the Shit. This Is It. This Is What We Need to Do.

While jam-oriented rock bands were starting to get bigger and bigger, a more avant-garde jazz scene was developing in downtown New York City. Clubs like CBGBs 313 Gallery and the Knitting Factory were hip to booking acts that didn't fit the traditional jazz sounds coming out of the Blue Note and the Village Vanguard. It was ripe for a crossover.

Billy Martin (Drums, Medeski Martin & Wood): It all comes from Bob Moses—legendary musician, composer, drummer. He took me under his wing when I was younger. Bob was a New Yorker and I played in his different bands as a percussionist, sometimes drums. He ended up moving to New England, to Boston, and teaching at New England Conservatory. And that's when I first heard about John Medeski and then Chris Wood as well. I knew from Bob's description that John was going to be an extraordinary player. Pretty much anybody that Bob talks about is gonna be great. I met John Medeski at a club called Johnny D's, somewhere in Boston, where I was playing with Bob Moses. John introduced himself after the show—he had a long beard and was wearing overalls.

John Medeski (Keyboards, piano, Medeski Martin & Wood): Billy was very much a New Yorker.

Chris Wood (Bass, Medeski Martin & Wood): Those guys seemed quite a bit older than me. I was like the younger brother.

Billy Martin: We were very much in admiration of each other already. It was like, "Yeah, I guess we should get together and play." I told him I live in Brooklyn and he said, "Well, I have a friend in Brooklyn and I go down there sometimes. So next time I'm down there, I'll call you." That happened weeks or months later, I don't know. John brought his Korg organ, which had drawbars and everything. He plugged into my amp in my loft—I had a funky loft in Dumbo, under the Manhattan Bridge in Brooklyn. And we played for two hours. We went everywhere under the sun and beyond. And it was really a powerful meeting, the duo. It was such a relief to play with a like-minded person who's super creative and can groove that you don't often get with one person.

Chris Wood: I was just ambitious, practicing a million hours a day and just whatever trying to make the music thing work and got noticed by some local Bostonians . . . this guy named Russ Gershon hired me to play in his band. He had this great group called the Either/Orchestra and he did all kinds of bands. John was in that band. He was a very striking individual. I mean, he's one of the healthiest humans I'd ever seen at the time. He was living in the Berkshires and doing yoga four hours a day and eating a macrobiotic diet. And he just had endless energy and crazy sharp blue eyes, and was fierce at the piano. One thing led to another and we ended up on this tour in Israel with drummer Bob Moses, who was integral to getting us all together. So John and I really got to know each other on this crazy tour in Israel, which was during the same time that Saddam Hussein had invaded Kuwait, and it was the precursor to the whole Gulf War in '91. Scud missiles were coming into Tel Aviv and people were preparing for chemical warfare. And it was just such a weird scene. But we were having this incredible little bizarre tour in Israel playing strange jazz music with this Israeli sax player and Bob Moses. I ended up coming to New York and doing gigs with John. Real straight-edge jazz. We decided to just get a place together in Manhattan. So I basically dropped out of school, and headed there.

John Medeski: For several years I was doing these two-week stints at the Village Gate—piano and bass duo. I would do them with different people.

Billy Martin: They had the cabaret laws there, where there was no drumming.

Chris Wood: It was sort of a glorified cocktail lounge.

Billy Martin: He was doing duos with Reggie Workman, and then Chris Wood would come down because they had played together at the Conservatory a little bit. He's like, "I'd like to introduce you to Chris Wood, he's a really great player, a little younger, and he's played with Moses, too." And I heard stories from Bob Moses about Chris and how amazing he was. So John brought Chris over to my place in Brooklyn. And our first notes we played, Chris just laid a bass line down, and I started playing a groove. And that was "Uncle Chubb."

John Medeski: Billy was not a jazz drummer. We were not trying to play straight ahead.

Chris Wood: Billy was heavily into hip-hop, he was heavily into Brazilian music, Brazilian percussion, along with rock and roll and R&B, but he could improvise, like a jazz drummer. So he's a unique musician in that way. He was also a visual artist. He had this weird loft in Dumbo when it was just a dangerous, desolate place. That was the first time we all played together—in his crazy weird art loft under the Manhattan Bridge in Dumbo. The second we started playing together, we were just improvising and it immediately turned into a song that ended up on our first record called "Uncle Chubb." The way Billy played . . . he could make people dance. And as a musician, playing with a drummer like that, he makes you dance. It's just making me feel this rhythm and this bass line in my bones. Something about the combination of that rhythmic feel, the feel of his eighth note, and then the flow of improvisational jazz vocabulary that John and I had that made for what was at the time I think a unique sound.

John Medeski: I got it together to do the first recording—*Notes from the Underground.* The very first thing that happened was Billy played a groove, Chris played a bass line, and we started playing and the tune "Uncle Chubb" was the first thing we ever played together. I transcribed it for the record and turned some of the stuff into horn parts. It's kind of like that magic.

Billy Martin: It was one of those lightning bolts. You get hit, you see a new path, and you're like, "This is the shit. This is it. This is what we need to do."

John Medeski: It instantly went from me trying to record some tunes to a collective.

Billy Martin: It was pretty instantaneous. *Notes from the Underground* I think was a one-day session. And we were prepared. There was a lot more on John to have certain music written out because we had a horn section on quite a few things. John had some more hashed-out arrangements, like "The Saint" or "Uncle Chubb." I set up the recording. Through Bob Moses, I knew David Baker, a great recording engineer, who was really good at recording a chamber situation. You get the sound of the room and he had a lot of access to different studios. Knowing David for many years, working with him, in a lot of different situations, I knew that David was the man to do this job. The assistant to David Baker was John Siket.

John Medeski: Nobody had money to go in the studio for a long time. So it was like, boom, boom, boom. That left for a lot of spontaneity. There was no mixing, no overdubbing. It was all live. We decided to use it for promo and to get some gigs.

Billy Martin: We were so used to one-day recording sessions, three-hour recording sessions, to get a record. You got to hit it like a performance. And the fact that you have three hours, that's like three sets. David and John mic'd everything and because I knew David, we got a crazy good deal. That was the beginning of our recording career with David Baker. I remember being excited to introduce Medeski to Steven Bernstein and Thomas Chapin because I had been working with Steven Bernstein in the Lounge Lizards and I had been working with Thomas Chapin and playing in Ned Rothenberg's

Double Band. We just kind of threw down. We were already well-oiled. So it was just a matter of capturing that.

Chris Wood: Baker can act fast. So if people are inspired and something's happening, he just gets it. This was the early '90s, so way before computers and Pro Tools and any of that stuff. And I just remember witnessing him cutting tape for the first time. And so we were working on one of the songs that had horns in it. And I think we'd done a couple of different versions or maybe there was a section we wanted to cut out that we didn't feel like was needed, and he just whipped out a razor blade and cut it out. That blew me away. It was just as good as a Pro Tools edit.

Billy Martin: I had been working with Bob Moses and John Lurie and other band leaders from the downtown scene . . . I watched how they worked. I saw what they did and how they created—whether it was a flyer about the band or their own independent deals, like making their own records. So I was already keen to that. I was very confident. I played venues on the East Coast—college towns, alternative clubs, that were open to exploratory music.

John Medeski: He was set up at his dad's place with his printer—so we started printing up press kits.

Billy Martin: You could pick up *Musician* magazine and look at their touring musicians guide. I was on two Knitting Factory tours that had the Jazz Passengers and Samm Bennett's Chunk—I was in a band, and we were on a tour bus. It was very unusual. We had started touring three bands on the road, down south, around the country. They were all alternative, college-town rock venues mostly. From that experience, I knew, "We gotta play this place. These people are into this stuff. They're into experimental stuff, as well as groove music and everything else."

John Medeski: We had another name when we started: Coltrane's Wig.

Chris Wood: John Lurie suggested, probably half-jokingly, the name Coltrane's Wig. Okay, that's kind of hilarious and kind of like, "No way," because people are going to take that as a disrespectful thing. I don't even know how that happened, but one of the press kits that got sent out, to try to book these shows down south, went to Knoxville with that title. I remember pulling into Knoxville and seeing posters for Coltrane's Wig all over the place and just being horrified.

John Medeski: We got in the van, and we just started touring. We would do our gigs back home with the Lounge Lizards or whatever it is we're doing to make some money and then go out on the road and invest into this project.

Billy Martin: There was a certain point where we had to devote ourselves 100 percent to the trio. I was making decent money playing with John Lurie in the Lounge Lizards and in the John Lurie National Orchestra, which was a trio. I was very busy with that. Later, we got gigs playing with John Zorn's different combos and Chris got gigs playing with Marc Ribot . . . but we maintained our connection and eventually we're like this is it 100 percent—we got to get on the road.

23

Who the Hell Let John Ride a Motorcycle?

Brendan Hill: I've been riding motorcycles since I was seventeen. I got my first motorcycle and didn't tell my parents for a year. I was just riding around back country roads in New Jersey. I used to keep the motorcycle at a friend's house—Rob Lester, who also drove the band van after we graduated. John—his thing was, in high school, he had a moped and he decked it out with a gas mask over the front headlight and all these tassels . . . he was a big fan of *Mad Max*. Any vehicle he has will probably have a secret compartment in it, with a button. He used to ride this thing just to school and he had his camo vest and he'd pull up and then he'd think he was the coolest guy in the world. But you know, it's 50 cc.

Fast forward like four or five years. John buys a motorcycle from a friend of the band. We were playing the Warfield in San Francisco, and somebody brought a motorcycle for John to buy. In the back of my mind I'm like, "Oh my god, John's gonna have a motorcycle? Okay." It turned out to be not a full-fledged motorcycle. It was a Hondamatic. I'd been carrying around my motorcycle in the back of a tractor trailer. I had a Shadow 700, the same one I got when I was seventeen. I had this little spot in the truck for it. Traveling the country is the best thing in the world—you may pull your motorcycle out, and drive around the country, bring it back, put it back in the truck, play the gig. Go on to the next city, do the same thing. John wanted to do that too. He got this Hondamatic. It's got a brake, obviously. But it's got basically a throttle on the right side . . . it's like a two-speed bike. But there's no clutch, there's no downshifting. You're dependent on the brake.

There was one time we were in Vegas, and we were like, "Let's go out to the Hoover Dam." So we rode out there in the blasting hot sunlight. We get out there and they didn't really have super security. There's a little parking area for authorized vehicles only and so we just parked our bikes in that spot and started walking along the Hoover Dam. We turn around and there are two federal cop cars, right next to our bikes. John, I think, didn't have his full license yet. And they busted him. It was kind of for fun—these guys let us go.

Then that following February or something that we went down to Bogalusa, Louisiana.

Rich Vink: They were out in the boonies.

Grant Cowell: We're down there at the New Orleans place. They've got horses, they've got ATVs, we can go out, we can run all around. John's big into guns, right? I have quite a few guns also. So we're sitting there and there's a wraparound couch, facing outside quadruple sliding French doors. We would sit on the couch, drinking, and then shoot out the back door. God forbid a deer or somebody walked by—they would have gotten blasted.

Chris Barron: He always had several guns on him.

Brendan Hill: We started practicing in this house—it was about thirty miles away from the studio. We were in this house for like a month. You know, it's not that exciting riding around Bogalusa, Louisiana—it's long Louisiana roads. We started doing sessions and we started working in the studio . . . and this record, we were producing ourselves. It was our timeline, we have a month in this house, just rehearsing and then we did a month in the studio. Bob would drive the van to the studio and start working, and I rode my motorcycle to the studio, and John was on his own clock. And so he would ride his bike to the studio . . . and we would get set up, we'd work on a song, get the basic tracks ready, and then John would arrive and then work on the track until evening. And it was this long stretch of road and you could go sixty-five, seventy miles an hour and you wouldn't think. We were probably almost done with a record—we'd done maybe ten of the tracks. Chan, Bob, and I were recording "Manhattan Bridge"—we'd done a take and it was good and we were just waiting for John to show up. And we were sitting in the studio, and over the headphones, it said, "You guys want to come in here? It's the Sheriff's Department. I think your boy's been in an accident."

I was like, "Oh, shit."

It was the sheriff.

"Your boy is here in the ditch. He's all kind of messed up. I don't know what happened to him, but we're gonna take him to the hospital."

You could hear in the background, "Ahhhh."

I called his mom's phone number. It was the same phone number from back in the day.

"John has been in an accident, we just found out. He's alive. But we haven't seen him yet. But I just want to let you know."

Rich Vink: Of course, my first thought was, "Who the hell let John ride a motorcycle?"

Grant Cowell: You don't put that guy on a motorcycle.

Michael Barbiero: They had just lost Bill Graham, who was their mentor. And they were very much shaken by that. And I commiserated with them about the loss of their manager because I was a big fan of Bill Graham as well. He was a legend in his own time. I'd been at the Fillmore East, many, many times. They told me what they didn't like about the sound of their last album—that they thought they were better live than in a studio; that everything was very sterilized in the studio. And it wasn't the first time I'd heard that from bands. So the record company suggested, since they didn't want a producer on this particular album, that myself and Steve Thompson would mix the album for them. And we would keep track of the recording process to make sure it was progressing along proper lines; that it was professionally done.

The first time we flew down to Louisiana, where they were recording *Save His Soul,* we went together. The second time I went alone. First time, I just checked out the studio that they were recording in and it looked like it had all the proper equipment and had some great mics, a Neve console, so I knew it was going to be punchy. They hadn't really started recording—they were in rehearsal. At that point, we just hung out with the band and let them know that we were going to check out the facility and make sure it was professional enough for them to make a decent record, which it was. The second time I went down alone. I got off the plane and I heard an announcement in New Orleans International Airport: "Michael Barbiero, can you please come to the information desk." Which, you know, is kind of weird to hear that in an airport. And they told me that John Popper had been injured in a terrible motorcycle accident and was in the hospital.

Brendan Hill: I walked into the emergency room. John was on a gurney and his leg was in an impossible position. His back and his arm were twisted. They hadn't fixed him yet. I turned green—we all walked up to him and I put my hand on him and said, "We're here, man." And he was just super out of it from the morphine.

Patrick Clifford: I didn't see him in the hospital, but when he got out, he was confined pretty much to bed all day long.

Dave Frey: I was back in New York. And John was always a prankster. He calls me and it's like ten or ten thirty or something.

"Dave, I'm on a gurney. I was just in a motorcycle accident. I'm really fucked up."

"How can you be calling me from a gurney?"

"They wheeled me over next to the payphone. They're taking me in and about to knock me out."

"Yeah, right."

And I hung up on him . . . but I couldn't go back to sleep. So I call the number and say, "Do you have a John Popper?

"That's a patient we just admitted."

I got on a plane and flew down there.

John Popper: I was facing death at that point. I remember thinking to myself, "Oh, this is what it's like to die." There was just a lot of times after that where you were just constantly facing "You might never walk again. You might never function again. You might die."

Dirk Stalnecker: I'd pick him up in Princeton and then take him to physical therapy. He was in a dark place—in a lot of pain.

Grant Cowell: We got a place in Princeton that was handicapped accessible. I think Dave Precheur was the one that was helping him in the beginning. And then they called me; I think I was second. They called me and asked me if I would be interested in doing it. And like an idiot I said yes.

Dirk Stalnecker: *Save His Soul* had some real heavy shit on that. I remember hearing the demos coming out of the studio, and I'm like, this is Traveler 2.0.

Chan Kinchla: The following year, we ended up touring and he had to do it in a wheelchair. It was at the same time that the Rolling Stones did the *Steel Wheels* tour so we call this "The Steel Wheelchair" tour.

John Popper: Definitely there were temper tantrums. The thing about our job is if I break a kneecap, I can't gig.

Grant Cowell: I took care of him up until the Backyard in Austin, Texas. Sheryl Crow was opening up for us. We were doing some drinking and I think I was sitting there in Chan and Bobby's room. John called up and was like, "You know, you need to get down here." When I got down there, he was furious. Basically stabbed a sword in the bed and then gave me some shit about I'm dehumanizing him and that's when he threw a bottle of piss in my face. I basically walked out of there at that point, said, "Fuck you guys. I'm getting on a plane. I'm out of here." And that's what I did.

John Popper: I give him credit. He could have just upended my chair and kicked the crap out of me. It was pretty terrible.

Patrick Clifford: One time in Breckenridge, on that tour, a friend of mine and I walked into Popper's room and I made a comment saying like, "Popper's in here manufacturing an atomic bomb, I'm sure." And we walk in, he shot a crossbow at us.

Grant Cowell: I guess they talked me into coming back. They were doing a show in Memphis or Knoxville, Tennessee, I can't remember exactly where. We started having a lot of feedback. And it was low bass, like low rumbling, and it was basically shaking the stage. But it was coming from the front-of-house. There's two different sound systems, right? There's what the band hears and then there's what the crowd hears. So I can't control what the crowd hears—that's Rich, that's out front. But it was feeding back up underneath the stage. John's flipping, flipping, flipping. Finally, he's screaming at me, off to the side. He used to carry guns underneath his harmonica belt. So he has a little .22 pistol, comes over, points it at me, and says, "You better fucking fix this shit right now or else I'm going to shoot you."

John Popper: That's the dumbest thing I've ever done with a gun.

Grant Cowell: There's other people around, hear it, see it. It goes around fast. So here comes Dickey Betts. Dickey Betts walks up to me and says, "That's not a fucking gun. Here's a gun. Go back up there and leave this on top of the monitor console." So he handed me his .357.

John Popper: I had to apologize to the entire band and the Allman Brothers crew.

24

I Walked Out of There, Stepped into a U-Haul, and Drove

Back in Buffalo, moe. were starting to have bigger aspirations than the confines of Western New York. They made a ramshackle recording space to lay down the tracks for their debut Fatboy. *But they also faced an unexpected bump in the road.*

Ray Schwartz: I loved what we were doing. Leaving had nothing to do with wanting to go into a different direction. It didn't seem like any record labels were lining up in Buffalo.

Al Schnier: Grunge happened before our eyes, while we were all making music and playing music, and everybody was so creative. There was this real zeitgeist of bands expressing themselves with anything and everything . . . taking mixed-media onstage and using video projection, but mixing all these different elements like funk and metal, rap, country, ska, blues, whatever.

Ray Schwartz: When I finally did graduate, it's like, "Well, I've graduated now, I'm supposed to do something . . . I'm supposed to be an adult, I'm supposed to get a job." My parents had expectations and that was weighing on me. We'd only played one show outside of Buffalo . . . we were in it really all by ourselves. Self-promotion, word of mouth, taping, playing as many shows as we could, writing as many songs as we could.

Al Schnier: We saw bands like the Chili Peppers, Jane's Addiction, Primus . . . all of these alternative rock bands were now suddenly having songs on the radio. Bands that were super edgy and underground now forging their way into the mainstream.

Rob Derhak: Ours was a sloppy mess that leaned more towards Frank Zappa and Fishbone than to any of the grunge stuff that was starting to become popular.

Al Schnier: We just saw this whole grunge thing pop up out of Seattle. And there's this whole other wave of fans that came out of that same scene. The Buffalo music scene was thriving so much that it definitely seemed that there was this parallel thing at the same time. It was another blue-collar city in many ways . . . I know people don't think of Seattle that way now, but at the time it very much felt like that—we were just on the opposite coast.

Ray Schwartz: We had already been in this grind. And I'm like, "Well, do I want to keep going?" My girlfriend at the time, who's now my wife, had graduated. We had already been apart for the better part of a year at that point and the question was "Are you leaving Buffalo? What are we going to do? What is our situation?" The prospects of the band were probably not good—not based on what they were doing. They were doing great stuff. But it was based on how the music business was and how we had progressed up until that point. We hadn't got a record contract, or national exposure.

Al Schnier: You had Ani DiFranco, Goo Goo Dolls, and who knows—maybe Monkey Wrench or Green Jellö. It felt like the Buffalo music scene was on the verge of having its own label, having its own scene.

Fatboy was our first real recording experience. We did it in somebody's apartment. But it was still such a big deal to us. We recorded to tape on a multitrack tape machine with a guy who really knew what the hell he was doing.

Rob Derhak: We recorded them on a fifteen-track because it was a sixteen-track recorder with one of the tracks busted.

Al Schnier: This apartment was above a vintage guitar shop—Topshelf Music in Buffalo.

Rob Derhak: The guitar tech for the Goo Goo Dolls was a friend of ours. He made a recording studio in his apartment, which was above our local used guitar store, where we would go and hang out and not ever buy anything until they got sick of us and kicked us out.

Al Schnier: We could only work after business hours because it was in a commercial area. So we did all of our recording from seven p.m. until two a.m. every night. We had to set up all the instruments scattered around the house. I'm pretty sure Rob's bass rig was set up in the stairwell. We did our best to isolate all this stuff.

Rob Derhak: We did my bass in the entryway down the bottom of the stairs to try to turn it into this giant bass trap or whatever.

Ray Schwartz: There's cables running everywhere.

Rob Derhak: Al worked a day job so we had to wait till he was done working. Basically we would show up with a case of beer, ready to go. It probably took us a week to maybe do?

Chuck Garvey: I think two.

Rob Derhak: We started experimenting with vocals. We did a vocal for "Time Ed" where we hung the mic outside the window . . . it was like two o'clock in the morning. We were checked out at this point and I'm trying to do the vocal and sing out there and cars are going, "Why?"

Ray Schwartz: For "Long Island Girls Rule," I remember all of us standing around a single microphone in a circle and singing the "Hava Nagila" part and being really into it . . . arm in arm or something. Maybe even dancing a little bit.

Al Schnier: I didn't realize that it was Ray's intention to leave Buffalo or quit the band after we finished the recording. He was very transparent with us and told us . . . so it wasn't like he withheld that information. But when he told us, I was surprised. I think I had blinders on and thought, "We're all just doing this, right?" I forgot the part of "he's graduating and moving on with his life."

Ray Schwartz: I was young. I didn't really know how I was going to support myself. All of those pressures were just too much for me. I was like, "I think what I'm supposed to do now is leave Buffalo and start a new life." I guess my parting gift to the band was that I gave them all of my drum tracks, and vocals, and just made sure they had all the raw material that they needed. And then I walked out of there, stepped into a U-Haul, and drove.

Al Schnier: We did find ourselves in a situation where we were like, "Okay, we just made the studio record. And now one of the guys is gone." Fortunately, we auditioned Jim [Loughlin], who was a mutual friend, and it didn't take long to realize that he was the guy.

Jim Loughlin (Drums/Percussion, moe.): They came over to my house and gave me a copy of *Fatboy.* A bunch of Rob's bass lines just jumped out at me. We played in my basement for about two and a half hours. We did songs from *Fatboy,* I think a couple of covers, and a bunch of improv jamming. Probably a week and a half later was my first gig with them.

Ray Schwartz: They found a great drummer.

25

A Late Breakfast and Scotch

As the early '90s were in full swing, so was Phish's touring presence: National tours were common, performing in clubs and small theaters while continuing to showcase the antics they had developed on stage at Nectar's years ago. Humor was at Phish's core in the early '90s, yet MTV and radio stations looked at more "serious" music that came out of the grunge movement. Still, they were signed to Elektra and began releasing studio efforts. For Phish's major-label debut, A Picture of Nectar, *they teamed with Kevin Halpin, a producer out of New York who had never heard the band.*

At the time in 1992, I was doing a lot of work for a New York City studio called JSM. They did a ton of commercials. We were working with some of the best studio musicians on the planet—the same guys that were playing on the commercials during the day would be playing on Steely Dan or Paul Simon records at night. One of the assistants at JSM was Jon Altschiller. Jon was big into the jam band and taper scene. He was tight with the guys in the Spin Doctors, Blues Traveler . . . and Phish. One night after a session, he mentioned to me he was talking to someone with Phish and said that they were getting ready to record their first album for Elektra and were looking for an engineer/producer . . . or maybe it was just an engineer who could help them along with producing the record. I'd never heard of 'em. I asked him for a tape to see what they were about. He gave me either *Junta* or *Lawn Boy.* I gave it a listen . . . and didn't dig it. It wasn't really my thing. I told him I was gonna pass. He said he'd get me another tape to listen to; probably a live gig. I liked this even less . . . Jon *loved* this band and was intent on getting me involved. I remember him saying something like, "Dude, the way you feel about The Beatles, that's how I feel about Phish—we gotta do this record."

He took me to the Capitol Theatre in Westchester to a show. The first thing that struck me was they had some *serious* fans. I didn't wanna stand on the floor so we went up to the first row of the balcony. The band came on and started playing and the balcony started bouncing up and down . . . literally. I thought it was gonna collapse. What struck me most was that Trey, Page, Mike, and Jon were *musicians.* And they didn't have a set way to play each song . . . the songs just developed, like live jazz tunes do. I was pretty impressed.

After the show, Jon brought me backstage to meet the band. We sat, had a drink, and chatted for a while. I got on well with the guys. They were friendly and I felt comfortable. The next thing I know, I was hired to work on *Picture of Nectar* in 1992. They wanted to stay close to home in Burlington, so we worked at White Crow. I believe they did their other records at Dan Archer's studio, and White Crow was a step up. We recorded on twenty-four track two-inch tape and mixed down to half-inch two-track.

The first thing we recorded was "Llama." When we finished the track, Trey wanted to redo his solo. Page had played his organ solo live. When we finished Trey's solo, we realized he played over Page's. Page didn't realize either. They both loved the arc of Trey's solo, so we just ducked the beginning of the organ solo till Trey's finished. I had no idea what the hell Trey was singing about . . . and he was singing fast.

"The Landlady" was one of my favorites. It reminded me of a Santana kinda thing—especially the solo—I love the way it comes screaming in. I got a kick out of hearing it played one afternoon at Yankee Stadium.

"Tweezer" . . . we did quite a few takes of this and each one was completely different except for where the vocal sections fell. Jon Altschiller told me this was their opus—the fans loved it.

"Chalk Dust Torture" . . . I had an idea to have Trey sing it while the track played faster, so on playback his voice got deeper and creepier. We tried one and he loved the idea. I was kinda proud of coming up with that. Now, I wish I was able to get that effect at the time after recording the vocal at normal speed, but I didn't have access to the piece of equipment that did that (an Eventide Harmonizer). We only had one track left for the lead vocal and after hearing the rundown of the vocal with that effect, the guys were really into it. We never thought we might wanna change it. Over the years, I found people either love it or hate it. I've seen in print people ask who actually sang it . . . and reviews that said it was a horrible idea. I take full responsibility.

We recorded another song for the album, "Runaway Jim." I really liked the song and thought it was gonna make the cut instead of one of the others.

Trey's dog Marley was a constant companion in the studio. At the start of the sessions, Trey would ride his bike to the studio. After a few days, I started picking him up with my car and that's probably when Marley started coming in.

While I was mixing one day, Jon Altschiller recorded the guys singing as a barbershop quartet in the lounge, direct to DAT. "Sweet Adeline" . . . I think they had just started experimenting with that kinda four-part harmony. That never made the album, either.

As far as a "radio hit," there was no talk of that. I suppose they picked the most radio-friendly song of the bunch with "Chalk Dust Torture." Elektra decided to remix it for the "single" with Frank Filipetti—a wonderful engineer/producer. When I heard it, it didn't sound much different to me. I bet they thought that they could take that "effect" off of the vocal. Looking back, it being the first time the general public was gonna hear Phish, it was probably even more of a reason not to have affected the lead vocal that way when I recorded it. I met Frank at a Phish show at Roseland in New York City right around the time of the remix. He said something to the effect of, "That was a pretty ballsy decision."

I was kinda surprised to get a call to work on the next record, *Rift*. We had a great experience with *Picture of Nectar*, but I thought it was a one-off project for me. I was told that I'd be working with a producer this time—the legendary Barry Beckett. He was a member of the famous Muscle Shoals rhythm section and an independent producer. He had won a Grammy for Bob Dylan's *Slow Train Coming* and played on countless classic recordings.

When we started the sessions, Barry sat beside me at the board and was interacting with the band, mostly with "groove and feel" stuff. This went on for a couple of days and then Barry told me, "You know, you and the band have a good vibe. You know what you're doing and everything is sounding great. I'm gonna let you work with them and I'll be in the lounge if you need me." He stayed in the lounge a lot playing Nintendo Tennis. He would walk in and out to see how things were going, but for the most part, he left it up to us. When they wanted another opinion, they'd turn to Barry. After the sessions, Barry, Jon, and I would go to a Denny's and have a late breakfast and scotch.

The arrangements the band came up with for this album seemed much more complicated to me than on *Picture of Nectar*. In the short time, they progressed in their musicianship and blew me away how easily they were able to pull 'em off. I think I always looked at *Picture of Nectar* as my favorite of the two, probably because it was my first experience with them and they relied on me more. But now I think *Rift* was a better record and really locked into what they were about. *Nectar* was all over the place genre-wise—which is one of the reasons I enjoyed it so much. It was fun shifting "recording" gears song to song. These arrangements made me think of prog stuff—I was a big Emerson, Lake & Palmer fan. The playing, singing, and production definitely grew with this record.

There were times I couldn't understand how they could each play their parts while listening to the other guys—they were so complicated . . . and yet perfectly intertwined. They did this kinda stuff easily; they were a pretty tight unit in the studio, especially on this record. We didn't do as much "punching in" on tracks to fix parts. I forget which track it was, but Fishman was playing four different time signatures with his four limbs.

Trey and I were hanging out one night, talking about music, and he asked me what my current favorite was. He was impressed that I had a huge CD collection, about a thousand at the time, which quickly grew to five thousand before I was finished buying CDs. I told him the current XTC record, *Oranges & Lemons* was incredible . . . great songs and amazing production. I was blown away by it. I gave him a copy. Now, after getting called to do their second Elektra record, I thought there was a good chance they'd bring me back for the third. I shouldn't have been that surprised when I found out that the *Oranges & Lemons* album team, producer Paul Fox and engineer Ed Thacker, were brought in for *Hoist*. I might have talked myself out of a gig.

26

We Became an MTV Band

Chris Barron: In terms of a jam band credibility, there was a backlash. Our commercial success knocked us out of the jam band club.

Aaron Comess: When H.O.R.D.E. started, all of a sudden "Little Miss Can't Be Wrong" was on MTV and our record was going off the charts. It was kind of weird, because we were the one band on that tour that all of a sudden had a Top 40 hit. Three to six months after they released "Little Miss," the record was platinum.

David Sonenberg: We did the "Two Princes" video, and MTV went to town on it.

Peter Denenberg: You literally could sense that a switch was flipped. And suddenly, it was on the freakin' radio and you could drive around, tune the dial, and find it playing on three radio stations at once.

Dave Frey: If you couldn't get into the mainstream type of media, you were probably doomed in lots of ways.

Joan Osborne: Labels will front you the money and then it comes out of your eventual royalties if you make them. Unless you're automatically the next big thing or Guns N' Roses, they're gonna wait to see how your record is doing at radio before they put any money into it.

Trey Anastasio: People were thinking about making videos before they made songs. People were starting to tell you, "You got to make a video or you can't be a band." Videos are great, there's nothing wrong with videos. But it was starting to become you have to make a video if you're going to be a band. People weren't caring about what music sounded like anymore. All they wanted to do was look good. It was messed up.

Aaron Comess: As the band got bigger and got more popular in the mainstream, we had an interesting dilemma with our gigs, where half the crowd was the Deadhead jam band types, and then the other half were these MTV kids who just wanted to hear "Little Miss" and "Two Princes."

Chris Barron: All of the tripping college kids that were our original fan base are coming out. And also we've got ten-year-olds and twelve-year-olds with their parents coming out to see us because of the MTV thing.

Dave Frey: When cable came out in the early '80s, that really changed a lot because suddenly there were sixty channels.

Joan Osborne: There was the expectation that you would make a video and try to get it on MTV. MTV and VH1 were the only game in town. [Spin Doctors] got a lot of heavy play on MTV and VH1. And that was a huge part of them breaking and having hits.

Chirs Barron: College kids are like, "What the hell's going on here? I came here tripping my balls off, and there's a bunch of kids hanging out!" We ran into a bit of cognitive dissonance between these two fan bases, and I don't know how well we navigated it. I don't know how else we could have navigated it.

Aaron Comess: It was an interesting problem but at the same time removed us a little bit from the center of the jam band scene. The hits eclipsed that.

We got offered to do the Lollapalooza tour. I mean, we got offered to do everything that summer—it was one of the biggest records in the country. We decided we wanted to do our own tour and MTV wanted to sponsor it and slap on that name "Alternative Nation."

Eric Schenkman: We became an MTV band.

27

I Should Have Had More Class

By 1993, Aquarium Rescue Unit was growing: They'd gained more exposure through the first H.O.R.D.E. tour and signed a record deal with Capricorn, following Widespread Panic. Yet that growth was hard to reconcile with.

Jeff Sipe: All flowers bloom and decay. Some last a long time. Some don't last a long time. And particularly for groups who are really intense, the lifespan is pretty short.

Jimmy Herring: Bruce and Phil Walden had known each other for many years. I mean, Phil liked us as a band. And he had heard all of Bruce's bands, and he really liked us. And he was really cool to us. Two of my favorite bands were on Capricorn . . . the Allman Brothers and the Dixie Dregs. I'll never forget looking at those albums being on my turntable saying "Capricorn" on them.

Matt Mundy: Capricorn signed us—they gave us a thirty-thousand-dollar bonus. For a twenty-year-old, a five-thousand-dollar check is pretty nice. We bought Widespread Panic's van because they had stepped up to a bigger van. There was miscellaneous algae growing in different corners of the van. It seems like the steps were laid out pretty good for us.

Jimmy Herring: We weren't going to have a hit. We weren't going to get played on the radio. Jeff Sipe, Oteil, and Matt Mundy . . . these guys could do anything. Could they play radio hits? Absolutely they could if they wanted to.

But they could also not do that. The group had options and Johnny Sandlin was producing us. The question came: Okay, you guys gonna make a record? And we all said, without even batting an eye, we need to be recorded live. We knew that we were not going to be able to do our thing in the studio. We're not all set up on the same stage together . . . you know, might have to be in a closet over there, the drums would be out there and the bass player be in the control room, you know what I mean? You can't play that kind of music under those situations . . . at least I didn't think so. And so we told Capricorn, "We should really be recorded live." They had us go to Johnny Sandlin's, and we did some demos. And then they listened to some live tapes of us playing and they came to the conclusion that yes, you guys are definitely a live band. And they found a way to kill two birds with one stone. They were recording Widespread Panic at the Georgia Theatre with Billy Bob Thornton producing the video for the show. And we opened the show for them. Capricorn could just record us audio-wise. We played three shows opening for Panic. It was September of '90. And then the record didn't come out until '91. None of us got any input on what material was chosen to make the cut for the live record. But that's okay. We were being produced by Johnny Sandlin. We played it, they did everything else.

Jeff Sipe: How broken do you need to be to hit the bottom? And how hard do you have to hit the bottom to bounce high enough out of that? It was a check and balance on intention, philosophy, motivation. The money started getting good . . . and then it just crumbled.

Matt Mundy: It gets down to what kind of person you want to be. I don't feel like the trucker mentality was for me.

Jeff Sipe: Matt Mundy decided he didn't want to have anything to do with the music business. He wanted to go back to sacred music, play with his family, play with the church. It wasn't about music as a commodity. He thought that was pollution of the sacred music. So he bowed out. And then the music started changing a little . . . a little bit more funky, less experimental. And then Bruce decided that he'd had enough. He also had some health issues and wanted to get off the road for a little while.

Matt Mundy: You're gone Thursday through Sunday of every week. So maybe that was too much for me. I was twenty-four when I left the band and I've apologized to each guy a million times for doing so. I blamed it on getting too loud. And Bruce would say the same thing: "We gotta turn it down, we gotta turn it down." Well, when you're playing in front of a Blues Traveler crowd, you really can't turn it down. They're here to hear an in-your-face rock and roll type thing. I think I should have had more class in leaving.

Jeff Sipe: Six months after Mundy split, Bruce called it quits.

Jimmy Herring: I can't speak for anybody else. I just think Bruce never liked to sit in one place too long. Most bands he was in didn't last that long. There were things expected of us. The minute there were expectations of a certain thing that we did, he started to lose interest, because he didn't want that. And then people would be expecting a certain thing from us when they came to see us live. He wanted it to be ever-changing. Bruce wanted us to keep it together. He wasn't trying to break up the band. He was just done. We were having to do really stupid things like two hundred shows a year or more and a lot of that time being spent with three to four people in a hotel room. He was just over it. And I don't blame him at all. Bruce didn't like being led around by the nose by a management company.

Jeff Sipe: Management decided Bruce can be replaced, and you guys could sound better. And you got two weeks to get it together. And here's a bunch of people who want to be the singer. Here's the rehearsal space and the audition times and go. We had no time to mourn or think about it . . . we were dug in deep and being pushed to just continue. Of course, that's in the best interest of management. They don't want to lose money by a band off the road. So they're just pushing us and it was the wrong feeling for me.

Jimmy Herring: We decided we'll have to audition some new singers. And I was just going along with the flow. I wasn't trying to push anything. We tried two people, and one of the guys already knew all the songs. He was a fan. There was a lot of hope that we could write together with him. And then we hit the road. But there would be people there who really missed Bruce.

Jeff Sipe: I wanted to see what we could do with it. Six months after Bruce left, I decided, well, this is a different thing. It's not the essence of what it was. It was becoming something completely different. Plus, I was convinced it was absolutely the wrong management. It was just a vibration thing. I couldn't be around them and so I split. It was the hardest thing I've ever had to do—tell my brothers.

"I love you guys and I love the music. But I can't be around this dude."

Zach Newton: A lot of bands were doing it for girls or the drugs. We were all in it for the music. And for the movement forward of the greater good. I don't know if that's too idealistic. But we really were.

Jeff Sipe: You got a lot of respect from players. Not a lot from critics. Not a lot from the lay listener. But musicians recognized that we were really trying.

Oteil Burbridge: Naivete is crucial, maybe, after all. Because it knows no bounds. It's the best time in your life to be a superhero—you're the most deluded.

28

This Is the Ultimate Wake and Bake Record

John Bell: We were catching a pretty good stride with our touring because we were pretty relentless.

Buck Williams: I had all the doors that could be open. But that doesn't mean they're right for that particular artist.

John Bell: You get a seven-year contract with some dollar figures behind that—then all of a sudden, that's the first time you go, "Wow, this has some legs to it." We weren't going day to day . . . this was an obvious step up with some stability. And another team to help, work with the record industry. And it was major label status. So that was a bigger game than we'd been playing before.

Buck Williams: You weren't moving everywhere at one time, which in the pop world, you would maybe do. Their world was so specific to particular fans. There was very little radio help. They didn't get MTV. There were markets that we could step up and we stepped up, but we did it carefully. Sometimes you're going for more people, maybe you have to go for a little less of a ticket price, but you don't want to ever be stepping down in ticket prices. So you've got to measure and weigh the attendance, the ticket price, and you look always at the history of what they've done and make sure that they've cleaned up the club before you move to the ballroom, so to speak.

WXRT in Chicago wanted Widespread to play their birthday party. I don't believe in birthday parties for radio stations. I don't tell the radio station that—I told them I'm just not available for some other reasons. But when we went to Chicago, I left a day off where I could call the station and say, "Hey guys, we're sold out, I've got sound and lights. We're sitting here twiddling our thumbs. How about you just throw a party at the Aragon." That really got radio excited, which got an audience that wasn't really our core audience.

Jeff Cook: 96 Rock was the big station in Atlanta at the time and I knew we had to start there to build our radio story. I came up with the idea of a contest, that if the station would play the lead track (I believe we released "Send Your Mind") then Panic would do a private concert in a listener's backyard. I doubted the band would be too thrilled with this idea, but they kindly agreed. One other promo idea I had was for the band to help serve Thanksgiving dinner at the Atlanta Union Mission, which got us a ton of coverage at press and radio. It was also much more in line with the band's values.

John Bell: We'd already been doing our thing for five years and we were pretty determined to stick with what. And we thought variety was better, you know?

Buck Williams: We would never do things for radio, until radio had done something for us. When you'd go and do something for a radio station—some party or something—and they said, "We're gonna give you this many spins." . . . Well, they'd give you that many spins at two o'clock or three o'clock in the morning. So when a radio station really helped us, we'd go back to help them unsolicited, to help them do things that they want to do, even if it's just a band play.

Dave Schools: Capricorn did a long-form documentary video. That was Billy Bob Thornton's first directorial effort—*Live from the Georgia Theatre* with interviews and some live performances.

Domingo "Sunny" Ortiz: Capricorn was trying to shut that whole concept [of fans taping shows] down. Phil Walden would say, "How do you boys expect to make money if you're letting these people make bootleg tapes at the shows?" And we said, "The quality of the tapes sucks, you know? I mean, it's a cassette tape." That was our way of distribution. Distribution was only limited because of our resources as a band.

Buck Williams: They butted heads with the label about not playing the hit every night.

Dave Schools: We were always having these philosophical battles with Capricorn. They'd be like, "We got you a single on the radio. Why don't you play it every night?" We'd be like, "Because it'll drive us insane and it won't have any grease under it if we play it to death!"

John Bell: The only thought of that is record sales are out the door. Taping was definitely a way that we earned some fans. People can hear us. And then they'd come to the show. It helped us get to a point where the record company actually noticed us. The tapes cost money, but the music was freely traded. And I have no doubt that that mindset hurt us with record sales. So, they had a point. We started it. Shoot, we were trading tapes. I had a brief stint of exploring the Grateful Dead and seeing that taping world. We were taping our own shows and trying to get it out there as early demos, too. You just kind of balance it out.

Domingo "Sunny" Ortiz: Our first San Francisco show wasn't through a promoter. This bar/club owner in Haight-Ashbury was given a tape of us by one of our fans, and he dug it. He contacted our management and said, "Hey, I hear you manage this band called Widespread Panic, I'd like to hire them to play a show in my bar in Haight-Ashbury in San Francisco." So our management said, "Well, that's great. But we got to be able to work from Athens, Georgia, to San Francisco." So our booking agent made us a tour to where we could go from Athens and we finally got to San Francisco. It was just a little dive, but it was so much fun. The fans that were there, they knew who we were because of cassette tapes.

Dave Schools: "Why do you let these people come in here and tape your concerts? It's cutting into record sales!" It's like no, no, no. These people that tape concerts . . . they've already bought the record; they want more.

Domingo "Sunny" Ortiz: Next thing we know, we're getting phone calls from Europe, Mexico, and Canada . . . but our management was going, "We got to be able to get from point A to point B, we can't just drive straight there. It costs money. It's a business, unfortunately." But we never looked at it as a business. We looked at it as this is our thing.

Jim Bickerstaff: By the time we got to *Everyday,* they were dialed in on the sound they wanted from the guitars. Mikey bought a Soldano stack and totally wiped out a new set of tubes during the record.

Dave Schools: Muscle Shoals . . . we were there for like eight or ten weeks, literally, living in some hotel room, about ten minutes away in the next town over. I can't remember what town it was. David Hood and Roger Hopkins are there every day.

"You want to see the vault?"

"Okay. Yeah, sure. I'd love to see what's in the tape vault. Oh look, it's Lynyrd Skynyrd's *Street Survivors.* Let me pull up the tracking sheet on this. Oh, there goes Robin Simon." Watching Johnny Sandlin just coax the cool vibe of that record out of us . . . a lot of my friends at the time were like, this is the ultimate wake and bake record.

John Bell: There wasn't much to do. There were a couple of bars and we would pretty much eat at the hotel. Patterson Hood—his dad was running the studio. I think he swiped one of the cassette demos. He was just a little sprout at the time.

Jim Bickerstaff: Someone taped a sheet of paper on the door that goes into the main studio, wherever we were. It was a list of recommended or suggested titles for the record. Everybody contributed, and some of them were pretty damn funny.

Dave Schools: We were there all fall, it was insane. I remember skedaddlin' because Christmas is important to me, it's really important to my mom. It's the day before Christmas Eve and I'm like, "I gotta get out of here." I got on some little prop jet thing and flew through a thunderstorm to get home.

Todd Nance said, “Well, maybe if we sacrifice Christmas to finish this record, it’ll be like Christmas everyday.” And that’s where the title came from.

Jeff Cook: The release of *Everyday* was a turning point. The single “Wondering” was radio friendly and I remember the stations also played “Hatfield” and “Pleas.” You could feel the momentum, you could see sold-out show after sold-out show on the books, and now we were getting airplay across the country.

29

Well, I Think Our Master Tapes Are Going to Be Thrown Into the Mississippi River

A 1994 New York Times *feature on God Street Wine said the group had been calling themselves the "best band unsigned by a record company" for years—and with relentless touring and spots on the '93 H.O.R.D.E. tour, they had a point. Tickets were selling, and the band had their first independent release,* Bag, *behind them. It was only a matter of time . . . before hair-metal impresarios found them?*

Dan Pifer: We saw Spin Doctors take off, Blues Traveler take off, Phish. We thought we could do this, but we also really wanted to have our music on the radio. We should have focused on one thing or the other, like building a touring base like Phish did or going for radio.

Jon Bevo: Radio was the path. We all wanted that.

Scott "bullethead" Reilly: For me, God Street Wine was all about touring.

Lo Faber: This scene was never as interesting to the label as the alternative rock scene. There was definitely interest, but it was really overshadowed by the world of Nirvana, Pearl Jam, and Soundgarden. So our little jam band world was not as exciting to the labels—but it was there.

Aaron Maxwell: Major labels were top of the mountain . . . what you thought would get you fame and stardom and money and success. We didn't really quantify what we wanted, other than we wanted to be successful, have radio play, but also through the music that we wanted to do.

Matt Busch (Merchandise Manager, God Street Wine): It always confused me to be quite honest that bands like Blues Traveler, Spin Doctors got that kind of commercial success . . . I always thought God Street Wine wrote songs. That's what separated, for me, a lot of the jam bands . . . both the songwriting and the harmonies. There was just such a focus on vocals that a lot of jam bands didn't have at the time.

Dan Pifer: When we signed up with bullethead, we told him, "We want to get signed to a major label, we want to go for this."

Scott "bullethead" Reilly: I remember driving down Seventh Avenue, past Madison Square Garden. Somebody said, "You guys will probably play there." I think it was Tomo who said, "That's exciting. But it'd be much more exciting to hear us on the radio driving past here."

Jon Bevo: We're getting two options at that point. We had the guy who signed Spin Doctors at Epic versus this imprint with Doc McGhee and Geffen.

Tomo: The McGhees heard us through a lawyer who was coming to see us at the Nightingale Bar who befriended us. An amazing guy and very, very high-end music attorney. He started bringing his friends and one of his friends was Scott McGhee, the younger brother of Doc. And Doc got curious, saying, "Who is this band that's unsigned and filling these places?" Here's the next big jam band kind of thing was his thinking.

Dan Pifer: We were really a road band at that point; we hadn't really spent a whole lot of time in the studio other than making *Bag*.

Tomo: Geffen owed him a favor.

Lo Faber: They flew us out to LA, put us up at the Mondrian, we went to their offices on Sunset Boulevard . . . it was this whole rock star moment.

Aaron Maxwell: 11 Records was actually a co-venture between Doc McGhee, who had been a manager for Mötley Crüe and Skid Row. They wanted us to be the first signing. He came and saw us play at some college in Pennsylvania and took us out to dinner—the only place to go was Shoney's. I ordered spaghetti and meatballs.

Lo Faber: They gave us $250,000. You're supposed to spend all the money on the record, but of course nobody did. We were gigging so much that we couldn't even interrupt our touring schedule to sign the actual deal. We had a gig in Boston at the Paradise. They flew up the McGhee brothers—Doc and his brother Scott—and our attorney and a couple other label people. They stayed at the DoubleTree in Boston. We did our soundcheck at the Paradise, rushed over to their suite at the DoubleTree, signed six copies of the record contract, took a bunch of pictures with them holding the contract up, and then went and played our gig. It was very fun. We were fucking rock stars now. Geffen Records. John Lennon's *Double Fantasy* was the first ever to come out on Geffen! It was a very cool feeling.

Jon Bevo: It started going south pretty quickly. David Geffen left the company and this guy who took over didn't like Doc McGhee for probably a hundred different reasons.

Aaron Maxwell: He hated Doc McGhee. He had no desire to help anything Doc McGhee was doing.

Tomo: We had three producers to pick from. And in true God Street Wine fashion, we chose the least reputable.

Lo Faber: One of my all-time regrets in the path through life is that I turned down the chance to work with T Bone Burnett. The excuse I can offer is

I had been living in a total bubble. Literally, for five years, I had been doing nothing but driving around and playing shows, hanging out with other musicians who are also driving around with bands playing shows. And so I didn't really know who he was that well, except for the fact that he had just done the Counting Crows. Part of it was just my orneriness and he was the label's suggestion. And I didn't want to do the record label's suggestion.

Tomo: We chose the least reputable, the least commercially successful certainly, and the one who was going to turn out to be the biggest headache to work with before, during, and after the actual session. And that's not to take away from the brilliance of Jim Dickinson—because he was an amazing guy and a real character. We learned an awful lot from him. But it wasn't easy-breezy and we saw a good bit of madness.

Lo Faber: Jim would only work in Memphis. So that's why we went to Memphis.

Dan Pifer: We went down to Memphis. I don't know that any of us had really spent much time in the South before then, other than we had done a few tours. We were in a Holiday Inn and in a recording studio on Beale Street.

Scott "bullethead" Reilly: Jim smoked a lot of dope.

Dan Pifer: Bob Kruser was the main engineer. And him and Jim would pretty much smoke pot the entire day. Even though we were in the jam band scene, we weren't big pot smokers or really into drugs. It was probably more drinking than anything, but it's a very different vibe.

Scott "bullethead" Reilly: Jim was a genius and an otherworldly personality. The thing I learned from the God Street Wine sessions is when a major label's involved, Jim gets paranoid and thinks he's getting screwed. So he still can make the great record but then he goes a little crazy about the money and he thinks other people are getting pieces.

Cody Dickinson (Drums, North Mississippi Allstars): My dad was a big champion of the artists. He saw it as his job, as producer, to be a buffer between the artist and the label. So he was very protective, and even sometimes unnecessarily so.

Lo Faber: It was very difficult and stressful. Nobody came from the label to the session, nobody talked about creating a radio hit from the session. We fought a lot on the record. Jim was known as the real kind of rebel—really alternative. He worked with The Replacements. We liked the fact that he had a "fuck the system, stick it to the man" reputation. But just to be the "talent" is very hard for me. So I fought with Jim about that. And I also fought with Jim because I realized that Jim, even though we thought he had a "stick-it-to-the-man attitude," Jim got his opportunity to make a commercial record. We were working at cross-purposes. Jim wanted a band like Radiohead and sell a lot of records. We probably should have wanted that too.

Scott "bullethead" Reilly: Dickinson, at the tail end, was holding the tapes hostage.

Lo Faber: It culminated once we were back on the road, and Jim was mixing the record. It sounded like crap. The entire band and label thought so.

Dan Pifer: I remember listening to them and being like, "What the hell is this?"

Lo Faber: I was the one who ended up having to tell him this in a phone conversation, at which point he threatened to take all our master tapes and throw them into the Mississippi River. He was telling me this when I was in a phone booth somewhere in Nebraska. And I had to walk back to the van and tell the boys, "Well, I think our master tapes are going to be thrown into the Mississippi River."

Tomo: He had first go with the mixes of the album. We immediately got on the road and started a six-week run across the States. And at some point, a cassette arrived of the rough mixes, and we put it on in the van and it was awful. It was as if somebody had tried to intentionally mix the worst album they could. Everything was all over the place and weird effects on things that had no business being affected.

Dan Pifer: Lo ended up doing a lot of the work to remix with a different engineer in New York.

Aaron Maxwell: We were getting a lot of airplay on Triple A and college radio. The song "Nightingale" was starting up . . . and they wouldn't do a thing. I remember the quote getting back to me was, "These guys would be better off working at a gas station."

Scott "bullethead" Reilly: I went two nights back-to-back at the Palladium in New York. I went to see Hole when they played and it was sold out. The VIP area was so jammed, you couldn't move. The next night, I went to see Dave Matthews Band, who sold out two nights, no advertising; it was a real phenomenon. And there was almost nobody in the VIP area. The myth was these hippie bands can't sell records . . . and the industry wanted to keep that myth because so many people didn't like that kind of music, so that's not what they wanted to support. But there were these bidding wars for these bands that never went anywhere, that they spent a fortune on. If they invested a fraction of that on the hippie bands, many of them would have broken, too.

Jon Bevo: We were in the Midwest somewhere doing a radio station thing and the DJ's like, "You know, people are calling up, they like your song—we're supposed to play Weezer."

Scott "bullethead" Reilly: WDHA in New Jersey started playing the record and played it a lot. We had stations in Long Island playing it . . . all these stations playing it a handful. The label flat-out told me, "We think Doc McGhee is paying to get that done because he had a radio guy on staff. That's not legitimate play." I got to WDHA and they are playing the record. He tells me the guy said Geffen was just here and asked me to stop playing God Street Wine and start playing "Sweater Song" by Weezer.

Aaron Maxwell: The best thing Doc McGhee did after that was getting us out of the deal.

Tomo: I think we lost the masters for *$1.99 Romance* to Geffen for a number of years . . . but it was fairly painless to get off the label.

Lo Faber: I never had a lot of bad feelings about it. Look who was making it at Geffen . . . we were there with Nirvana, Whitesnake, and Weezer.

Scott "bullethead" Reilly: Doc could have just locked them up. And he just said, "Go."

30

Things Got Weird Very Quickly

Billy Martin: John Zorn is the Mother Goose of the New York downtown scene. He would create these residencies at different clubs, like the Knitting Factory. In protest for the new Knitting Factory, because they were really selling out, Zorn was like, "We need a new home. Let's all do gigs at CBGBs Gallery." It was a small bar with a stage for singer-songwriters, and also an art gallery.

Liz Penta (Manager, Medeski Martin & Wood): Everybody played the Knitting Factory and the Gallery.

Billy Martin: We were so into what we were doing. I had a passenger van, and we ripped the seats out of the back and threw the equipment in the back of the van and we hit the road. Some venues would let us sleep upstairs in the apartment or wherever in the club. Or we would find friends that would put us up, or even fans sometimes had spaces where we could sleep on their couch . . . avoid the hotel costs, if we could. In the beginning, it seemed like nothing could get in our way. We had solutions to everything.

Liz Penta: I was dating Sim Cain, who was the drummer for the Rollins Band, and Marc Ribot hired Sim to play drums on tour with him in Europe. He also hired Chris Wood to play guitar. I went to visit them on tour in Europe. And that's how I met Chris Wood. He was telling me about his band, and

I was like, "Wow, it sounds great. You should come play CB's Gallery." And that's how they first came to play there.

It was very obvious to me that they had this really special chemistry. I wrote them a note of appreciation, just saying how thrilled I was, and I think I figured out what their take from the door was and I wished there was a lot more money. They always talked about that note.

Billy Martin: Liz really loved our music. And she wanted to get out of CB's because it was becoming just an organized mess. And she didn't want to be associated with it anymore. She wanted to move on.

Chris Wood: We were living in the East Village. We were scrappy. We were young, we were opinionated, we had a lot of energy.

Liz Penta: I had been at CBGBs for four years. I was originally hired as a bartender and somebody to assist the curator of the gallery, because I had a background in fine art. Eventually, I ended up taking over everything: curating all the exhibits, booking all the music, managing the business and bartending . . . because none of it paid. So I was ready to go. I was talking to Soul Coughing about going out as their tour manager. But their manager wouldn't hire me because I didn't have any tour management experience. And they had never toured either. He decided I wasn't qualified, even though they wanted to take me. At the time, I was also roommates with John and Chris in the East Village. We had an apartment on Avenue A between Sixth and Seventh. They'd just jam there. People walking by would hear and if there was a friend that they knew, then they would just stop in and everybody would play.

Billy Martin: My dad, who's a violinist and played in the New York City Ballet and opera, he had an Apple Computer and a database—and he would say, "Hey, I can print you guys labels. You can have a database of addresses and a mailing list and mail things out. I have a Xerox machine." He was like our office. We bought an RV at a certain point in Florida. I dumped my van. John traded an organ or a Wurlitzer or a Clavinet with this guy in Atlanta for my van. Then with the RV, we got a trailer. So we came back with an RV that we could sleep in and cook in. We needed a place to put it, so that was at my mom and dad's place in New Jersey, not far from New York City.

Liz Penta: Medeski Martin & Wood were like, "Why don't you come out with us? We can only pay you a hundred dollars a week." And I had to tour manage two bands: them and Lost Tribe. They were touring in an RV throughout the US, and then through Canada in December.

John Medeski: We were the booking agent. There was no booking agent. I had a friend living in Atlanta, Billy had some abstract connections with a guy in Chapel Hill, North Carolina. He was touring a bit down there with his band. And then we met this guy from Knoxville—he was a promoter there, which was the connection to Col. Bruce. So we just started going down, and really the truth is we went out not knowing anything. At that time in our peer musician group, the deal was you play in different bands, because no band can play enough in the city to make a living. We knew that if we wanted to work with this band to play this music, we needed to play every night. So the way we did that was by playing in different cities. I had toured with this band called Either/Orchestra from Boston. And that gave me a little taste of the fact that actually there's a small group of crazy people who want to hear some weird music.

We printed up our own press kit, did follow-up calls.

A big part of our decision was that touring in the Northeast sucks. Playing Boston double sucks, especially when your band is just starting up. When you have to drive yourself, unload your gear, you can't park anywhere, it sucks. What we started doing was heading down to North Carolina—we'd skip the whole Northeast Corridor. And we liked the scene down there—people were friendly, it was easier touring. There was this incredible, weird scene down there in the college market. People were showing up.

In early August 1993, Medeski Martin & Wood spent three days recording their label debut, It's a Jungle in Here. *The sessions didn't go as they had envisioned . . .*

Billy Martin: Because I was working with Bob Moses on a lot of Gramavision records, I was very familiar with the label owner, Jonathan Rose. And then some woman took over and her husband was a producer . . . Jim Payne. Getting that deal was who we knew. And we got to deal with Gramavision. Rykodisc bought Gramavision, and we had a bump up in the relationship.

John Medeski: We were very like, "Fuck everybody. Let's just do it ourselves."

Chris Wood: They came to see us. The owner was this real estate guy. The whole situation was so weird. Part of us was like, "Oh, great, exciting. We have a record deal, right?" We were young and never had that before and surprised that anybody even cared about what we were doing. But then things got weird very quickly.

John Medeski: We never tried to get connections. They came to us. So we said, "Yeah, we'll give it a try." We were skeptical, but we did it. And sure enough, it was an issue.

Billy Martin: They wrote into the deal that we had to work with Jim as a producer, and he was going to take a cut of the record. I don't know if we signed it and didn't read it or we were like, "Fuck it, we got a record deal. We got financial support." But then later, we realized this is not good. We didn't want to work with anybody. We wanted to produce our own record and also work with David Baker, the engineer—he's a producer himself, and can work with guiding musicians lightly. That was the first wake-up call.

Chris Wood: I think in their eyes we were just these young brats. And so they felt like we needed a babysitter.

Billy Martin: And then they were also dictating where we were going to record. Of course the studio was great. It was Sear Sound. But the recording engineer we didn't know. All of a sudden we couldn't work with David. This engineer started to tell John how to play the piano, so he could get a certain sound. And John just broke down into a fit. I mean it was an internal fit because

John's trying to figure out how this guy could say that. So that really threw a horrible vibe into the session. And the session was multiple days. We had a horn section in and then we added some other musicians—Steve Bernstein was still in, maybe Thomas Chapin. There was some tricky stuff like tricky rhythms that took longer for some horn players to learn. And just the friction of feeling like we no longer felt we owned everything on this record. And I don't mean "law" owned—I mean feeling like this is really our record and we're doing everything. We're in control. They weren't even listening to who we were, so it was tough. But we definitely made an impression. Ultimately our spirit came through, regardless of the shit we had to go through. But that was a tough one. That wasn't our proudest moment or best record. But still, those tunes and playing them out on the road was just a blast.

Chris Wood: He stops us and says, "Hey guys, I have an idea for the name for the record. It's going to be 'Function Junction' but with a K."

John Medeski: "Dude, you gotta be kidding."

Chris Wood: We didn't know what to say and we're like, "Oh my god, this guy's our producer! This is terrifying." This is our first record with a label. We were concerned about how we were going to be portrayed in the world; how this band was gonna be birthed. The next thing that happens is he hires this engineer for the session—we have no say—and it was this guy whose claim to fame was recording Manhattan Transfer. It was like, "Oh my god, this was not going the right direction."

Billy Martin: It's having these other, older adults in the room . . . they're supposed to have some kind of special knowledge or guidance and it was really not. We did not relate to them at all; whatever they said, it was just stupid. And we were also really into our relationship as a trio. They did not understand who we were, what we were . . . they just had an opportunity to make a record with us. We were also cocky, and really feeling the power of what we were doing. That was the problem—our egos and getting tricked into working with these people. We were starting to get a little more electric. And starting to get a little more groove oriented. We were going to treat all these sounds as individual sounds and mix them together. There are advantages to that and it's definitely the direction we were going.

John Medeski: I actually like that record. I think it's good. So I don't have any problems with it.

31

Oh Shit, This Is My Time!

In Southern California, a new sound entered the '90s jam band lexicon: an amalgamation of acid jazz, funk, and soul that was more rooted in '60s Blue Note boogaloo versus anything rock oriented.

Karl Denson: I was doing Lenny Kravitz from '88 to '93. We started touring in '89 and in '90 he kind of blew up and we were traveling the world. I always loved dance music from a Black perspective; I grew up with James Brown, and then Sly Stone and Michael Jackson. I always went to clubs, just to see what was going on. And I vividly remember being in Europe . . . hip-hop was already happening, so there was that influence—you know, Run-DMC, and Whodini and the earlier stuff. They were just starting sample stuff, but I think they were just starting to run into the problems with sampling rights and things like that. And I'd go to these clubs, and I just remember that sea change, where all of a sudden I started hearing things that were familiar for me as a jazz guy. Grant Green and the soul jazz thing that started happening, which they called "acid jazz." I remember hearing that and thinking, "Oh shit, this is my time!" I realized I needed to move on that because it was something that I was doing. In the acid jazz scene you had DJs using live musicians. That was the whole thing and I jumped right on it and started seeing what the scene was. I got back home in '92 or '91 when I met DJ Greyboy. He just happened to have showed up at a club I was at—a little nightclub in Orange County. And he heard about me through a friend of his, and he was an American DJ looking for somebody to collaborate with.

And we did that in '92. And I remember going back to Europe, and going out to nightclubs, and hearing my frickin' saxophone in the clubs! That was one of the most awesome moments of my life. In the middle of that, I got my jazz deal. I did four records for a German label, Minor Music, that were traditional jazz, quintet style. I started touring that and was playing with Fred Wesley at the time.

Elgin Park (Guitar, The Greyboy Allstars): I was coming out of a band called the Origin, which I fronted—singing and played guitar. I was pretty young at the time; I started as a teenager in that band. And we did a couple records for Virgin Records . . . we got a record deal very, very early. And that's where I met Karl because he was playing with Lenny, and we toured with Lenny during *Let Love Rule.*

Zak Najor (Drums, The Greyboy Allstars): There's more of a blend of culture, especially near the border. San Diego had this blend of culture. You're punk rock, but you have punk rock bands that speak Spanish.

Robert Walter (Keyboards, The Greyboy Allstars, Robert Walter's 20th Congress): I grew up in Southern California and San Diego. I played in punk bands around the Casbah record scene in that whole world. That was a real thing you felt a part of: All these bands interacted with each other. And it was an underground scene, but you felt excited; something was happening, and you knew you're in the middle of it.

Chris Stillwell (Bass, The Greyboy Allstars): I was a late bloomer. I came from a rock background, the tail end of hair metal and stuff. All the guys had long hair. I just kept my hair short. And then that sort of dissolved. My dad had a good record collection and I just wanted to get good on the bass. I locked myself in my bedroom for like three or four years and learned how to play. There was a band in town and Robert [Walter] was in the band—it was called Daddy Long Legs. They were the most interesting thing happening. They were more like Parliament-Funkadelic meets Frank Zappa. I was blown away by those guys. Robert was playing drums back then; he wasn't on keys. And I would just park myself at gigs and would try to talk to these guys.

Zak Najor: We all really looked up to Daddy Long Legs. A good friend of mine took me to this place called the Ché Café on UCSD's campus. It was very progressive. People lived in houses like twenty people deep. They had all-vegetarian meals. That's where I saw them the first time and my first experience of anything like that. They all switched instruments a lot. So the whole thing was just phenomenal. The reason why that band was so cool is because they all went to this high school for the arts. That's probably why there was such a high concentration of talent. They were playing funk and it was multicultural . . . white dudes and Black dudes playing together was different in that way.

Chris Stillwell: Eventually Daddy Long Legs broke up. And they were trying to get some sort of other thing going. And so I got a shoo-in from a guy at work. So we started this band called Schmaltz. And that lasted for maybe two years. And Zak Najor was in that band. That's the first time that I met him . . . and Robert. So we have three of the guys that ended up in the All-stars. And then DJ Greyboy had his thing going with *Freestyle*. And that was more in line with what we eventually became. Greyboy knew Karl. So you have that camp, and then our camp.

Zak Najor: We were playing Monday nights at the Casbah. We rarely had the same band and couldn't really rehearse that much. Nobody really was committed, but we'd play twenty-minute jam versions. We weren't really into the Grateful Dead or anything like that; we just wanted to have a band with a singer but couldn't get any buy-in from anyone in particular. So we had to do a lot of instrumentals.

Chris Stillwell: *Freestyle* was on the San Francisco tail end of the acid jazz type thing. We ended up coming to this club and put a band together playing James Brown, The Meters, that kind of stuff. We went to this club called Green Circle. We thought it was double-booked, because Greyboy was spinning. We got to talking and basically Zak and I ended up going to this guy's house and playing on a few tracks and stuff.

Elgin Park: I had come home and was living in San Francisco, to start something else. I ran into a friend of mine at a coffee shop down there and he was just like, "Oh, hey, you play music. My friend Andy has been making some cool stuff with some friends. He's a DJ, but they had some cool people over there. And maybe you should meet him." And I'm like, "Cool, I'm up for anything at this moment." I went over and I met Andreas, who was Greyboy. Karl happened to be there. And it was just like, "Whoa, this is crazy. What are you doing here? No, what are *you* doing here?" The record was almost completely finished and there was another guy that was playing guitar on that record named Marc Antoine. Chris [Stillwell] played some bass on it, Zak [Najor] played some drums on it. But it was mostly a sample-based record.

I kept in contact with Andy and shortly thereafter, it was like, "Oh, maybe we should put a band together. And you guys can play the record release party for *Freestyle*." And so Andy put this band together, which was made up of Karl and me and Marc Antoine as the primary guitar player, and Chris, Robert [Walter], and Zak had played in different configurations of different bands together, so they came as a trio. We learned a set of music . . . some of the stuff that Andy had made with Karl; we got a little rehearsal studio down in San Diego and immediately sounded pretty awesome. So that was encouraging.

Karl Denson: Back home in '93, I was doing well enough when it was time for me to leave Lenny, because we were having conflicts of scheduling. DJ Greyboy was releasing a record and he wanted a live band for it. And so I showed up in this garage, and it was the Greyboy Allstars.

Chris Stillwell: We ended up in the garage at Zak's house to rehearse for two days on these tunes. That first rehearsal tape is still around. And even then, it was immediate. It sounded great.

Robert Walter: It's all intertwined with DJ Greyboy's career. It was coming out of the hip-hop production model . . . and acid jazz at that time, which was going off in clubs in Europe and England, in particular. We started a live band and learned those tunes plus things that influenced it, which were covers of Prestige [Records], and Blue Note—funky jazz records, basically.

Elgin Park: I thought, "Oh this is cool, we'll do this gig. And then, you know, who knows what else." It was a very light commitment from everybody, mostly. But the band sounded really great. And then we ended up going up to San Francisco playing the *Freestyle* release party.

Zak Najor: We were playing consistently to nobody on Monday night. And then you go in front of this metropolitan crowd in San Francisco, where everybody's skinny.

Robert Walter: All of this happened with no knowledge of the jam band world. We were playing to kids that would otherwise be listening to DJs.

Zak Najor: None of us were in touch with that at all. No Grateful Dead. No Phish.

Chris Stillwell: We were all record collectors. So we started finding out these names and buying those records ourselves.

Robert Walter: A lot of the same things that happened, happened at a Phish show or Grateful Dead show. The first set, we'd play a little bit safer. And then as the night would go on, and people get more intoxicated, the music would expand a little bit . . . we'd stretch things out and get a little weirder in the second set.

Karl Denson: We were basically ecstatic that we were getting away with playing jazz in a dance club. And these kids were super, super into it. When we finally started touring, within probably three months from the beginning of '94, we were playing a club in San Diego called the Green Circle on a Wednesday night. Initially the club held about eighty people—little tiny room—and we'd run two, three, four hundred people through there on a Wednesday night, by timing our breaks correctly. All the college kids were coming to see us. And then the club expanded. And we'd run five, six hundred people through there every Wednesday night. And it was a madhouse. We were able to play San Diego probably five nights a week. And then we started going to San Francisco and Santa Cruz and San Jose. Everywhere we went, it was well accepted.

Zak Najor: We weren't trying to get money. Maybe seventy-five bucks here or there. We were so enamored with the sense of movement.

Chris Stillwell: We kept it West Coast for a while.

Zak Najor: It was received well, but I think you still had to work pretty hard to get people to like you at the same time. We got in front of one audience, and then we got in front of another audience. That's why it moved so quickly.

Robert Walter: It felt like the weirdest thing ever. But it had its own momentum. It was based on historical precedent: All this great music from the late '60s. People started to incorporate elements of soul music and R&B, and vice versa. We were students rather than just "check out my great idea." I felt like part of a tradition.

Chris Stillwell: No one was playing that kind of stuff. In San Diego, it was mostly the beginnings of smooth jazz, which has strong ties to San Diego—you know, the wine crowd. And this was raw, '60s boogaloo and funk. And the covers that we were playing, no one ever heard those types of tunes. We weren't doing "Brick House" or anything like that.

Zak Najor: I worked at Bank of America as a courier. Chris was working in Jimbo's, the grocery store. I was like, "Chris, you gotta get a clue, man. We're going somewhere with this." And he just hung up the phone on me. There was that transition where it was like, "Should we leave our jobs to do this?" It was like that, I want to say, for close to a year, maybe two. I remember having to play a gig in San Francisco, where I told the guy at Bank of America that I needed to help my grandfather clean out his garage because I was afraid to tell him that we had a gig in San Francisco.

Robert Walter: We got into the studio. Fred Wesley came in—Karl knew him from the road.

Zak Najor: You're trying to be on your best behavior.

Robert Walter: He was a hero of ours, because he had played with James Brown, and all that. So we felt really cool. I could barely play when I made that record. I was just learning. I had only played on the Hammond organ a few times ever in my life at that point. I was way over my head. But we were all like that together.

Fred Wesley (Trombone, James Brown, Maceo Parker): Back in the '80s, a call went out for musicians to do a beer commercial. I went to audition for it and Karl was there. They put the two of us together and wanted us to do a routine.

Chris Stillwell: I remember Fred saying, "You know, if it feels good, you don't want to play it to death; it loses all of its feel."

Fred Wesley: They didn't do tunes like A-A-B-A—first verse, second verse, a bridge and third verse. They all had a different kind of slant on how to write music.

Robert Walter: Greyboy wanted to start a record label. *West Coast Boogaloo* was 001 on Greyboy Records. His idea was that it was going to be an all-star group and everybody would release solo albums like in the model of Blue Note or Prestige Records, where everybody had a record and everybody played on everybody else's record. You buy a Wayne Shorter record and Herbie's on it, you buy a Herbie record and Freddie Hubbard's on it. A whole stable of people. This was gonna launch that.

Chris Stillwell: We booked a studio I'd never heard of in LA. It was this real discreet, wood-panel type of place. And I had heard that Sly Stone had recorded there or used that board. We just ran down stuff . . . what we were doing because we were going under the aesthetic of those jazz records—you look on the back, and it's like "recorded in one day" or there's two separate sessions, and it's like, two days. We were pretty well-oiled by that point, so we just played the tunes and ran them down. Being in the studio can be kind of nerve-wracking when you're not used to it, so there's a couple of mistakes there, but the mistakes turned out to be these cool things about the tunes.

Elgin Park: It was incredibly quick. It was very rough and ready.

Robert Walter: Supposedly, the first Ramones album was made the same way. They could afford studio time for a day and did it.

Chris Stillwell: We were all writers, so we would just come up with stuff. Robert was very prolific from the get go. He would come to writing sessions with five or six complete tunes.

Zak Najor: It's such a big part of my formative years as a musician, having someone tell me what to do. And when it sucks, to tell me—look you in the face and say, "That sucks." You better believe Robert Walter is like that, Elgin Park is like that.

32

We Sure Enjoyed Selling a Ton of Records and Making a Boatload of Money

With the Spin Doctors seeing explosive commercial success, and John Popper's recovery from his motorcycle accident in the rear-view mirror, Blues Traveler went into the studio to record Four, *their fourth album, in spring 1994. They reteamed with producers Michael Barbiero and Steve Thompson for what would be a massive commercial hit from the jam band community.*

John Popper: There's an ego you have as a performer. And to some extent, you need to be a performer, especially like a frontman. You need to be able to convince yourself, "Yeah, everyone's looking at me, this is all about me." And you develop this sort of paranoid arrogance that you never tell anyone about, like, "Is this about me?"

Chan Kinchla: Hair metal had kind of gone away. And grunge had its big explosion, but it had kind of gone away. So the mid-'90s was a very eclectic music scene.

David Precheur: It's very simple. Not only does every musician want to be a big rock star and have tons of money, any human with a brain wants to be a huge rock star and make lots of money. Because who doesn't want to make lots of money and be sexy when you're ugly and get up every day and play music?

Brendan Hill: You have to be careful on how early you hit. Because it really does change your trajectory if everybody's looking at you for what you're going to do next.

Patrick Clifford: It was definitely pushing a boulder up a hill. Believe me. And for some time as well.

John Popper: For many years as a band, I was convinced, "Maybe they recognize us? Are we famous enough?" The entire time we were thoroughly convinced we never were that famous. One day we're in an airport, and then people really *are* looking at you and you see the difference. You see the difference between your ego going, "Yeah, they probably might know who you are," to "Oh my god, they're looking at me." And even when it's happening, you're like, "Wait, are they? Or is it that I'm looking at them wondering if they're looking at me?" And you tell yourself, "Nah they aren't." And then you tell yourself, "Yes they are." And what you learn is about 50 percent of the time they do. And that's a safe bet.

David Precheur: It's important to keep everybody alive and functioning with having a strategy that works for them and for the business, without crashing people physically, mentally, and abandoning the crew.

Joan Osborne: If you had a record, whatever your touring schedule was, you were also going to build in visits to the different radio stations, because that was the main way that your music was gonna get heard. And MTV was certainly a part of it. You would also go by the radio station, talk to the DJs, make nice with them, get your picture taken with them, and perform a couple of songs live on the air.

David Precheur: There was a huge influx of revenue into these record companies that made their books look so fat and happy. They were showing record-breaking revenue because everybody was refreshing their collections from cassette tapes and vinyl to CD. I owned Bob Marley's *Legend* and *Dark Side of the Moon* seven times.

Brendan Hill: We toured *Save His Soul* for two years, from '92 to '94. We were in a tour bus—Bob, Chan, and I. We were playing these gigs, and we're getting bigger and bigger and bigger. The success was coming, because we had this popular fan base . . . not much radio play, but we'd been on *Letterman* a few times. And so people knew our name. And there were some radio stations that just loved us and would play whatever we gave them. We were at the point where people knew us, and so we wanted to tour and make money. John, to his credit, said, "Okay, let's go out there and make some money." And unfortunately he couldn't walk, so we did what a bunch of twenty-two-year-olds would do in that situation: We wheeled him around in a wheelchair, and we got him on stage, we put him in a special stool that he could sit in, with a table for his harps, he had a microphone right in front of him. And we would just play with him sitting down. Instead of getting on the tour bus, we had a van. And we paid somebody to drive this van—it was an emptied moving van, and we put a queen size mattress, and John would zoom off to the next gig.

The rest of us were drinking and carousing and having fun on this tour bus. And John was kind of isolated. When he got back home, he moved to an apartment in Princeton. He basically holed up there after we got off tour. That was his thing: watch TV, have his stuff around him, his swords, all that stuff. And he would just write prolifically. Song after song after song. By the time we were ready to talk about the next record, John had seven songs already, if not more.

Michael Barbiero: Before we did the album, I had to fly out to California and have a meeting with Dave Anderle, who was in charge of the A&R department of A&M records, about the forthcoming album. The first question he asked me when I walked into his office was, "You know, the last album did alright, but are we gonna get a radio hit?" And having heard "Run Around" prior to doing the album, I said, "I can guarantee you there's one hit on this album." He said, "Well, that's good enough for me."

David Precheur: Al Cafaro said, "Gimme a fucking single."

Patrick Clifford: I don't doubt that happened.

John Popper: He grabbed me by my head at some party and said, "We will break you this year."

Al Marks: We were getting very frustrated because we couldn't figure it out.

David Precheur: Listeners are not as complex as an artist's mind says. The master chef creates a seven-course meal, where you get hit with seven to twelve flavors in a single bite of food. Yet there's an entire nation of people that are very happy having hot dogs and hamburgers on July Fourth, and look forward to it. Al Cafaro was retiring on a fucking diamond parachute. And he turned to us and said, "I'm leaving, going to Hawaii for the rest of my life. I want to make y'all rich. So give me a goddamn hit." And that's when John was like, "Oh, we have a three-chord progression, 'Run Around,'" And then how about I rip off Pachelbel's Canon and do "Hook." He just took two ditties, and because he's a fucking genius, was like, "I know exactly what it takes to make a hit."

John Popper: One time I was in the DMV, getting my license, so I didn't have my ID on me. And this girl was whispering to her mom. And I noticed and she goes, "Sorry, you just look so much like him." And I go, "Well I am him." I wait to get my license back and I go and show the mom. And she's like, "Oh, I don't care." You feel like the biggest jackass.

Brendan Hill: We went up to Bearsville [in Woodstock] and by that point, John had healed enough to walk and get a cane. We did some songwriting in New York first, at one of those rehearsal studios on 50th Street or something. This was when we were getting big budgets: We had a couple hundred thousand dollars and we could afford to really flesh it out.

This was the height of the recording budget, so we had a month of preproduction. We went in, and all stayed up there in the Woodstock area in the fall.

There was only one little bar in Woodstock, so we'd go there. But the main thing was just working. Bearsville had forty-foot ceilings, thirty or forty feet across, sixty feet long—like this giant gymnasium. Everything was soundproofed correctly . . . it was designed for good sound. We were confident in the space. I had my drums set up, just in front of where the sound booth was; my back was to the control room. And then Bob was over to my left, Chan was to the right. And John had this little booth built for him in the middle, out of little partitions. And I think it was a hundred degrees in there every single day.

Dave Frey: "Run Around" was kind of like a throwaway song. They didn't know how to demo it. It didn't play well live. It was not even really on the list.

Brendan Hill: I remember recording "Run Around" and getting in the control room and seeing Mike and Steve look at each other. And it became a joke: "I smell a single!" But they knew from that moment on, we didn't know shit. We were just like, "Oh, it's kind of a light bouncy number." When John brought that song to us originally, it was much slower, on acoustic guitars. These guys just made it danceable. They knew, "Okay, this isn't just a throwaway record, we got to make every song have it so that the record company has ammunition to release a single, another one, another one." And that's the goal: to have four or five in a row.

Michael Barbiero: Steve and I came up with the idea of making Popper a bet that he couldn't sing "Run Around" in one take. I said, "We'll take you and the whole band out to Peter Luger's for a nice steak." Well that got Popper off the couch in a hurry. And he sang it in one take! That was the best bet we ever made even though we lost.

Al Marks: This one had Top 40 written all over it.

Pete Shapiro: There were not a lot of songs from the jam band genre as commercially friendly as "Run Around."

Michael Barbiero: The record company didn't think there was another single on the album and wanted us to record another song. That song was

"Hook." We booked a session at Electric Ladyland Studios on West 4th Street in New York. We did the "Hook" tracking there and the band was up against the deadline, and they had to go out on tour. So we had Warren Haynes—just Steve and I—in the studio. Warren came in and I was meeting him for the first time. Warren set up to play in the control room with us to be able to just hear everything on the big speakers, really loud. And he played a killer solo right off the top. And I was really excited about it. But Steve looked at him after the solo and said, "What would happen if you play this on slide?" And Warren liked the idea and pulled out a bottleneck slide classic that he told us belonged to Duane Allman, that had been given to him.

Al Marks: John didn't go out to write the Top 40 record. It was all his influences that he was listening to. Spin Doctors, Dave Matthews . . . everybody in that era was starting to move their criteria of how they wanted to write their music differently so that it would take on a different form, and they'd be able to expand it to a larger audience. I listened to *Four* and said, "Holy shit, this is terrific. We're gonna be able to break this."

David Precheur: I had the demo in my car and I remember tapping my hand and foot to it. And I call up Al Cafaro and said, "'Run Around' is the hit," and Al Cafaro, being a fucking monster-minded record guy is like, "Yep, and we're gonna release 'Hook' because 'Hook' also's got a catchy hook."

Patrick Clifford: I played them "Run Around" and they said this sounds like a Van Morrison song . . . like the girl who got away. And I said, "Guys, let me tell you, they wrote a song about you two guys." They didn't know whether to be proud or chagrined. And I said, they're tired of you guys lying to them. They feel left out.

Chan Kinchla: Our first single actually was "Hook," but we always knew "Run Around" was probably our best shot to get really good on radio. Our whole deal was like, "Let's not go out of the box with that. Let's save it for later." So we put out "Hook" and did a huge fall tour. We were killing it. Our numbers were just packed. We felt great, but the album dipped off the charts . . . we're like, "You know, it's just the same old thing."

Brendan Hill: We had a discussion about the color of the record, because now CDs were the main thing. So how do you differentiate your CD spine from other CDs? I think I wanted it to be silver. And Chan was just like, "maybe green." We went with the green thing and it was like this kind of vomit, neon green, but you could see that spine anywhere.

John Popper: One time somebody said, "Are you John Popper?" And I said, "No." I just wanted to try that out. And they looked so disappointed like I was the biggest dick in the world.

Chan Kinchla: January '96, "Run Around" came out. And then inexplicably I remember looking at the charts, and we reentered . . . in record company speak, that means the "track's reacting."

Patrick Clifford: The crowds got bigger and the audience changed.

Chan Kinchla: We spent the next year doing every Hot 100 radio show. That was some smarmy schmoozing ass kissing.

Al Marks: It got to a point where we were buying so many tickets for shows, the bands complaining that they were having to pay us back. We would give radio stations ten pairs of tickets to give away when they were coming in the marketplace. And we would have like eight radio stations giving away ten pairs of tickets. So it got to 160 tickets that we would have to buy at whatever face value was, and then ultimately that would get charged against the band's tour support.

Chan Kinchla: It was a culture clash at the shows. The crowd was all our hardcore fans and then all these fans that just liked the few singles.

Jono Manson: All of their back catalog went gold, and some of it maybe even platinum.

Patrick Clifford: Baseball cap–wearing crowd of guys and polished girls. It wasn't the hippie-ish early years.

Scott "bullethead" Reilly: Blues Traveler played one of the big rooms at South by Southwest and I'm in there with a bunch of young folks in the industry. And kids are kicking hacky sacks and somebody flat-out says, "It's our job to stop this thing"—meaning the jam bands—"These guys aren't cool. We want more Nirvana."

Dave Frey: I think a lot of people at A&M saw Blues Traveler as a favor of Bill Graham, because Bill cut the deal with Jerry [Moss]. And they were like, "Oh, we're stuck with this uncool band that we don't get, and we don't like very much." They're not cool like Soundgarden who got signed at the same time.

David Precheur: Then everybody's CD collections were satisfied and it went back to normal sales. And the corporations were like, "Whoa, whoa, whoa." Blues Traveler was in the middle of it. And we were probably one of the last bands to enjoy that kind of false bottom existence.

Dave Frey: I think it was John Sykes at MTV, the president, called me: "Why don't we have a video for this song? It's been number one and you've sold four million records." I said, "Why? You know we sold four million records without you, right? Why do we want to spend money?"

John Popper: You want to flirt with MTV. You want to come at it and give it a lot of lack of respect, but in a way that makes it want you more. I did my first MTV interview on our bus and I don't know quite what I was thinking, but I had a teddy bear held hostage at knifepoint the entire interview . . . like it was a hostage negotiation. And that's kind of the dance you want to do for them. As a new band, you always want to say, "I'm different. Check me out." But they also need to go, "Oh, you're different. Who are you like?" So I knew that I would have to deal with MTV, but I had a sense that MTV wasn't going to like me. So it always started with me trying to do something funny and absurdist or surreal. The very first interview, I just kept talking like we were in a hostage situation. The whole time I kept making the bear shake, like he's really scared. And I'm holding a knife to his throat. I never explained why I was holding a bear hostage and we would have to talk like that was incidental. Basically every other appearance on MTV was me talking about my ass or masturbating. At the same time if you're a new band, and you just do as you're told, they forget all about you.

Chan Kinchla: We weren't obsessed with MTV . . . the record company sure was. If you could get something on rotation on MTV, you were selling a lot of records. The Spin Doctors got on MTV. And Dave Matthews. So it was what you needed to do. We were a little less of a traditional kind of "good-looking frontman straight up rock." I mean, I was a little more dubious that we actually would pull it off but lo and behold, we were on MTV and VH1 all summer . . . us, TLC, Seal. It was hilarious.

Dave Frey: For the first time ever, they spent a shit ton of money on it. And nothing happened. It was dead, dead in the water. And so we were like, "Oh well, let's start working on the fifth record." In the meantime, John had guest-starred on "What Would You Say" with the Dave Matthews Band. Jerry Moss, you know, the "M" in A&M . . . I had a meeting with him and I was like, "What do you think? How come it didn't work the first time?" He's like, "Timing. It's about timing. What's in the market? What's going on? What's around it?"

"So why do you think it worked then?"

He goes, "Well, clearly, it's a summer song."

A summer song? What the fuck is that?

Chan Kinchla: We sure enjoyed selling a ton of records and making a boatload of money and getting a Grammy and *Saturday Night Live* and all that fun stuff that goes with having a hit.

John Popper: The one time that records actually get you some money . . . you get to renegotiate your contract. Everybody got a million bucks, we all got to buy houses.

Brendan Hill: It opened the next level of doors . . . we were opening for the Rolling Stones. The H.O.R.D.E. tour took off.

Dave Frey: We sold six million records.

John Popper: We were victims of our own success, because people think of us and they think about that time when that record was out. And the irony of "Hook" being a hit isn't lost on me. Had that not happened, the punch line of the joke wouldn't have worked.

33

We Really Went off the Rails

How do you follow up an album that sold millions? That was at stake for the Spin Doctors for what would become their second album, 1994's Turn It Upside Down. *Ironically, the album title became a metaphor for what actually happened.*

Chris Barron: It was really intense. And we didn't handle it super well.

Eric Schenkman: Everybody gets a big ego.

Aaron Comess: When you're in your twenties, and suddenly there's all that success and money and responsibility . . . you know, we're four very different types of personalities, and so the truth was, it was actually not a great time.

Chris Barron: We had some big hit songs . . . I think it sidelined us as a jam band. I don't want to say we paid the price or something like that . . . but maybe we did. Maybe we had a bit of a wipeout.

Eric Schenkman: You exchange the crowds, you exchange the expectations. And when you lose your core crowd, it's hard to keep the thread of that music alive.

Aaron Comess: We took six months off, because we had been going for three years.

Chris Barron: Our first single from the second record was "Cleopatra's Cat." It attempts to right that ship a little bit with something a bit more underground, subversive and strange. I don't think it was the right move. We should've kept the ball rolling and let the momentum carry us rather than quickly trying to get back into the weird good graces of the weirdos.

Aaron Comess: We could have made better decisions if we were united at the time. But it's hard. It's a lot of pressure and it's not something that everybody can manage that well.

Chris Barron: One of the things that kind of bugs me about the Spin Doctors' legacy is because we are known for two upbeat songs, "Little Miss Can't Be Wrong" and "Two Princes." People that don't really know us think that we're lightweights but we've got shit that's as heavy as any of that grunge shit.

Eric Schenkman: It's hard to hold on to the audience when you're getting on the radio. People don't really want to follow you around when that's happening, because you're playing the song predictably.

Aaron Comess: There were a lot of internal, stressful dynamics going on.

David Sonenberg: We had some internal strife.

Aaron Comess: We made the second record. And I gotta say, Sony was pretty cool about not being up our ass too much. We kept everybody away. They seemed very happy with the record and really liked the record. And obviously, it was not nearly the success of *Kryptonite,* but it did sell two million records around the world. Coming off ten million around the world, it was a big disappointment.

Eric Schenkman: For the [label], it was a straight business. And for management and for booking, same thing. A new record was necessary, and they're trying to take it to the next level.

Aaron Comess: Trouble started and the vibe internally was struggling. Eric left in the middle of the tour, and that was the beginning of things crumbling for a while.

Chris Barron: We didn't have the communication vocabulary that we needed at the time.

Eric Schenkman: We really went off the rails. And we never did rectify it. Blues Traveler rectified it by continuing to play. Phish rectified it by really growing into it.

Chris Barron: We kind of turned around one day and Eric was just gone.

Aaron Comess: He basically just quit after we did a gig in the Greek Theatre in San Francisco.

Chris Barron: It was a bit us being like, "Alright, well, you want to quit . . . off you go."

Eric Schenkman: I really didn't want to make the record the way we did . . . we started in Memphis, which is fine with me, but then [bassist] Mark [White] didn't want to work there anymore. And that was not fine with me. And then we went back to New York and we started with the same crew that we worked with on the first record, which is okay with me. But then when it got done, everybody seemed to want to have "Cleopatra's Cat" as the first single, which was not okay with me. We also wanted to go to bigger venues, which was really okay with management, but it was not okay with me.

Chris Barron: Aaron put it really well, right in the beginning of the formation of the band. Aaron was like, "We should play songs with different tempos, different rhythms and different tonalities . . . meaning we should play songs in major keys and in minor keys. We should play fast songs, slow songs, medium songs, and songs in even time signatures and songs in uneven time signatures." To me as the lyricist and as the frontman and the singer, that also meant having a broad, emotional palette . . . having songs that are angry and aggressive and also having songs that are upbeat.

Eric Schenkman: I'm a hothead by nature. I'm not really anymore. But once I hit critical mass, I was just like, "You know, fuck this shit." And so that's just the way I was and I actually dug my heels in on it.

Chris Barron: Metallica did group therapy. Later on, I found out that they did that, and I was like, "Jesus, that would have been fucking great! Somebody should have just been like, 'Here's a shrink!'"

34

We Were Just These Hippies, Running Around Half Naked or Sometimes Fully Naked

After the Fox opened in spring of 1992, the jam scene really started to take hold in Colorado. Already, bands had found national touring success: Big Head Todd and the Monsters and The Samples, to name two. But their sound was more straight rock and roll. As the mid-'90s hit, a melding of sorts started between, well, nearly every sound under the sun.

Kyle Hollingsworth (Keyboards, vocals, The String Cheese Incident): There's a great drummer in town named Dave Watts, the founder of a band called The Motet. He used to be in a band called Shockra out of the East Coast. Dave moved out here and he kind of became the chairman of the jam scene.

Dave Watts: In Boston, it was this competitive scene. And as a band, Shockra was an outlier to some of the bands that were happening back then. I decided to move out here and try and start a scene . . . and also because of the natural environment, I think a lot of people moved out here because they want to be close to the mountains and use that as some inspiration. Shockra was picking up on the steam that Phish had. We actually had a house and I suppose that was my inspiration for finding a house in Boulder. We had a house called Neptune that was in Newton, Massachusetts. And we would have parties there, and jam sessions there in the basement. Phish would come over and play with us in the basement after their shows at the Paradise. And so we started following their coattails. There wasn't a lot of jam bands back then, compared to what happened after I left Boston.

Kyle Hollingsworth: He lived on a kind of commune in North Boulder. All the bands coming through town, whether it was Phish or ARU, would stay at his place.

Dave Watts: I wanted to have a house that I could share with other musicians and artists. There was a group of us, maybe like three, four, five of us that were like, "Let's find a spot that we can all live and play music all day." That's all we wanted to do . . . play music all day, do gigs, and have a low overhead so that we didn't have to work day jobs. I was living with Don Strasburg, who ran the Fox Theatre at that point. And we just found this little house with a couple of outbuildings, a barn, and a little studio space. It was a little run-down, but kind of perfect for us. It was on four acres of land. Michael Travis from String Cheese was down in Telluride at the Telluride Bluegrass Festival, and he was talking about his new band String Cheese, and he had just added a hi-hat snare drum to his congas percussion setup. And he had a vision of what kind of drummer he wanted to be with String Cheese. He was talking about moving up to Boulder as well, with the whole band—String Cheese. And they wanted to start touring the country. After about six months of living at this spot that we called Double Dig, Travis moved in with us. Eventually Mike Kang moved in with us.

Bill Nershi (Guitar, vocals, The String Cheese Incident): Double Dig Ranch was a very heady place to hang out.

Keith Moseley (Bass, The String Cheese Incident): Several musicians were living there, and we would rehearse there. From time to time, they had a little outbuilding studio space.

Michael Travis (Drums, The String Cheese Incident): It was a wild situation. We were living on this kind of run-down farm.

Kyle Hollingsworth: I grew up in Baltimore. So for me, it felt like music and being out in nature and taking more chances and a little less strict to guidelines . . . was kind of the way you're living your life. It definitely seeped into the kind of music we we're playing.

Drew Emmitt (Mandolin, guitar, vocals, Leftover Salmon): I never went there. But our early bass player, Tye North, used to go there and hang out.

Tye North: It wasn't a commune . . . people just kind of wanted to do their thing.

Vince Herman (Guitar, vocals, Leftover Salmon): I didn't hang out there much. But it was certainly legendary on the scene with Dave Watts and the Cheese guys. I was married and had kids.

Dave Watts: We were just these hippies, running around half naked or sometimes fully naked, planting a huge garden and making music all day as much as we could . . . being weird artist types.

Bill Nershi: It was kind of like a commune. They had a garden out back and they were growing vegetables. And they had a garage that we would rehearse in . . . I think there was a possum that had died in that building. On a hot day we would be driven from the practice space and had to go to the house. My favorite memory was coming back to Double Dig and the ladies that lived there were in the garden; it was a beautiful, sunny summer day. And they were gardening topless. And I just felt like I had woken up in nirvana.

Michael Kang (Mandolin, vocals, The String Cheese Incident): We were surrounded by this housing development encroaching on us . . . for lack of a better term, hippie enclave of musicians that really are just dedicated to living life and doing it.

Michael Travis: This landlord was planning on tearing the whole thing down and turning it into a subdivision, which he eventually did. But it was a big farm that he bought, for very cheap I'm sure, on like twenty, thirty acres.

And it was his grace that let us stay there because he could have gone for the dollars right away. He let us just hang out and do the crazy music hippie ranch thing for a good long time.

Dave Watts: They would leave their tour bus that they called "Bussie" in our driveway. They would rehearse eight hours a day in between tours.

Keith Moseley: We would just crash on the floor there until we went back out again.

Keller Williams: The first night I met Keith Moseley from String Cheese, I gave him a ride from Colorado Springs to the Double Dig where he was parked. It was ground zero of the jam.

Michael Travis: Me and my girlfriend built a tent in the woods near the edge of the property.

Dave Watts: Mike Kang took over the living room and put up some walls and made a hideout in the middle of the house. I was living with my girlfriend in the studio and someone was living in the barn. There was a teepee, a little RV . . . there was probably about fifteen or sixteen of us living there at one point. And there'd be a jam session in the house going on, there'd be a jam session in the barn, I'd be working on something in the studio . . . it was just a really creative space that everyone could just count on at any hour being able to play some music at some point.

Michael Travis: I finally moved out when a tree fell on the tent.

Jamie Janover: It had an outbuilding where there used to be a horse barn, and an outbuilding that was used by a prior tenant to be a telemarketing conference center. So it had all these telephone lines put in. Dave lived out there—no bathroom or sink or anything; he had to come into the house to do that stuff. But he had his music studio in his bedroom in the outbuilding. And that's when String Cheese said, "Hey, Kyle, do you want to audition for String Cheese and come jam with us at the Mountain Sun?" The

Mountain Sun holds like a hundred and something people and it was sold out. And people were standing on tables. And at the end of the show, Kang was like, "Hey, we're thinking of just asking Kyle to join the band. You think he should join the band?" And people freaked out. So that was the beginning of Kyle getting that gig.

Keith Moseley: Colorado in general has been a super fertile music environment for a long time. And some of that is due to iconic venues like Red Rocks . . . bands from everywhere have always wanted to play Red Rocks. But it's also a really thriving music scene with Telluride Bluegrass and RockyGrass and all the other festivals that show up here in the mountain towns and in the cities.

Keller Williams: Colorado was more of a magnet for young, open-minded, hairy people. The winter is what got you there and summer is what kept you there.

Dave Watts: When I first moved to Boulder, there was a jazz trio playing in the parking lot of Alfalfa's or something. And they're killing it. I'm like, "Whoa, I moved to the right place. There's jazz in the parking lot of a grocery store." There were so many opportunities for musicians in these random little ways that we didn't need to be headlining the Fox. You're happy to do some little coffee shops.

Tye North: Michigan Mike started doing these Monday night Nederland Acid Jazz gigs at a couple of different bars in Nederland. When I would come home from tour, I would call Mike or Mike called me and tried to get a bunch of guys together. So that would be a couple of guys from String Cheese, couple of guys from the local jazz scene.

Michael Travis: The scene in Crested Butte was small. Our big influence was Leftover Salmon—they came through all the time. They lit us up as far as what the band could do and how much fun a band could have. They were our first big influence for sure. There was a 150-person club called the Eldo and in one winter we got to see Phish, Aquarium Rescue Unit, and Widespread

Panic all in that venue. The guy didn't care about making money. He just cared about getting cool bands in there.

Bill Nershi: I had skied Telluride for twelve years straight, and I wanted to ski a different ski area for a season. I was going to have one last ski bumming winter before I got my shit together. I drove my school bus from Telluride to Crested Butte to park it at Keith Moseley's place. I met Keith at different bluegrass festivals—we had a couple of beers and played some music. He said, "Yeah, you can park your school bus in the back of the house," and I gave him some money for taking showers. I drove my school bus to Crested Butte . . . it caught on fire on the drive. There was a fire coming through the floorboard. I had to stop along the way to put out the fire.

I was asking around because I wanted to do some kind of ski show that I could do like a once a week and get some food. People told me about Mike Kang and I met him and we started playing.

The ski area would get really long lines. They wanted somebody to entertain the people in the lift line. So me and Mike would every so often go up to the ski area, get our instruments out, play a couple of tunes, and that's how we got our ski passes for the year.

Keller Williams: In Steamboat Springs, I got a ski pass from what was BW-3's at the time. And I played for fifty dollars and dinner every Thursday.

Michael Travis: I was living in Crested Butte in the winter, and I had jammed with Kang and Keith previously on some other side projects in the summer. I was working for the Forest Service when Bill Nershi moved his school bus into my backyard and started camping out there. The tenants were fine with it. And so I came back and the guys were like, "This guy Bill living in your backyard is awesome, let's jam." And we jammed in my house there for the first time and that was it.

Keller Williams: My first job in Colorado in '95 was at the Telluride Bluegrass Festival. String Cheese Incident were playing in a basement bar as a four piece, an after-show type of thing. And what got me was Michael Travis on the drums, playing full percussion with one hand, and then full kit with the other hand and legs.

Bill Nershi: We played this variety night in Crested Butte along with a bunch of other acts of different kinds. That was December of '93. For some reason, it really clicked. Keith learned how to play the bass, but he was a guitar player. We got done and were like, "That was cool, that was fun." I didn't really think it was any different than any of the other shows we're doing. But people started coming up after the show and everybody was amazed, asking, "How long have you been playing together?" I laughed and thought, "About three hours."

Keller Williams: The now infamous Mishawaka Amphitheatre, just outside of Fort Collins . . . back then they were known for being a roadside bar and grill with lots of animals like peacocks and goats. String Cheese definitely had their own little PA—the speakers on stands. I just remember there being maybe thirty or fifty people there and just a bunch of crazy peacocks and goats.

Michael Travis: We were living pretty frugal. We had a game for a while where I was like, "I'm poor. I don't want to spend money on food." So you build any bite on the table and I should try to eat it no matter how disgusting. Then you buy my dinner. I got a lot of dinners! Kang did one where we put a weed roach on top and he ate it. And I'm like, "Okay, I'm out."

Drew Emmitt: I grew up in Boulder. I was there first, before Vince showed up. And I was raised there in the '70s and '80s. I was always trying to get into the Boulder, quote-unquote "music scene," which seemed like a big deal if you'd get into the Boulder music scene. I managed to get in some bands and the last band I was in before Leftover Salmon was Left Hand String Band, which was part of why it's called Leftover Salmon. And we had some steady gigs around Boulder at JJ McCabe's, the Walrus, the Gold Hill Inn.

During the '80s and early '90s, there wasn't a Boulder Theater or Fox Theatre yet. There were some local bands starting up—Big Head Todd and the Monsters, The Samples, Acoustic Junction. And of course, there was Hot

Rize playing bluegrass. And there were some festivals like Telluride Bluegrass Festival, the Rocky Mountain Bluegrass Festival, that were happening. So we were already getting in on all that stuff. And so Vince shows up in Boulder. He drives out from West Virginia with a friend of his and came into Boulder one night—it happened to be our regular Tuesday night gig at the Walrus. He shows up there and it says "Bluegrass Tonight" and it happened to be Left Hand String Band playing there. He came to the show and we met that night and then ended up going to a picking party where we picked and hung out together and partied.

Back then, there was a really awesome local picking scene, fed by both Telluride Bluegrass Festival and the Rocky Mountain Bluegrass Festival. A lot of great pickers and parties and things like that. We ended up in a lot of those same circles. Vince actually ended up playing with Left Hand String Band for a little while, before he went off to start his own band, the Salmon Heads.

Béla Fleck: It was New Grass Revival (before I joined) that really bashed the doors open. When I joined, we continued to develop and folks in Colorado accepted us for what we were . . . and were not disappointed that we were not more traditional. Telluride Bluegrass Festival and RockyGrass brought in enough talent to build a significant audience for the traditional scene too.

Mark Vann (Banjo, Leftover Salmon): My mother played guitar and piano, and eventually we had a family band: Dad played guitar, my brother played mandolin, my mother played upright bass, and I played banjo. And we always had other instruments—recorders and autoharps and ukuleles and clarinets. Mostly it was what we did instead of watching TV. After college, I went to a cabin in the piney woods, in Virginia. A "cabin on the hill," with no electricity, and the lamplight in the window, for almost three years. No telephone, no nothing! Basically, I worked a few hours a week—as little as possible. I had no bills. I had an old car, and that was about it. It was a great way to learn to play the banjo. Really woodshedding, I guess.

Drew Emmitt: In Telluride, we all got together and we all got [in the festival's] band contest. We just met Mark Vann at the campground.

Mark Vann: The picking hadn't been that great that particular night. I was kind of bummed out. I went to bed early, around eleven, in the tent, but woke up about an hour later and heard this picking about forty feet from my tent that was just awesome! I threw my clothes on and ran out there. It was Drew and Vince, and a bunch of others getting all wild and crazy, and we just clicked.

Drew Emmitt: And so we ended up in the band contest as the Left Handed Salmon Spankers, because it was the Left Hand String Band, the Salmon Heads and the Chicken Spankers. We got like thirteen of us on stage with the intent of trying to lose the contest, and just trying to make a big mockery out of the whole band contest thing. And we ended up playing some gigs in town during the festival. One gig was at the Roma, and the Fly Me to the Moon was another one. And Mark came out and sat in with us.

That next winter, the Salmon Heads were booked to play some shows around Colorado, one of them being here where I live in Crested Butte at the El Dorado Café, but some of the band members really didn't want to come all the way up here. On the way up to the gig, Vince just blurted out, "Let's just call it Leftover Salmon." We ended up doing the gig and that turned out to be the new band.

Mark Vann: The first gig was literally an accident. We were just a bunch of guys thrown together, trying to figure out songs we all could play. I ended up playing banjo on calypso tunes and Cajun tunes, and Drew played electric guitar or mandolin, depending on which fit the song.

Vince Herman: The next day we had five other gigs after that first night. All the club owners were really tight and they talked all the time. So when they heard how well that night went, other venues were calling up the next day. It just kind of took off on its own.

Drew Emmitt: There were some more rock-oriented bands and then there was the bluegrass scene. Our concept was what if we did both? That way not only could we play bluegrass in the summertime, but also in the winter, we could go play ski areas because we had a drummer, and we got some electric instruments.

Tye North: Nobody did the electric bluegrass thing yet. Salmon were the first band to do that. We would do twenty to thirty songs a night.

Vince Herman: It was unusual to make a living playing bluegrass. We had a whole lot of ski town work. And some of those gigs were four or five days in the same place. Often we'd play a happy hour set, and then come back a couple hours later and play a night show.

Tye North: You could probably play ten different ski towns in Colorado in the period of a week.

Drew Emmitt: It was met with some resistance, of course. "Bluegrass with drums? And electric mandolins and banjos and stuff . . . that sounds really weird."

Tye North: Mixing the bluegrass thing and putting it through a high tempo with crazy loud rock and roll and you've got a recipe for people to really go nuts.

Jon O'Leary: I met Leftover literally right after I made it to Colorado. I was a big Deadhead but I just got done seeing a whole bunch of New Grass Revival shows. And then I saw those guys. And I was like, "Holy shit. This is exactly the type of band I would want to have." They called it "Cajun polyethnic slamgrass." That's exactly what it sounded like. And it was amazing. I made friends with them instantly, just by walking up to them and hanging out with them.

Michael Kang: Colorado became the hotbed of not only touring bands, but just also the music fan base.

Drew Emmitt: The Boulder scene was mostly bands playing locally around Boulder and Colorado. People weren't really touring yet. The Samples had just started touring. Big Head Todd had started touring, Acoustic Junction had started touring. But we were still just playing around Colorado. But the thing about the Colorado music scene was that there was enough work, where you didn't really have to tour. People didn't really know how to tour back then. Unless you had a record deal, it was kind of pointless to try to get out on the road. We bought a school bus and just started putting out our feelers to see if we could get some gigs out of state. Slowly but surely, we started to get gigs. Mostly we started on the West Coast, up in the Northwest. We played up in Seattle; Portland and Eugene; Moscow, Idaho; Boise; Jackson Hole; Salt Lake City and California, and then eventually branching out more and more and just getting on the school bus, driving around playing gigs. We had no idea what we were doing.

Keith Moseley: DIY is always the way we've rolled, and we've got a lot of strong, independent-minded band members. "Let's go out and conquer. Let's go out and create our own destiny."

35

The DJs Always Knocked Us Out Cold

Robert Walter: Our first tour was not in the States. It was in Europe. We'd play in San Diego and maybe go up to the Bay Area . . . that was a little California circuit. But other than that, we just would fly to Europe and do a few weeks there. We did that for the first couple of years.

Karl Denson: I met Stephen Miner in Cologne, Germany. He offered to make my records. I was always writing music, so I had material and the records were received well, and they were my own gigs. And I was like, "You know, this is a no-brainer." With Lenny, I wasn't playing that much. It was one of those rock and roll gigs where you're playing, but you're not really stretching out—you got your little moment in the sun here and there, but you gotta worry about your chops. You get home and go to the club and get your ass whooped by a twenty-year-old.

Elgin Park: Karl had a booking agent from his jazz thing.

Zak Najor: Europe, it was a lot of hard work. Even though they like to dance, you had to win people over.

Robert Walter: The audience was receptive and they knew the references. We were obsessed with all this '60s music and in the States it was like, "Oh, what's this weird thing?" But over there, you played a Grant Green record or Reuben Wilson song . . . they got where we were coming from. When we first went, I think *West Coast Boogaloo* wasn't even out. We were touring on Greyboy's success with *Freestyle* and he had a hit with "Unwind Your Mind," with Karl playing on that track.

Karl Denson: We were playing dance clubs, kind of hipster joints.

Elgin Park: We went to Rome the first night. And I remember being struck, because we'd been playing the Green Circle and it was packed. And so we were like, "Okay, we're gonna go all the way to Europe and somehow, there's gonna be people that want to see us." I had disbelief. When we ended up dropping in on Rome, we were super jet-lagged. I think we got there in the evening and then we drove to the club and played late-night. And it just sounded great. I mean, it was crazy. And it was packed. I couldn't wrap my head around it . . . it was all just rare groove and acid jazz.

Zak Najor: You're co-headlining with a DJ and you're sort of involved in the house-techno world. So it was hit or miss; I mean, we were developing something. And there's a lot of hype, but honestly, if we had kept on that path, I don't know if it would have been sustainable. The DJs always knocked us out cold.

Elgin Park: We continued to move through Europe—insane, ridiculous places. I think we played an ice cream parlor. It was comedy. We didn't have any equipment—we just had our guitars and sax. Robert would be playing on these absurd keyboards or I would be playing through a terrible, miniature heavy metal amp. We had to be loose about what we were doing. And prior to this, we were tone conscious, all vintage. Everything was very purist. And then once we ended up in Europe, we had to become a little bit more flexible.

Zak Najor: Once in a while, we got lucky and it was a crowd who wanted to dance. But a lot of times it was seats and people just sitting there listening. They wanted to hear avant-garde jazz, they wanted to hear America's export of the highest level. When Erik [Newson] started booking us, that's when we were playing to a completely different audience. Before, if we didn't play to the top of our ability, it would suck. And somehow the people knew.

Elgin Park: Really, the only other band that was around at the time that was even slightly funky was Medeski Martin & Wood.

Robert Walter: At some point, people started to come and tape us from that other scene. A couple people suggested to us, "You know, if you played in front of that audience, they'd love you." It made sense right away.

Elgin Park: Erik came on the first or maybe the second of our European things. He was like, "Hey, I want to work with you guys. Let me do something." And we're like, "Okay, well, you can come, but you have to pay your own way. And you have to be useful." And so he made these hats that he was going to sell in Europe and those are the black Greyboy Allstars hats with the star.

Karl Denson: He asked if he could tape, and we're like, yeah, we need somebody to tape. And he started taping us.

Robert Walter: He was familiar with all this. And I do have to give him some credit for having that vision to be like, "There's no reason why this should be in front of these people other than it seems to work." Nowadays, there's self-identifying jam bands. At that time, I don't think any of us thought that . . . all the bands in the scene were weird bands that didn't have another place to be.

Karl Denson: I go, "No, we don't need a manager, we need a booking agent." And so he started finding gigs, and he got us onto the East Coast. He managed to finagle more money out of them than I ever would have thought to ask for. He eventually became our manager.

Zak Najor: When we got into the jam band scene, it was a funny feeling that they liked everything we did, even when it was bad. Or even when it wasn't at what we considered the top of our ability. So that transformed our mind about things—we don't have to try as much, which is kind of bad, but it's kind of good, because now we can be more comfortable.

Elgin Park: We started putting a lot of our *West Coast Boogaloo* record in snowboard movies, and skateboarding videos. We would play in Tahoe, we would play in Colorado. And that was right when the snowboard thing was starting to hit. That subculture embraced us, too. We were trying to find a foothold spot we could play at in New York, and we were playing Irving Plaza, and we played a bunch of different places. And then we started playing Wetlands. And Wetlands was really the spot. From there, it started circulating out.

Karl Denson: There was a little bit of snobbery, you know, from some of the band, and some of the bands in general—a little bit of like, "This is not my crowd." I've seen that from tons of these bands in our circle, where they were like, "This is not my genre." I'm like, "Yeah, it is your genre, this is what you do and the people that like you the most, so shut up and appreciate it."

36

Everything Started to Cross Over

Billy Martin: It was growing. We were playing clubs and making repeated visits back to places. We came back with a new record, *Friday Afternoon in the Universe.* And this logo showed up on the record cover, and then the font that I designed ended up with a T-shirt. And I remember that being part of this culture of "We're going to silkscreen our own T-shirts, we're gonna sell them, we're gonna have mailing lists." When you see the logo, you see, okay, now this is who we are. This is our image, we decided . . . this is it.

John Medeski: None of the business people were taking this scene seriously.

Billy Martin: The only thing that Gramavision had to our advantage was a publicist to send out press releases to all of the writers. And they had respectable writers who were paying attention. The thing about Gramavision was that it had a very unique roster. They had John Scofield, they had Jamaaladeen Tacuma, they had Bob Moses. Just really important musicians that grew up in the '60s and '70s that were really doing something different with jazz. Jamaaladeen played with Ornette Coleman. People were really paying attention. That was part of the marketing that was really advantageous to us: get this to the journalists that really cared about new music.

Kristin Wallace (Tour Manager, Medeski Martin & Wood): A lot of people weren't willing to take a risk on an all-instrumental band. People didn't get it.

Billy Martin: But we purposely refused any tour support. We didn't want to owe the label anything more than the advance that they gave us for making the record. Marketing-wise, they weren't really savvy or hip at all to what we were doing, where we were going. And honestly, we were in the moment. I was into art, into silkscreen printing. I knew these wholesale places and we started doing that self-promotional stuff. That paid for our gas.

Kristin Wallace: Once they started taking off, we started getting lots and lots of inquiries, obviously. But at first, it was a lot of trying to convince people: "Just trust me, just trust me, it's gonna be good." And then once people saw them, they were like, "Okay, I get it, but I don't know how to market to this crowd."

Billy Martin: We had a gig at the Cooler. The Cooler was on 14th Street in the Meatpacking District, which was starting to change a little bit. This Cooler club was a meat cooler, but it turned into this cool basement venue for alternative gigs. So we had the occasional gig there. And around this time, we were starting to make more of an impression. And our manager Liz Penta was like, "Hey, can I bring these guys back? They're in the back dancing . . . they're big fans."

Trey Anastasio: There was a second room at CBGBs—The Gallery. And we stumbled in and saw them.

Liz Penta: We kept hearing that Trey [Anastasio] was mentioning them in interviews. And people would show us a quote in a magazine or something. People were like, "They're a big band, this is a big deal." We were like, "Okay, cool." We didn't really know what that was about.

Billy Martin: They were faceless to me because I didn't know them. There was nothing about how they looked that made me think, "Oh, wow, that's Lou Reed or David Bowie!" It was just four dudes.

Chris Wood: We were clueless, we had no idea.

Billy Martin: The next day, someone said, "Did you look at the paper?" We met these guys in Phish, and they sold out Madison Square Garden in fifteen minutes.

John Medeski: That's when we became aware they were a big phenomenon. Everything started to cross over.

Liz Penta: I certainly knew about Grateful Dead culture but the guys didn't really know. They were really coming from a different place, even though they were all kind of hippies in a way . . . they were really coming from jazz and classical and experimental . . . that world.

Chris Wood: It was very surreal. We felt like we're emulating, in our own weird way, Charles Mingus and Sun Ra, Sly and the Family Stone and James Brown and Hendrix, but like Cecil Taylor. And [the audience] was relating it more to Phish or the Grateful Dead. We didn't really know what to do with that.

Trey Anastasio: When I started hanging out with them . . . Sun Ra was playing a lot in the '80s, and, you know, [drummer] Bob Gullotti . . . they shared a love more than anybody, more than any of the H.O.R.D.E. bands, for those kind of musicians.

Billy Martin: That was the beginning of a new shift to people showing up at our gigs. "Wow, that doesn't look like our normal fans." It was growing and influenced by Phish's fandom.

Chris Wood: The biggest marketing for us was Phish.

Liz Penta: Then we started hearing they were playing Medeski Martin & Wood during their set breaks.

Billy Martin: Some friends of ours were like, "Oh, I love Phish. You don't know about Phish? I've been following them for years." So they would tell us about it. And then we would talk about the Grateful Dead phenomenon.

"You gotta go to the show. You can't listen to their records." That's what people would say about us, too.

One show in particular in New Orleans—we opened for Phish. Jon Fishman and I were hanging out . . . there was a lot of people hanging out backstage, in the greenroom, whatever. We started playing duets; he was making sounds that normally would buzz and twang in a way . . . you want to avoid those notes and he would just lean into that and those notes. It was kind of hilarious.

John Medeski: We were on this tour, which was very parallel to Phish's. And we played in Madison, Wisconsin, and it was a night off for Phish. Three thousand people showed up.

Benjy Eisen (Journalist): I remember being shocked. And there's this thrill of like, "Oh my god, look how many people are here for this band that nobody heard of just a month ago."

37

It Was Another Thing to Commune With Real Musicians

Luke Smith: Phish was always present in the air and in the consciousness of any musician in Burlington, whether they wanted to admit it or not.

Brett Fairbrother: Burlington exploded because of the Phish thing—the vibe was incredible. But you also had Wide Wail, The Pants, Chin Ho! Belizbeha. All these other genres represented on an elite level. I knew that it was the real deal. Trey was sitting in and going to Pants shows. Wide Wail was doing the indie-rock thing, Belizbeha was doing the R&B-jazz-rap thing. And you had Strangefolk doing the CSN jam thing.

Andre Gardner (Tour Manager, Strangefolk): It was thriving.

Jamie Janover: Fishman would have these crazy parties at his dome house in Burlington and we'd go there and jam all weekend.

Luke Smith: Club Toast, which doesn't exist anymore, was a nightclub, across Main Street from Nectar's.

Reid Genauer: I think I was living off two hundred bucks a month, at that time, and I was making more than that . . . two to three times that for every gig. And I felt like I was rich.

Luke Smith: Anne [Rothwell] gave us the slot opening for Dave Matthews Band.

Reid Genauer: We started to become embedded in the music scene in Burlington. It's a nuance that a lot of people don't even realize. We had blind self-confidence, but then you start meeting guys like Jamie Masefield of Jazz Mandolin Project and Dave Grippo and Gordon Stone. These guys were working musicians. They had wisdom. It was an Obi-Wan type relationship we started to build in the community in Burlington. It woke you up, because it's one thing to play a gig at a fraternity, or even at a club where a bunch of your buddies are just getting loaded, dancing, and celebrating you—it was another thing to commune with real musicians.

Andre Gardner: All the touring acts would come through Burlington and play Club Toast and the Metronome . . . later Higher Ground.

Reid Genauer: We started sending, like Phish, a monthly newsletter. We got to a point where that thing was costing us twenty-five thousand dollars to publish and send each one.

Sam Ankerson (Promotions Manager, Strangefolk): Through our newsletter, we would encourage people to get in touch with us if they wanted to help us put up posters in advance of shows, try to coordinate in-studio radio plays, trying to coordinate in-store plays, and all around trying to get what recorded music was there, out there. And focusing almost always on colleges and independent music shops.

Andre Gardner: I went and saw them and became hooked. I just kept showing up at their shows and helping out wherever I could. Eventually I lived with Reid and Luke—they had graduated from UVM and I was finishing my senior year. When I graduated they said, "Any chance you'd want to do this full time?" And I said, "Of course, it beats getting a real job." It was a gradual process of hanging around long enough that I became useful.

Sam Ankerson: I moved up to Vermont in fall of 1995. Jon was my best friend from high school. We went to a boarding school in Massachusetts. I went up to visit him on what was going to be a couple weeks' visit. The band was living in a farmhouse in Waterbury. Right when I got there was when they were graduating from just being around Burlington bands to playing in other parts of New England. They needed a hand to help on the promotional front to help get press releases out and posters out—try to get people to their shows. And so I raised my hand for that. It really was a two-week plan to visit that turned into five years.

Reid Genauer: Keep in mind, we didn't think of it as marketing . . . we didn't know what the fuck we're doing. Phish had a newsletter, and it would tell you where they were playing. The way we used that, and even Phish bootlegs, was figuring out where to play—so in part by how Phish came up and in part by looking at how other bands that were doing it, were playing. We had an address sign-up clipboard at every show. And that was more important than anything . . . just getting an address.

38

August 9th, 1995

Pete Shapiro: Jerry died in August '95. I remember going to Central Park—Strawberry Fields, just to see. And I remember right away being like, "Fuck, these people are not gonna go away."

Dave Schools: I had been to the dentist. And I was all sort of numbed out and I was walking down the street. I went to our office, which was across the street from the Georgia Theatre. And our office assistant, Mary Armstrong, looks at me: "Oh my god, I've got terrible news. Did you hear about Jerry? He passed away." And my first thought was Jerry Joseph, the bad boy that I knew that we were close to. She's like, "No, no, Jerry Garcia." I had just seen the show the spring before in Vegas. I had actually stood on stage with Chris Robinson and watched the show.

I was shocked and heartbroken. But I wasn't that big of a fan of the Vince era; I was a big Brent Mydland fan. Almost every single show I ever saw was during the Brent era, including that famous "Dark Star" from RFK Stadium in 1990. Who's got the balls to play in front of forty thousand people a forty-five-minute improv with a drum solo in the pouring rain! Those guys do. It really struck me and I couldn't listen to a lot of Grateful Dead for a long time after that. And for some reason, the song that really got me was "Crazy Fingers." That was really hard for me to listen to.

Dean Budnick: The Dead scene was deteriorating at that time. And the music—I don't think anyone will dispute that in 1995 the music wasn't what it once was.

John Bell: I remember being sad. Jerry Garcia was a big inspiration on me experiencing improvisational rock and roll. He sang Robert Hunter's lyrics with such sincerity.

Oteil Burbridge: The Grateful Dead was not huge on my radar at that time. But a lot of the people that I knew, people that were fans of ARU, I remember them just being crushed. It was terrible.

Chan Kinchla: Obviously, he was a very important figure for all of us. But the scene was off and running. We had opened up for the Jerry Garcia Band. But us, Phish, and Widespread and a lot of bands similar to us, like Aquarium Rescue Unit . . . we were already trying to carry that torch. Perhaps more Phish and Widespread—they were more of the Dead perspective. We were a little more like Jimi Hendrix and Led Zeppelin with some Dead influences. But I think when the Grateful Dead disappeared, that did leave a hole that a lot of jam band fans looked for.

Dean Budnick: There were bands that were anointed after that. There was no question that people would have more time and energy. I do think it opened something up. Unquestionably Jerry's passing contributed to it . . . I don't want to overstate it because it was already in motion.

Jon "The Barber" Gutwillig (Guitar, vocals, The Disco Biscuits): It definitely made Phish huge, there's no question about that.

Dirk Stalnecker: Phish took the brunt of that, which really put a lot of pressure on them with the parking lot scenes.

Jon Topper: Some people were obviously looking towards Phish.

Trey Anastasio: Just for the record, we have to remember that we were already selling out the Garden before Jerry died. We were cooking with gas.

Pete Shapiro: Jerry's death led to, in a weird way, the further development of the jam band scene.

Trey Anastasio: That was a tricky landscape to navigate. It was really kinda confusing. We were out there with lots of other bands, including the Dead. They were playing. We were playing. We had a completely original song list—"Maze," "Split Open and Melt, "It's Ice." It doesn't sound like anything you've ever heard before. We thought we were completely in our own realm. And we were. We didn't just think it. We actually were. It's true—"It's Ice" does not sound like any other band. We were fucking proud of it. We would walk off and be like, "There's nobody doing this right now. Nobody." That's how we felt. So after Jerry died, when that element was like, "Well, we'll just move over to Phish," it's like, "Well, you're not gonna like it dude."

Vince Herman: We were at Barley's in Asheville, North Carolina, when the word came. It was an intense moment for sure. The impact of the Dead on our culture . . . you can't emphasize enough.

John Moore (Tour Marketing and A&R, Mammoth Records): I think Garcia going sped things up. Fans wanted to see as much music, of course.

Tye North: When Jerry died, that changed a lot. People had to find a place to go and bands around benefited.

John Popper: Bobby looked at me and said, "I don't want to capitalize on this."

Dave Frey: We got the Black Crowes and Ziggy Marley and Sheryl Crow for H.O.R.D.E. '95. We get to Portland, Maine, and we've got a day off. And on that day off Jerry Garcia dies. I got a call from the promoter: "I need help. Can you give bodies to me?" So I got people up there, including myself. We helped sell tickets all day. And it sold out. All these people that were going to Dead shows came to H.O.R.D.E. Where we were going at twelve thousand tickets the day before we sold out at twenty thousand. And there were more that couldn't get in. And I told the promoter: "Just let these people in because they're gonna break your fence. They're coming in, whether you let them in or not." So suddenly, we've got a whole new set of issues—we're completely sold out everywhere we go. Deadheads just needed something else, you know, that's the closest thing to it. Same thing happened to Phish. And bang, the rest of their tour sold out. I think they got more of the criminal parking-lot elements.

John Popper: We were torn because us, Phish, and Widespread were the big touring bands out there. And it made sales go through the roof because everybody who was on tour with the Dead needed to go somewhere.

Dave Frey: All the numbers were exploding.

John Popper: We felt guilty about it.

Dave Frey: And we had a whole new set of problems. We didn't have enough comp tickets for people because we hadn't held tickets. Security and working with police on how do you mitigate people showing up who can't get in? You always have problems. You just hope you have good ones to have.

Pete Shapiro: I did see there would be a healthy scene post-Jerry of people who wanted to dance for three or four hours.

Dean Budnick: There were already younger people who were drawn to those bands who may or may not have been Deadheads. But certainly those acts got a little bit more attention, which probably did help them.

Trey Anastasio: In '93 or '94, I walked offstage with pride. When Jerry died, there was a lot of that "Let's go over here." Well, this isn't what we want. I don't go to a Cranberries concert and expect them to play like King Sunny Adé.

Warren Haynes: We played Jones Beach. And it was obviously a really sad, somber day. It's got that big, enormous backstage area. I remember getting there early and some of the guys in the Black Crowes were gonna come in. I remember seeing Chris Robinson walking across the backstage area—he was normally an upbeat, energetic person, and just the look on his face being so sad and subdued . . . we hugged each other. And there wasn't much to say. We dedicated the show to Jerry that night. And I think there were a lot of magical moments that came out of that sadness that everybody was feeling. When I got home that night, I wrote "Patchwork Quilt," which was the song that I'd written about Jerry that stemmed from that whole thing.

Derek Trucks: Obviously, I knew who they were and was familiar with it, but it wasn't where my head was. But I remember how seismic that feeling was to everyone around me.

Warren Haynes: I never did meet Jerry. And of course, the opening line to "Patchwork Quilt" is, "I never knew you, but then who really did." I had three opportunities to meet him. And each time, I was like, "I'll meet him next time. I don't want to be in the way." And it was a valuable lesson to me, because there wasn't a next time.

Dean Budnick: The day that Jerry passed, I was at that Bob Weir show that took place up in New Hampshire. The Hampton Casino is a big GA place. I was sitting on a chair, towards the back of the room, but when I stood on the chair I was about the same height, eye-contact wise, as Bobby. I remember a lot of that night I was locked with him. You could really see what he was going through, and why he was there and what he felt he needed to do. I wouldn't say that the music itself was the most profound that I've ever heard relative to RatDog. But the night was unbelievably deep. I do believe Jerry would have wanted that . . . that that's what music is for, to draw people together in that day of deep sadness. Between songs, I'll say that people were respectful. People weren't calling out "Jerry!" Everyone was there to be with Bob and to listen to Bob.

Shelly Culbertson (Internet and Ticketing Manager, Phish): I don't know if I would say there was a big influx of fans. Before then and after, there are the Deadheads who liked Phish, Deadheads who didn't care for Phish, the Phishheads who liked the Dead, the Phishheads who weren't into the Dead. The fact that unfortunately Jerry passed . . . that didn't really change people's tastes in music. It might have given them more free time and disposable income, depending on who they were following.

Jon "The Barber" Gutwillig: I think that the Dead are a unique Americana experience. You got Michael Jackson, Madonna, and Jerry Garcia . . . there's very few artists that I think were on his level.

Pete Shapiro: Jerry's death led to the super growth . . . you can go to any of these bands and there's a similarity to how they approach the music and how certain people want to experience live music.

Marc Brownstein: Is there anybody more influential than the Dead on music in America?

Trey Anastasio: Nobody ever is gonna sound like Jerry Garcia.

39

No Offense to You, but I'm Going for It

Along with Blues Traveler and the Spin Doctors, the Dave Matthews Band also started to see some viable commercial success after the release of their major-label debut, Under the Table and Dreaming, *in October 1994. The lead single "What Would You Say" featured John Popper on harmonica, and the album peaked at No. 11 on the Billboard 200 on June 10, 1995. ('90s icons Hootie and the Blowfish's* Cracked Rear View *was No. 1; Live's* Throwing Copper *was No. 2, with the top ten featuring an eclectic mix of White Zombie, The Eagles, TLC, Boyz II Men, and two soundtracks:* Friday *and* Forrest Gump.*) The band had a choice: Compete with Hootie or go back into the studio.*

Dave Matthews: One of the reasons we chose Steve Lillywhite for the early sessions was when he spoke about recording, he said, "I just want to get what you do on stage."

Steve Lillywhite (Producer, *Under the Table and Dreaming, Crash, Before These Crowded Streets, Billy Breathes*): I went to Irving Plaza and I saw the band and I saw the scene as well. The scene was as important as the music. And what was weird about the scene was that the audience dipped in and out of the music . . . it was as much being there as it was listening to the music, because the music would rise and fall.

Bruce Flohr: We released our record and Hootie and the Blowfish released theirs around the same time. And there was a little bit of competition, certainly within the labels, of who's going to do better. We were almost neck and neck. And the decision was made: Go back in, make another record, and put another record out when we were still pumping on *Under the Table and Dreaming*. That decision was one of the most important ones because we could have taken *Under the Table and Dreaming* to ten million units. And I think could have burnt out the audience, and the band. But by putting out another record while Hootie was still working the first record, it added fuel to the fire, another batch of songs, and one of the band's biggest songs.

When we went to pick producers for the first record, we generated a list that we felt would be right for the band. The names that we submitted to the band was: T Bone Burnett—him and I flew to somewhere in the Carolinas and saw Jeff Buckley open for Dave Matthews, and we had a meeting with Dave afterwards until four in the morning talking music. Steve Lillywhite and Jerry Harrison, because Jerry had just done the Live record [*Throwing Copper*].

Steve Lillywhite: Jerry Harrison is at the gig. I had produced the Talking Heads a few years earlier. So, we were mates. I said, "Hey, Jerry, good to see you . . . no offense to you, but I'm going for it."

Bruce Flohr: I never saw the Dave Matthews Band as a jam band. It wasn't a scene that I was familiar with.

Steve Lillywhite: Bruce was just the guy who would come in and put his credit card down.

Bruce Flohr: I was not a Grateful Dead fan. I was a U2 and R.E.M. fan. And one of the things that those bands have are songs. And one of the things I noticed with Dave Matthews were the songs. Certainly the playing was great. But there were songs already there. We brought in producers who had made successful records that were song-driven and then we brought in a mixer that made the song sound competitive . . . the same guy that was mixing the rock records, Tom Lord-Alge. Dave Matthews Band records sounded competitive to Pearl Jam, Nirvana, Soundgarden because we were using the same people to help make those records.

Steve Lillywhite: I was very aware, mainly from growing up with the Beatles, and then my work with U2, that you try not to repeat yourself on your next album. The idea I've always thought is that you want to take the listener on a journey.

Dave Matthews: "Crash" is odd because it was a love song. And I've dribbled on about what it was about, but it was very, very much at the beginning of the partnership I'm still in. And that's where it came from, there's always a funny regret that I have, because there's this throwaway line that, while recording, that I jokingly at the end of the song—about a skirt—that I threw in there in one take as a joke.

Bruce Flohr: I remember being in Woodstock at the studio and hearing "Crash Into Me" for the first time, going, "That's the one." And it wasn't because I was some genius. If you look back, "Crash Into Me" was the third single released from that record. "So Much to Say" and "Too Much" were the first two singles. We wanted to challenge the audience . . . to make them think Dave had gone electric. Because on the first record, I don't think they played any electric guitar. We wanted to fuck with people a little bit.

Steve Lillywhite: The band had a little bit more of a swagger about them, because they'd been validated by record sales. The album did well.

The Spin Doctors perform at Columbia University, New York City, April 1989. (*Steve Eichner*)

Widespread Panic's first promotional photo, shot in 1988. (*Flournoy Holmes / Courtesy of Landslide Records*)

Phish perform at Wetlands, New York City, June 9, 1990. (*Steve Eichner*)

A show flyer for God Street Wine's first performance at Nightingale in New York City, December 13, 1988. (*Michael Weiss / God Street Wine*)

A flyer promoting Widespread Panic's gig on January 13, 1989, at the Uptown Lounge in Athens, Georgia. (*Provided with permission courtesy of Brown Cat, Inc.*)

John Popper, David Graham, and Bill Graham in conversation backstage at Roseland Ballroom in New York City, 1991. (*Steve Eichner*)

The late-night scene at Arrowhead Ranch, in Parksville, New York, summer 1991. (*Steve Eichner*)

Phish perform at Arrowhead Ranch, Parksville, New York, July 1991. (*Steve Eichner*)

Arnie Lawrence, John Popper, Rene Lopez, Mark White, and Aaron Comess perform as Wasabi at Nightingale, August 1991. (*Steve Eichner*)

Strangefolk's first performance, opening for Acoustic Junction on April 29, 1992, at the University of Vermont in Burlington, Vermont. (*Unknown photographer / Courtesy of Jon Trafton*)

(ABOVE, LEFT) Colonel Bruce Hampton and Jeff Sipe perform with Aquarium Rescue Unit during the 1993 H.O.R.D.E. tour on August 12 at the Walnut Creek Amphitheatre in Raleigh, North Carolina. (*C. Taylor Crothers*)

(ABOVE, RIGHT) Oteil Burbridge performs with Aquarium Rescue Unit during the 1993 H.O.R.D.E. tour on August 12 at the Walnut Creek Amphitheatre in Raleigh, North Carolina. (*C. Taylor Crothers*)

Widespread Panic perform at the H.O.R.D.E. tour at Red Rocks Amphitheatre in Morrison, Colorado, July 3, 1993. (*AJ Genovesi*)

Dave Matthews Band perform at the Flood Zone in Richmond, Virginia, on August 10, 1993. (*C. Taylor Crothers*)

Phish perform at the Bender Arena in Washington, DC, on December 28, 1993. (*C. Taylor Crothers / © Phish, Inc. / Used by permission*)

John Popper and Bobby Sheehan perform on New Year's Eve 1993 at the Roseland Ballroom in New York City. (*AJ Genovesi*)

Phish and Dave Matthews jam together at the Lawrence Joel Veterans Memorial Coliseum on April 21, 1994. (*C. Taylor Crothers / © Phish, Inc. / Used by permission*)

Widespread Panic perform on March 10, 1994, at Irving Plaza in New York City. (*AJ Genovesi*)

Trey Anastasio and his dog Marley backstage at the Glen Falls Civic Center in Glen Falls, New York, on October 31, 1994. (*C. Taylor Crothers / © Phish, Inc. / Used by permission*)

INFORMATION FOR
NORTH CHARLESTON COLISEUM FROM PHISH

Phish Fans,
In an effort to address growing concerns about our impact on local communities, we are creating information flyers for each show. Please take the time to read this flyer thoroughly. With your cooperation we can leave a positive impression with each venue we play, and in doing so, preserve the vitality of the Phish community. We ask that you please respect the rules of the venue and local community so that we will be welcomed back in the future.

- No cameras or video; audio taping with taper ticket only.
- Beware of scalpers selling counterfeit tickets!
- All vending is prohibited on the premises.
- The sale of alcohol is strictly prohibited.
- The sale of nitrous oxide is strictly prohibited.

Some facts about Nitrous Oxide:
- Nitrous oxide cuts off the flow of oxygen to the brain.
- Numerous medical emergencies have occurred due to its ingestion, ranging from concussions (falling down after passing out)to, in extreme cases, death.
- Some confiscated "nitrous" tanks actually contained other gases such as argon, automotive nitrous, etc. which are extremely dangerous.
- Remember, if you purchase nitrous oxide, you are likely to be supporting people who care nothing about, and contribute nothing to the Phish community.

- The Phish Green Crew will continue their efforts to keep the parking lots clean. Please help by disposing of your own garbage properly, and lend the "G. Crew" a hand whenever possible!
- Please make your after show plans with friends before going in. You will be asked to leave the parking lots a half hour after the show. Please cooperate with us on this issue.
- Please help us discourage people from coming to the parking lot of a sold out show without tickets. Parking is limited, and legitimate ticket holders may not be allowed access to the lots if they are partially filled by non-ticket holders. Also, people coming without tickets increases the cost of security staffing, which ultimately leads to higher ticket prices.
- Please pass along this information to others.

<u>SHOW INFORMATION</u>
- Parking lots open at 3:30 pm. (PLEASE don't come earlier, because you <u>will</u> be turned away)
- Doors open at 6:00 pm. (PLEASE plan to go in early so that we can avoid a crush at the door.)
- Show begins at 7:30 pm.

(ABOVE) Dave Matthews in a hotel lobby in Stockholm, Sweden, March 22, 1995. (*C. Taylor Crothers*)

An informational flyer given out by the Phish organization to fans at the Charleston, South Carolina, show on November 18, 1995. (*© Phish, Inc. / Used by permission*)

(BELOW) R–L: Chris Wood, John Medeski, Liz Penta, and Billy Martin at the *Shack-man* photo shoot, New York City, July 1996. (*Michael Macioce*)

Walton, Williams & Lick

CAMPING
The Clifford Ball
Plattsburgh AFB, I-87 exit 36
Plattsburgh, New York

Camping area opens noon, Thurs., Aug. 15, 1996
Camping area closes 10 AM, Sun., Aug. 18, 1996

No alcohol No vending No open fires
Please recycle or dispose of trash properly
Ticket admits one vehicle and **does not include concert admission**

ADMISSION $20.00
NO REFUND - NO EXCHANGE
GENERAL ADMISSION
TKT. NO. 902

A ticket stub that allowed for camping at the Plattsburgh Air Force Base, the site of Phish's Clifford Ball, August 15–17, 1996. (*© Phish, Inc. / Used by permission*)

A flyer made by *The Pharmer's Almanac,* given out at the parking lot during Phish's Clifford Ball festival, August 15–17, 1996, weekend in Plattsburgh, New York. (*Courtesy of* The Pharmer's Almanac / *Used by permission*)

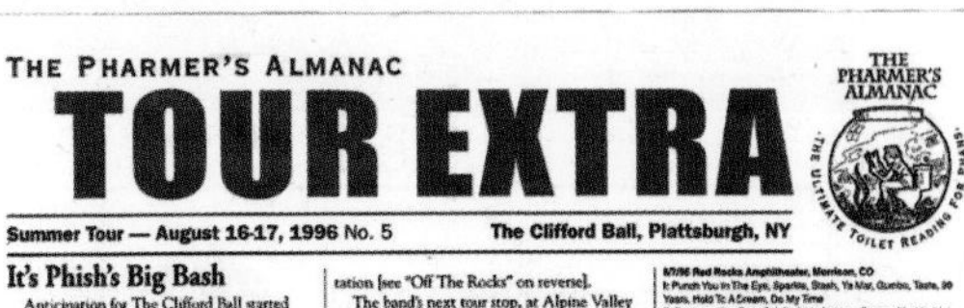

THE PHARMER'S ALMANAC
TOUR EXTRA

THE PHARMER'S ALMANAC
THE ULTIMATE TOILET READING FOR PHANS

Summer Tour — August 16-17, 1996 No. 5 **The Clifford Ball, Plattsburgh, NY**

It's Phish's Big Bash

Anticipation for The Clifford Ball started building from the moment Phish announced their summer tour dates in May. The band's American Tour, which began in Utah on August 2, now finally winds its way after two weeks to upstate New York for these final two shows.

The Clifford Ball — named in honor of a deceased aviator by the name of Mr. Clifford Ball, who is remembered by a plaque in a tiny West Virginia airport honoring him as "a beacon of light in the world of flight" — promises three sets of Phish each day, numerous special guests, and a level of activity the likes of which the town of Plattsburgh, NY has likely never before seen. Over 100,000 Phans are expected to arrive in the area for the concerts, making these shows by far the largest Phish concerts ever.

Phish has not disappointed the Phans who elected to follow the tour on its way east. The four-night stand at Colorado's Red Rocks Amphitheater provided breathtaking high and low points for Phans and the band alike. Musically, the shows demonstrated Phish's ability to share the wealth — each show was solid in its own right, and Phish repeated no songs during the stand. Off the stage, however, controversy swirled after a Police-Phan confrontation [see "Off The Rocks" on reverse].

The band's next tour stop, at Alpine Valley in Wisconsin, saw Fishman uncork his first version of Whipping Post since April 1993. And Phans at Deer Creek in Indianapolis saw a

Continued On Reverse Side...

8/2/96 Wolf Mountain Amphitheater, Park City, UT
I: Ya Mar, Down With Disease, Guelah Papyrus, Poor Heart, Foam, Theme From The Bottom, Golgi Apparatus, Tweezer, Ragtime Gal, Possum
II: Runaway Jim, Simple, Taste, Free, Fluffhead, Prince Caspian, The Horse > Silent In The Morning, Run Like An Antelope
E: Punch You In The Eye

8/4/96 Red Rocks Amphitheater, Morrison, CO
I: Chalk Dust Torture, Funky Bitch, Guyute, Fee, Split Open And Melt, The Mango Song, The Sloth, Maze, Loving Cup
II: AC/DC Bag, Reba, Scent Of A Mule, Sample In A Jar, David Bowie, Sweet Adeline, Slave To The Traffic Light
E: Rocky Top

8/5/96 Red Rocks Amphitheater, Morrison, CO
I: Wilson, Poor Heart, Guelah Papyrus, Divided Sky, Wolfman's Brother, Foam, If I Could, Julius, The Squirming Coil
II: Also Sprach Zarathustra > Down With Disease > It's Ice, Halley's Comet > Jam, Waste, Talk, Train Song, Strange Design, Amazing Grace, Mike's Song > I Am Hydrogen > Weekapaug Groove
E: Cavern

8/6/96 Red Rocks Amphitheater, Morrison, CO
I: Makisupa Policeman > Rift, Suzie Greenberg, Simple, Theme From The Bottom, Lizards, Dinner And A Movie, Ham, Run Like An Antelope
II: The Curtain > Tweezer, Prince Caspian > A Day In The Life, Big Black Furry Creature From Mars, Purple Rain, Harry Hood > Tweezer Reprise
E: Johnny B. Goode

8/7/96 Red Rocks Amphitheater, Morrison, CO
I: Punch You In The Eye, Sparkle, Stash, Ya Mar, Gumbo, Taste, 99 Years, Hold To A Dream, Do My Time
II: Runaway Jim, Free, Col. Forbin's Ascent > Famous Mockingbird, Possum, Life On Mars, You Enjoy Myself, Ragtime Gal
E: Bouncing Around The Room, Golgi Apparatus

8/10/96 Alpine Valley Music Theater, East Troy, WI
I: My Friend My Friend, Poor Heart, AC/DC Bag, Fee, Reba, I Didn't Know, The Horse > Silent In The Morning, Rift, Bathtub Gin, Cavern
II: Wilson, Down With Disease, Scent Of A Mule, Free, Fluffhead, Whipping Post, Harry Hood, A Day In The Life
E: Contact, Fire

8/12/96 Deer Creek Music Center, Noblesville, IN
I: Ya Mar, Split Open And Melt, Esther, Chalk Dust Torture, Waste, It's Ice, Dog Faced Boy, Taste, Oh Kee Pa > Suzie Greenberg
II: Timber Ho, Sparkle, Simple, Prince Caspian > McGrupp, Run Like An Antelope, Ragtime Gal, Golgi Apparatus, Possum
E: Sample In A Jar

8/13/96 Deer Creek Music Center, Noblesville, IN
I: Divided Sky, Tube, Tela, Maze, Fast Enough For You, My Old Home Place, Punch You In The Eye, Llama, Glide, Slave To The Traffic Light
II: AC/DC Bag, Lizards, Mike's Song > Lifeboy > Weekapaug Groove, Waste, Train Song, Strange Design, David Bowie
E: Sleeping Monkey, Rocky Top

8/14/96 HersheyPark Stadium, Hershey, PA
I: Wilson, Down with Disease, Fee, Reba, Mango Song, Gumbo, Stash, Ragtime Gal
II: Runaway Jim, You Enjoy Myself, Horse>Silent In The Morning, Cars, Trucks & Busses>Tweezer, Theme From The Bottom, Cracklin' Rosie, Sample In a Jar, Tweezer Reprise
E: Julius

KEEP THE SCENE CLEAN! RECYCLE THE TOUR EXTRA, OR PASS IT ALONG TO A FRIEND... PRINTED ON RECYCLED PAPER

A mail-order ticket stub from The String Cheese Incident's May 1, 1999, show at Tipitina's in New Orleans, Louisiana. (*Courtesy of The String Cheese Incident / Used by permission*)

40

Acoustic, My Ass!

In the early winter of 1996, Widespread Panic played a series of ski towns in Colorado and Utah for three weeks . . . nontraditional venues, where the premise was that it would be a bit of an unplugged, acoustic experience. That quickly changed.

Dave Schools: For some reason, we always had luck in Colorado. We'd set up shop in these little ski towns and we'd ski and make friends and play our weird rock and roll and have a good time.

Mary Dugas (Operations Management, Widespread Panic): The premise behind the Sit-n-Ski tour was for them to play acoustic in smaller venues and relax a little bit. They had been hammering the road for years.

Domingo "Sunny" Ortiz: The boys would trade tickets for lift tickets. You had to get up to the mountain. Well, the ski lift tickets were not cheap. So the boys would say, "Hey, you know, if you give me a lift ticket, I'll let you into the show tonight."

John Bell: We were hitting it pretty hard. We were skiing, we were partying. And so I really enjoyed the sitting part.

Domingo "Sunny" Ortiz: Our manager hated this concept because he knew what was going on. He knew that there were a few of the boys in the band that could ski.

Ted Rockwell (Founder, *Everyday Companion*): They were trying to figure out how to fill out their repertoire. In '95, they were looking back at old tapes, looking back at old performances, to figure out: Are there any songs that we wrote, or any covers that we really love, that we've just forgotten about and haven't played . . . and what would those be?

David Blackmon: We scaled down. There were no buses, everybody traveled in a van, all that kind of stuff. We could get to the smaller ski resort areas and play ballrooms.

Dirk Stalnecker: We had two vans, and then we hired a trucking company to drive a box truck with all the equipment because we didn't want to roll with the trailer.

John Bell: Some of the cats knew how to ski. I don't think the band members knew how to ski. We'd done a little bit, but I don't think we took lessons. But it's crazy we were doing that because, you know, it's so easy to mess yourself up and lose a gig.

Buck Williams: In those days people partied a little bit.

Domingo "Sunny" Ortiz: I didn't ski. I can pretty much guarantee that Dave Schools is not a skier. Mikey probably would get on a set of skis, but JB and Todd had no hesitations of jumping on the slopes. They tried to beg me, "Come on man, you gotta get on, you got to put on a set of skis!" And I said, "Man, as quick as I put them on, I'm gonna just fall flat on my ass." I didn't have any ski gear, nor did I want to spend my money to rent gear and then I wouldn't have any money to bring home.

Dave Schools: We decided before the fans called it "Sit-n-Ski" it was supposed to just be an acoustic tour. And literally halfway through the first show, Mikey's like, "I hate this. I'm gonna play electric. But I'm just gonna sit down." And JB's like, "Well, I'm gonna play whatever, but I'm gonna sit down too." And I'm like, "Acoustic, my ass! I'm just gonna stand." And it wound up just being pretty much a regular rock and roll Panic show.

Mary Dugas: "Acoustic, my ass" really is what it turned into.

John Bell: I might have still been playing acoustic, or at least playing it half the time. And so it kind of resembles an acoustic set, but we were just sitting down playing our instruments. And these were for the most part ski resort kind of venues—conference halls. And you'd create a space, bring in a little stage, and it was kind of a good look for the place.

Dirk Stalnecker: We were trying to do it acoustic and that blew up on the first show at the Fox Theatre in Boulder. Mikey just wasn't happy with it. And that's when he first started sitting down. And then he never stopped sitting down.

Ted Rockwell: At that point, they were really starting to feel like they gelled and that they could pretty much pull off anything onstage they set their mind to. And so going acoustic, I think that was a part of that thing—the band's responding to hearing a song in a different arrangement.

John Bell: We played some places where balconies were moving and all of a sudden people were getting a little worried. They were there to dance, not just to watch a band.

Ted Rockwell: Spreadnet was really in full swing at that point . . . and so people were able to give updates or get updates on what was happening. People were out there recording and soundboards were leaking, either by accident or on purpose, depending on who you are.

Dave Schools: The one that freaked me out—we were playing in Vail, Colorado. And it was up on the third or fourth floor of the structure. People were dancing so hard and the floor was bouncing—Sunny's chimes were constantly just chiming.

Dirk Stalnecker: It was very fucked up. And we went through three or four rolls of duct tape trying to secure everything.

Buck Williams: This happened a couple of times—the room was so crowded that the floor felt like it was gonna cave in. And I was really nervous.

Dave Schools: And at one point, they went into a drum break. Underneath was a parking deck—directly under the floor of the dance floor. And I ran down there to smoke a cigarette because they wouldn't let the smoke on stage. And so the drums were just pounding away. The audience is dancing, the floor is flexing. And it's creating so much pressure that it's opening and closing every door in this parking deck. It was like, "Wow this is just physics at work. The floor's about to collapse."

Buck Williams: I went down to look at the floor when it was on top of a garage to see what it looked like. It had steel I beams across it so it was never going to give in. The sprinkler system in there was shaking and the sprinklers were coming out of the concrete. You could see movement of I'd say a quarter of an inch or so—barely visible, but it was visible. I went back up and I stood—not in the middle of the floor but I got up next to a wall, just something.

John Bell: The plaster was crumbling down and pipes were moving.

Dirk Stalnecker: I was pretty free to float around during the show because I didn't have a job on stage. I went underneath in the parking garage and the floor was absolutely undulating. It was going up and down to the beat of the music. They didn't really tell us that when we got there, but it is a thing. It's the way the floors are constructed.

The kids had already found out what our vans looked like . . . these kids were all into it. There was never enough tickets. There was never enough capacity.

41

A Rite of Passage to Becoming Royalty in Town

By the mid-'90s, the jam band was a full-blown national movement. One city in particular became a new de facto home for improv and live music: New Orleans. Of course, it already had a rich history of musical traditions, dating back from the early days of jazz to being spearheaded in decades prior by The Meters, the Neville Brothers, and The Radiators. A young funk group called Galactic started to carry that torch and almost immediately found an audience in the jam band scene . . .

Robert Mercurio (Bass, Galactic): The genesis of Galactic was started with me and my lifelong buddy, Jeff Raines, guitar player. We moved to New Orleans from Washington, DC, in 1990. We had been playing music together in DC and then we got totally entrenched in the New Orleans music scene. The brass bands, the New Orleans folk, The Meters, all that stuff was just totally blowing our minds. We were just in our dorm rooms learning that kind of music.

Stanton Moore (Drums, Galactic): There was this guy, Rob Gowen, and he was a guitar player. I was at Loyola University. And Rob was in the music program. I was studying music there and studying jazz . . . and we weren't able to just have some fun and play some funk. Rob was like, "I met this bass player. He's fun. He wants to play some funk." His name was Robert

Mercurio. I didn't know who Robert was. So we got together in a bedroom at Rob Gowen's house and the three of us played together. We were laughing and having a blast. A few months later, I bumped into Robert Mercurio at Tipitina's.

Robert Mercurio: Tipitina's was very much the center point for music. Everybody would roll through there at some point; you'd cross paths with so many different kinds of people.

Stanton Moore: He said, "This is Jeff Raines, he plays guitar in my band that I was telling you about—Galactic Prophylactic. Do you know a drummer who would want to play some funk with us?" I said, "Oh, man, I wanna play some funk."

Ben Ellman (Saxophone, Galactic): I played in a band with Stanton Moore called The New Orleans Klezmer All Stars. Stanton was our drummer. Stanton was actually a fill-in for Mean Willie Green, who was our regular drummer—he was the drummer for the Neville Brothers at the time. So for a klezmer band from New Orleans, we had this crazy good drummer playing klezmer music.

Robert Mercurio: I believe it was on Christmas break '93, we had Stanton over at our apartment and that was the first time we played together and the first time that it really clicked with a drummer where we were like, "Okay, this is our guy."

Ben Ellman: Everyone seemed to play in a lot of different bands. It was a very commingling group of musicians. There was also a really killer rock scene in the '90s in New Orleans. I was playing in a jazz-punk band. Stanton came from a punk band out of Metairie called Oxen Thrust, which was a heavy band in the '90s.

Robert Mercurio: We had a more college, kind of jokey, vibe to us. Our singer was hilarious. He couldn't sing very well, but he wrote hilarious lyrics, like him being infatuated with the checkout woman at the Winn-Dixie. It was very funny, but not as grown up. Stanton was in another band called Entourage that was a progressive jazz band. But he truly just loved playing funk and the New Orleans Meters stuff, but he hadn't found any contemporaries to play with.

Ben Ellman: There were all these older cats who were a part of the history of rock and roll that were playing these little clubs and were hanging out with young musicians and taking them under their wings. Older horn players that played with Fats Domino's band—horn players from the '50s who were still living around there. Wayne Bennett, this guitar player who was Bobby Bland's guitar player forever, lived in town—he was this incredible guy who would hang out with anybody and talk your head off at the bar all night, throwing wisdom at you. There was also lots of opportunities to explore your music and play in venues—maybe not big venues, but coffeehouses or cafes or whatever. It felt like back then we all had weekly gigs that we were playing with different bands.

Stanton Moore: There were a good amount of bands playing original music, playing gigs all over New Orleans—clubs like Café Brasil, Dream Palace, and Dragon's Den.

Ben Ellman: I got here in '89. And it felt like it was still stuck in the late '70s. Rent was cheap as shit in New Orleans. It was easy to rent a big house with a bunch of rooms and stay there with your friends—so you always lived in houses with other musicians. My first job in New Orleans was at Tipitina's. I was a cook there. And I worked two days a week—I got paid once a month for my hourly salary. And I took that to pay my rent. My rent was like two or three hundred dollars for a share. I'd get in for free anytime I wanted at Tips, I ate there for free, I made some tips, and then I also hustled and played all these gigs. I played with a brass band and we played in Jackson Square and I made tips out there.

Robert Mercurio: Tipitina's was *the* club. There was no House of Blues, no Howlin' Wolf, the theaters hadn't been renovated. It was really the center of the music scene.

Ben Ellman: Tipitina's would put a thousand people in there. And there were no other clubs in the city that were at a thousand capacity, so it got all the national acts to roll through. But it was a big room to fill for a local band. And the bands that were doing it were the Neville Brothers and The Radiators. For a smaller band like Galactic, it was always a great gig to get but we wouldn't get the gig on our own, because we couldn't put eight hundred people in there.

Robert Mercurio: To get to play there as a band . . . you made it. To sell it out was a rite of passage to becoming royalty in town.

Stanton Moore: Pretty quickly we developed a good following in town. We realized if we wanted to go any further, we'd have to get a little more serious, so we pared the band down to just me, Robert Mercurio, Jeff Raines, and Rich Vogel.

Robert Mercurio: The impetus of us changing our name and maturing our sound was when we met with our producer, this guy Dan Prothero, who started Fog City Records. He was from San Francisco and came to New Orleans to scout out some bands to work with. We were one of the bands that he found and he recorded this one song with us in our living room and put it on a compilation.

Stanton Moore: This compilation was called *Is That Jazz?*—we recorded a song called "Black Eyed Pea."

Robert Mercurio: At that point, the record label, which was called Ubiquity Records, suggested that we lose the "Prophylactic."

Stanton Moore: We couldn't think of a name fast enough before the deadline, so they just put Galactic on the record.

Robert Mercurio: Dan Prothero did a great job recording a song in our living room. We were like, "Wow, let's see what he could actually do at a studio!" So when it came time to make *Coolin' Off,* our first record, which we did in the summer of '95, we hired him to be our producer. We went into Sea-Saint Studios, which is Allen Toussaint's studio—so many amazing records were recorded there, from The Meters, Dr. John, Neville Brothers—any Allen Toussaint project was pretty much recorded there.

Stanton Moore: My mom made red beans and rice and brought it to the studio.

Robert Mercurio: It was a super funky studio; we went in there for two days and cranked out *Coolin' Off*. That set us up to be the band that started touring nonstop.

42

Wildlife on a Safari

Capturing these bands in photography was no easy feat: These were not rock stars in the traditional sense. Here, famed rock and roll photographer Danny Clinch explains what it took to get the best shots back then.

My girlfriend at the time, who's now my wife, Maria, went to FIT. She went to study Shakespeare with her class. In my family, nobody had gone to college. My mom had gone to nursing school, but certainly on my dad's side, no one could go to college. So I had no idea you could go study abroad. I was like, "Wow, you're going to London to study Shakespeare?" I was like "I wanna do something like that!" I found a workshop, which was the Ansel Adams Gallery workshop. One of the instructors was Annie Leibovitz. It was Annie Leibovitz and David Hockney. I befriended her assistant and he said at one point, "Annie told me to keep my eye open for someone who might be able to intern at her studio in New York City. You think you're available for that if she were to ask you?" I became an intern and worked my way up to being one of her main assistants to traveling with her all the time. I learned a lot from her and worked with the top people in the industry, whether they were producers or stylists, makeup artists, assistants—everybody was top game.

I spent many years sneaking my cameras into shows at the Stone Pony, at the Spectrum in Philly, wherever I was going. My real break was the community of friends I made through working with Annie . . . a group of friends that I still hang out with to this day. One was working a job for *Spin* magazine as an assistant photo editor. She helped me get my foot in the door there and I did a shoot for *Spin,* photographing 3rd Bass, the hip-hop group. I felt like I did a good job. I think part of my skill is getting along with people and getting them to feel comfortable. I hit it off with the band and got some really good photos; there were several options that they could have used in the magazine. And they were really happy with it. Not so far down the road, I got a call from MC Serch from 3rd Bass. He said, "I have an artist that I'm helping produce and just got him signed to Sony Records . . . and I think you're the guy to shoot the album packaging." He handed me the cassette and it said Nasty Nas on it. And so it was the Nas *Illmatic* record on a cassette. I did the Nas *Illmatic* shoot and I took those images and the MC Serch images to Def Jam.

I said, "I'd like to work with you guys. Can I bring my portfolio in to show you?" And that was the difference maker right here.

"Well, we look at portfolios on Wednesday. So drop it off Tuesday, pick it up Thursday, we'll let you know what we think."

"Actually, I'd like to come in and say hello, show my face, meet you guys."

"We don't really do it that way."

"Well, I just photographed 3rd Bass."

"Alright, well, bring them in, and we'll look at them."

I rolled up and went into Def Jam. The Drawing Board was the name of their creative agency at the time and they were my age. We were kids! I was like twenty-four or something. I started to shoot for Def Jam—my first album packaging that I had ever done for a major label was a freelance job they got me for Atlantic Records—Lord Finesse's *Return of the Funky Man.*

I started to do all this hip-hop stuff. And the hip-hop stuff turned into a good thing for me. My style of photography at the time was very documentary in a sense, I liked to capture the moment, I liked going on location. For *Spin,* I shot the Smashing Pumpkins, Blind Melon, the Chili Peppers, and Jane's Addiction. They all loved hip-hop, whereas mainstream just thought hip-hop was pretty much a fad. They would see my portfolio and I would have Public Enemy, Nas, LL Cool J. They were like, "Shit, this is cool. Let's work with this guy!"

Spin gave me my first assignment with Phish. I met the band up [in Boston]. The first moment I spent with them, I just realized how quirky and kind of strange and different these guys were from the rock bands and hip-hop artists

I was photographing. We found this fire pit out in a field and someone found a sneaker . . . and Trey put the sneaker on the end of a stick and was holding it over the fire like a marshmallow or something. And they all just thought that was the funniest thing ever.

I ended up going out to Philly to photograph them as well. I had been to Dead shows and stuff so I was kind of familiar with that kind of scene in the parking lot. I remember just wandering around the parking lot and taking photos of people inhaling nitrous, people selling grilled-cheese sandwiches. My assistant at the time bought some goo balls off of somebody and we ate them and that was it. I was done for the night. I was like, "Holy shit, what have I got myself into?"

After that, they started to hire me.

I met Dave Matthews in '96. I photographed him with the Chet Atkins Gibson for *Guitar World* magazine. He came by himself. We got along real well and just down the road I got a call from RCA and they're like, "Hey, Dave really liked you for that guitar magazine . . . would you do some publicity photos for us?"

Labels would see the portfolio, there might be a creative brief: "This is the album, this is what it's called, this is what they're looking for, we chose you for this reason." Publicity pictures had to be a simple, clean image where you could see everybody, and they look good. My approach was always doing these simple portraits but then also just finding really crazy light, or backlight or silhouettes . . . stepping back and having the artists be very small into the frame; having a lot of atmosphere and room in case that it was a poster, or inside the record where they're putting the titles of the songs. I would shoot with these crazy different cameras—plastic cameras, double exposures, Polaroids and solarizing Polaroids. I was just always giving people a bunch of different options.

Some people love having their photos taken. Some people hate it. Some people are just super nervous and they just get stiff. That was the challenge for both of those bands—you've got four or five guys, all different shapes and sizes, and you're trying to arrange them in a way. They weren't showing up in leather pants and cool hats. The challenge was: How do you bring some of their personality out? Phish was: Have a good time, distract them a little bit. You get them in a good mood, you could see it in their faces. Dave could cut loose every once in a while and be silly in a fun way. It was all about keeping it loose, and looking for a moment where you could shoot five rolls of film on one thing. It just depends on when you were able to get that moment where everything came together—everyone looked relaxed, someone didn't blink, someone wasn't yawning or talking. It's like photographing wildlife on a safari.

43

Our Clubhouse in the Jungle

Billy Martin: Bob Moses had already been to Hawaii and had a connection there. Every other year they would close their eyes and put their fingers on a world atlas. They landed in Hawaii and hitchhiked and were picked up by Carl, who's the guy I call Shack-Man. He lived in a tree house. I met Carl in New Jersey. He showed up at my house one day, because Bob Moses and I were recording a duet record called *DrummingBirds,* in my dad's basement . . . my dad had the equipment and I was still living at home, so we decided to record the record in my basement on eight-track. Carl was in town, because one of his cousins was getting married in Chinatown. Carl showed up with all these beautiful tropical flowers and a huge bag of amazing weed—homegrown in Hawaii. He said, "Hey, you got to come to Hawaii . . . anytime." So I did. That was a few years before meeting John and Chris. So I made a couple of trips out there in the late '80s.

Chris Wood: Rykodisc were willing to take a chance and let us really do what we wanted, which was to go into the jungle of Hawaii and record a record off the grid. The whole idea with the record *Shack-man* . . . it was supposed to be solar powered.

Billy Martin: The sound of the Shack is really special.

Liz Penta: It took a lot of convincing with Gramavision on that concept.

John Medeski: I was very concerned, because the record label had just gotten a brand-new head and he didn't understand what we were doing. But he was stuck with us, because we had one more record on our deal. We were trying to get more money in the budget, because we wanted to do the solar power thing. And they were not going for it. I'm sorta the guy in the band that's more concerned about that stuff.

Liz Penta: Very small budget. Probably around twenty-five thousand dollars or something.

Chris Wood: The only friction came when we liked the idea of taking Billy's reel-to-reel eight-track and recording the whole record on eight-tracks in the Shack.

Billy Martin: Some studios are great and you want to go to Electric Ladyland. But wherever you feel comfortable and where it sounds good, you bring the studio there. You bring your equipment there so that's what we did and what I encouraged. It took a while to convince everybody but I was like we've got to record there.

Chris Wood: The record company was like, "No, no, no, you've got to do it on sixteen tracks, at least." So instead of just a reel-to-reel eight-track, they convinced us that we had to take to the ADA digital eight-tracks and you put them together, you get sixteen tracks. First day of the session, one of them dies and we're back to eight-tracks for the rest of the record. We had just enough of a budget where we could add a little extra renovation so we had enough room to fit the band in the Shack—literally a plywood shack with a tin roof. And then solar panels, some converters, the batteries . . . that was our dream, to really record off of just solar power. It's the cleanest energy—sonically, not just environmentally; it's supposed to be the best clean electricity for recording. Turns out the record budget wasn't quite big enough to afford enough solar panels.

Billy Martin: I was like, "You know, I have a friend there, we could stay at his place . . . he offered." And when we got there, we were like, "Holy shit!" There was this broken piano that kind of sounds cool, a Guatemalan xylophone, amps, a drum set, congas . . . all kinds of things laying around we can play.

John Medeski: We were transposing this life in Hawaii.

Liz Penta: They ended up using a generator for a lot of it, because that was the only way to do it. Which was against our whole concept, but you didn't have a choice, because otherwise it wasn't gonna get recorded.

Chris Wood: We had to borrow from a friend, this World War II Willys flathead generator. We brought in a Bobcat. It was so heavy; we had to stand on the back of the Bobcat while we drove it up the driveway. And the thing's really noisy. So we had to run it during the day and go swimming and, you know, be in Hawaii . . . and then at night, we'd get about five hours of recording time off of the batteries.

Billy Martin: We brought our girlfriends, invited other friends, some of our other friends would jam with us. A lot of our close friends and family would come visit us and we'd just have these vacation hangs. It was our clubhouse in the jungle.

John Medeski: The guy who owns the Shack had to build a separate room. We had to find an organ. We found this organ and I brought it to this guy to get fixed up. And he got the dates wrong, so it wasn't ready when we got there.

Chris Wood: There was this freak out, like, "Oh my god, we don't even have an organ . . . what are we gonna do?"

John Medeski: We saw a classified ad and there was a speaker with pulleys in it—seventy-five bucks. We went and looked at it and sure enough, it was a Leslie speaker, so we got that . . . I gave him a hundred bucks.

Chris Wood: Word of mouth, we found out that there's some dentist who lives in Hilo who has a B3 organ.

John Medeski: I went over there and played it a little and talked to him. I remember the look on his face as we had his organ in the back of the pickup truck, driving it out to the jungle.

Chris Wood: I think that took about a week before we were able to actually press record and start the record.

Billy Martin: There were no neighbors within earshot, except for birds, a dog barking or something, rain on the tin roof. Isolation between the instruments—there wasn't much. But we did put Chris in a closet type thing. It's really just a plywood shack with a tin roof and glass on one side where the rain would come. It was very quiet there. It was actually an advantage, the way things sounded and bounced off things. You can hear it on the record.

Philip Harvey (Live Sound Engineer, Medeski Martin & Wood): The toilet was an outhouse.

Chris Wood: On previous visits, we'd spent a lot of time jamming and rehearsing in the Shack, and it was like playing inside a speaker cabinet. It had this magical sound, not to mention the humidity and just the jungle around it . . . there was a reverberance to the property and to the actual Shack itself in the way everything rattled.

Billy Martin: We'd go way out of our way to get really good fish. And John is a gourmet cook. So we would be doing all these amazing things cooking, like cooking the fish on banana leaves on the fire or making special rice combining with Japanese food . . . eating really unusual tropical fruits, breadfruit in the fire, sashimi. Music or not, that was so incredible. And the swimming water was incredible; we'd go to the volcano and watch the lava flow down in the middle of the night. And then we had instruments there and started to accumulate enough stuff that we could just play when we were there.

After the second or third visit out, we made a deal that we wanted to rent it year-round so that we could have it at least for a couple of months every year. The rent was three hundred dollars a month. So we split the rent—a hundred dollars each. We'd stay there for two months or we could send our friends there. We did that for many, many years. We lived there, we slept, we had blow-up mattresses and mosquito nets inside the Shack; we had a little kitchen that had a propane stove and a propane refrigerator and an outdoor shower that collected the rain. The temperature was always anywhere between the sixties and the eighties—sixties was cold.

John Medeski: We would basically spend a couple of months in the winter there because touring in the winter was really brutal.

Billy Martin: It was just paradise. We didn't want to leave.

Chris Wood: I think Rykodisc was pretty happy with it. When we mixed it, it was one of my first experiences seeing someone work with Pro Tools. I remember hearing, "Oh, someone from the record company is coming over to listen." John and Billy were like, "Do you have any ideas for a sequence?" And so I just quickly threw together some stuff that basically ended up being somewhat close to the sequence of the record. And it just flowed beautifully.

John Medeski: I don't think they knew what to make of it when we delivered it . . . and then it did really well for them. Then we were gone.

44

That Kind of Touring Ages You

Back in Westchester County, New York, God Street Wine were picking up the pieces after a rather disastrous first major-label attempt with Geffen. They went back to basics and self-recorded their third album, Red, *while continuing to tour. And it got them noticed . . . again.*

Tomo: Two things: I don't think we were ever asked, or ever really pushed, to produce a single. And I also think we were assholes. We were difficult.

Jon Bevo: We got seduced. McGhee is a big personality. He's a guy that will suck the air out of the room. He had charisma . . . the total wrong charisma for a God Street Wine kinda band. He made it seem like he wanted to be the center of attention. He flew us out to Malibu, to a restaurant in a private room on the beach.

Matt Busch: It is a huge surprise to me that something like "Nightingale" never had the same type of radio success that "Run Around" had.

Aaron Maxwell: We made phone cards—calling cards—for our fans. We actually made it into *Rolling Stone* for that. But the label didn't really get behind it enough and it's the worst feeling.

Tomo: Labels really didn't know what to do with jam bands, even going back to the Grateful Dead. Warner Brothers didn't know what to do with the

Grateful Dead until they made *Workingman's Dead* and *American Beauty*. We were never a three-minute single kind of band, not that Lo couldn't have written that kind of thing. Even if there hadn't been that strife between Geffen and the McGhees, I'm not sure that Geffen would have known what to do with this band. The shortest song on the record is five and a half minutes long. We were playing to dancing college kids and hippie skirts and ball caps.

Jon Bevo: We sold out Irving Plaza, and backstage our lawyer's like, "Take a look at this . . . because this is gonna be an intimate closet." You want to believe it, you know?

Dan Pifer: We felt like we got screwed. We were actually getting played at AAA radio, we were killing ourselves on the road, too, doing all the radio shows at 7:30 in the morning, after playing until four in the morning. That kind of touring ages you. And we were doing it. And having a label actively trying to kill it, even while it's going, was just really sad. I remember driving to Philly for a gig and listening to the radio in the van and "Nightingale" comes on the radio and it was like, "Yeah, this is amazing!" It was the AAA station in Philly, but it still was getting played.

Tomo: When people started talking about jam bands, I hated that term. I wanted to get songs on the radio and I was really conflicted. I liked playing the stuff we were playing, but I also wanted to be bigger and more popular and make money and not be worried about paying rent. We just couldn't, whether we didn't have muscles or we had two lead singers that made it confusing. I don't know how likable our front people were. Not to disparage the guys in our band, but they would probably say the same thing.

Dan Pifer: [When we left Geffen], I think the vibe was we were a little down. We had a feeling we could work at radio. We also did a 180. Instead of doing a record in a studio, we had a bunch of songs we wanted to record but we were going to record them in our house. We set up a multitrack studio using ADAT machines—it was like an eight-track digital recorder that kinda looks like a VHS tape that you popped in. We had four of those, so we could get thirty-two tracks. And we had a big Mackie mixing board, which is all we could afford, and a bunch of outboard gear. We recorded about a year and a half after the Geffen deal.

Jon Bevo: It was more experimental.

Aaron Maxwell: We ended up getting signed to Mercury, because Danny Goldberg became the president.

Jon Bevo: He had Joni Mitchell, Nirvana, and everyone else back then. Just a ridiculous roster.

Aaron Maxwell: He came and saw us and fell in love with our live show.

Scott "bullethead" Reilly: He came to see them open for the Allman Brothers at the Beacon Theater. I had gone to see them at Jones Beach two nights before. And I thought God Street Wine did not put on a great show at Jones Beach. I think Lo came out without pants on . . . they put on a great show for their fans at the 712 Club. This was Jones Beach, in front of people who didn't know who they were. There were inside jokes, there were obscure songs. They did not knock the audience out the way they could on their best nights. Backstage at the Beacon they asked me what did I think, and I told them that. And they all got really angry. They played their set and they all walked off stage and said, "Was that good enough for you?" And it was. Danny Goldberg wasn't sitting in a seat—he was in the back of the thing and was like, "I want to sign this band," from having seen them that one time. They put on a great show. When I went to meet with them, they held up the Rusted Root marketing plan that was like twenty pages thick. And it was a six-month plan: "This is what we're going to do for you." Unfortunately, I don't think they ever did a marketing plan like that again. They were putting out fifty records a year, which was unheard of for a major at the time. The band had made their own record in the band house, *Red,* which has some great stuff on it. But Danny Goldberg was so anxious to get things he had signed into the marketplace, he just took it as is.

Jon Bevo: He's like, "You know, I came from management, I'm not a record label exec guy just throwing shit against the wall." He sold us on that.

Lo Faber: They gave us $250,000 for a record that was already made.

Scott "bullethead" Reilly: He should have made the band go back and finish the record in a way that would have upped their tier. No band wants to do that. A band is always satisfied. It's up to the record company to say, "We can do better than this."

Jon Bevo: Mercury probably would have pushed something they were more involved with, as opposed to just taking on one that existed. We probably shouldn't have pushed for *Red*. That was the pet project we did in our house.

Aaron Maxwell: It was the same host of problems.

Dan Pifer: *Red* wasn't a cohesive record. It comes out on Mercury, and it didn't do very well. The single didn't really get any traction. They did give us a lot of marketing attention, a lot of tour support. We got into a bus and we started touring around the country in a bus.

We got Matt Bongiovi, who was Jon Bon Jovi's youngest brother . . . he, at the record company's request, became our tour manager. It was fun, but we also came out of that tour with like fifty thousand dollars in debt that we ended up carrying for years afterwards.

Lo Faber: I don't like to be bitter. That's not a good place to be.

45

We've Been a Volatile Band Since Day Fucking One

The mid-'90s marked a new wave of jam bands in the scene . . . it was clear Phish was not only having an impact at driving ticket sales, but were also musical influences themselves. The templates for what became the Disco Biscuits were laid down in 1995 in Philadelphia, which ushered in a new sound in the scene . . .

Marc Brownstein: A whole slew of bands came out that were Phish influenced. Ominous Seapods, Strangefolk, Percy Hill, freebeerandchicken, moe. We were the youngest of that generation.

Aron Magner (Keyboards, The Disco Biscuits): We were all students at the University of Pennsylvania.

Marc Brownstein: I had a friend that was in sales—she sold everything. She had a slew of Grateful Dead T-shirts . . . you know, with the ice cream cone, and it said "Nothing left to do but smile, smile, smile." She asked me if I could help her sell them and I was like, "Yeah, of course. I'm a salesman." So I took a bag of these down into the quad, which was the freshman dormitory, and I just started going door-to-door, asking people if they wanted to buy these Grateful Dead T-shirts. At some point, I ran into Sammy [Altman], who wanted me to come back and hang out—"Hey, why don't you come back and do some bong hits in my room!" So we went up to what's called "The Nipple" . . . it's at the very top end of the quad at the University of Pennsylvania freshman dorm. It came out that we were both bass players.

Sam Altman (Drums, The Disco Biscuits): I think I bought weed from him. And he was kind of pompous.

Marc Brownstein: They were really . . . let's call it confidence. It didn't rub me the wrong way at first, but they were overly confident about themselves and I was just like, "Wow, these guys are super confident." He said he was the best bass slapper in the world. He certainly wasn't the best bass slapper, but he was damn good at slap bass.

Sam Altman: I was kind of pompous. He was talking about how he played bass. And I was saying I was better than—he was very into the Spin Doctors at that point, because they were a New York band and I'm sure he was used to seeing them at Wetlands—and he says, "You're not as good as Mark White." And I was like, "I'm way better than Mark White." And I don't even think I knew who Mark White was . . . I was just being kind of a dick.

Jon "The Barber" Gutwillig: We were all living in West Philadelphia and we had a little band, which was a precursor to the Biscuits. It was me, Sammy, and Marc. We would do covers of the Grateful Dead. Allman Brothers, Miles Davis, Phish. We did some Chili Peppers—I think we did "Give It Away." We didn't do the poppy stuff like "Under the Bridge" or something like that. We'd do the stuff that we thought was musically interesting. We'd play every bar in West Philadelphia and there were some bands doing ska and some bands that did pop music, Top 40—which was rock at the time.

Aron Magner: They would call themselves something different every fraternity party they'd play. I don't know why, or even if that's true.

Sam Altman: I had a little punk rock band in high school, and I got into the Dead a little bit. We'd play a lot in my bedroom. And then I got into Jane's

Addiction and Primus and Fugazi and the Beastie Boys. And so I was always playing drums and with Marc, we had a bass player and we needed a drummer, so I just switched to being drums.

Marc Brownstein: Phish came around on Thanksgiving weekend to play the Keswick Theatre. My grades had been going bad, like worse and worse, throughout the course of that semester. And I had tickets to this Phish show. It was the Wednesday of Thanksgiving, and my mother found out that I was basically about to drop out of college—that I was just playing music and hanging out with my friends. And she was so pissed off that she drove down to Philly, packed all my stuff up, and took me back to New York on the day of that Phish show. That would have been my first big jam band show. I decided that I was gonna go to the New School and study jazz. I wasn't really good enough at the bass at this point to get into a music school, but my bass teacher was in this band called The Authority that was playing at Wetlands at the time. He had gone to school and despite the fact that I kind of failed the audition, he talked to Reggie Workman, who is a very famous bass player, and said, "This guy's a quick learner. He's one of my students, is there any way we can make an exception here?" They actually had to go back into the pile of applicants and find three other people that weren't accepted because they weren't quite at the level yet—and that created a beginner ensemble for us. That began the journey of what it takes to become a professional musician, which is playing eight hours a day. February 5, 1993, Phish came back around to play the Roseland in New York City and we got tickets for that. All of my friends from Penn drove up and stayed at my father's apartment in New York City. That was a game-changer because I had been seeing a lot of jam bands in New York—Shockra, the Mexican Mud Band, The Authority—but nothing like that.

Jon "The Barber" Gutwillig: We had an original keyboardist—he quit.

Aron Magner: Legend has it the original keyboard player did not want to get his keyboard out of storage to rehearse and Brownstein did not like that lack of fortitude, and got mad at him and some sort of words ensued or he was just tired of him and fired him. Through a mutual friend, I was introduced.

I was introduced as "Yeah, he's cool, he's from Philly, loves jazz. You guys should have a lot in common, you should talk to him."

Marc Brownstein: July of 1995, the band coalesced into the Disco Biscuits with the lineup that became the band.

Aron Magner: The first time we called ourselves the Disco Biscuits was when I joined the band.

Jon "The Barber" Gutwillig: When we found Aron, we had a really good group of players.

Aron Magner: Marc called me up and I was a jazzer, so I was all about the hustle of gig to gig, rather than band formation. I also had never really been in a rock band. I was used to playing in complex colors. I really had to learn and listen to rock piano players . . . I was always into the Grateful Dead, but I never really listened to it as music that I was going to play in the band. Marc gets the impression that I'm this forty-year-old Black jazz keyboard player.

Sam Altman: A sixty-year-old Black jazz keyboard player. That's what I thought was happening.

Aron Magner: And I come in and I look exactly like a small white kid with a hat on backwards.

Sam Altman: Aron shows up and he's this little Jewish dude from ZBT.

Aron Magner: Very quickly some sort of fight ensued and Marc left the band that day. So the first day that I showed up, he quit. We've been a volatile band since day one. Legend has it the reason he lashed out at the band was just because he really wanted to go on Phish tour and he needed an excuse.

Marc Brownstein: I was like, "This band is crazy. I'm getting out of here and going on Phish tour." And I went to see Phish at Sugarbush. That was the night that everybody was climbing up through the woods and then storming the gates and they made the show free on the second night. They named the band while I was away in Vermont, and when I came back, I was like, "Alright, I'm feeling better. Let's do this, let's start a band together." And then we solidified our lineup as Aaron, Sammy, Jon, and myself.

Jon "The Barber" Gutwillig: We would do little tours around Philadelphia. And we would start to pick up gigs—we'd go out to Penn State, go out to Lancaster and other markets in Pennsylvania. We would do Penn State gigs in fraternity houses and they would talk—the fraternities between Penn and Penn State. So we'd play a great show at one house, and we would get a call from the other house, or we would ask them if they were connected with anybody at nearby schools. We would work that angle a bit . . . it was enough to survive.

Marc Brownstein: School became my second priority, and the Biscuits became my first priority. I was booking the band. I was marketing the band. Sammy was doing graphic design so we had flyers.

Jon "The Barber" Gutwillig: Seven hundred and fifty dollars was a good gig price. It was like two hundred dollars to play a bar. And then considerably more to play a frat show. We lived together for a couple years until the house exploded. A pipe just exploded. You could rent a house for seven hundred bucks a month, plus utilities. I drank a lot of tea and I ate Cup O' Noodles. That was where all the money went every week. And I would write and we would go play shows and then I would write and we've been playing those songs ever since. So there was a lot of value being created, but just wasn't being paid for up front.

Marc Browstein: We were really volatile.

Sam Altman: Extremely volatile.

Marc Brownstein: I take a lot of the heat for that volatility. There was the time that Aron ran across the room, jumped over the drums, and tackled Sam. It was Aron and Sammy, Sammy and Jon, me and everybody. Everybody was fighting, all the time.

Sam Altman: A lot of that has to do with personality—Marc and Jon at each other's throats. They're both strong personalities. They both had a creative vision. They both had ideas for the band, ideas for the music, ideas of the right way to proceed. Should we be focused more on the business side of things? Should we focus more on musical purity? Should we be focused more on inventing a sound? Aron and I were more on the sidelines in terms of that—the real creative forces of the band were Marc and Jon.

Marc Brownstein: We didn't know why that was happening. It was a harbinger of some of what was to come over the next ten years—a lot of tumult and a lot of fighting and a lot of not understanding the effects of different psychoactive chemicals and stuff . . . we didn't know, really, what we were getting ourselves into. We didn't know why we were feeling the way we were feeling every Tuesday . . . partying all weekend and then Tuesday would roll around and we'd feel like garbage. And people would have emotional breakdowns and it would turn into a fight the next day because nobody had any serotonin.

Sam Altman: I waded into the fray many times. I've had physical altercations with Marc at least twice. And I think Jon threw a glass bottle at my head one time. I got out of the van one time, skipped a bunch of gigs; Jon got out of the van one time, we couldn't find him.

Jon "The Barber" Gutwillig: One time we played this gig in Reading, Pennsylvania. We sold the place out and we really needed the money. And the bar owner didn't want to give it to us. And so he pulled a gun out on us and told us to leave the property with no money! We just sold his venue out. We don't know if he's gonna pull the trigger. We don't know how drunk he is or if he's on other drugs, which it seemed like he was. We ended up outside in the backyard, but we refused to leave. Marc was refusing to leave.

Marc Brownstein: I sat down on the floor of the venue and said I wouldn't leave until we got paid. And they said that I had to leave and then they called the cops on us because we wouldn't leave the building. Then the gun popped out.

Jon "The Barber" Gutwillig: And then he calls the cops and the cops show up, hear our story, don't care, and kick us off the property. I guess we could have gotten vigilante, but we didn't.

46

He Had to Whip Us Like a Rented Mule

Al Schnier: We would drive from Buffalo down to the city on a Tuesday, play Nightingale's, and then turn around in our cars and drive back that same night. People were trying to go to class on Wednesday morning, or get back to their jobs. We would do that probably every three or four weeks—keep making that drive over and over again.

Jim Loughlin: Someone had to be sober. We drank a lot of coffee. Al drank an excessive amount of coffee.

Steve Young (Sound Engineer, moe.): In the clubs, we were ending at one or two in the morning. After the show was over, we would break everything down and I pretty much drove all of it. We would drive a couple hours, and park somewhere at four or five in the morning and sleep for three hours.

Al Schnier: That was how we built up a following in the city. But we were doing the same thing in Akron, Ohio, in Rochester, in Albany, in Northampton, Massachusetts. We just kept chipping away at these markets. We basically went from playing every Friday or Saturday night to Tuesday through Sunday and had Mondays off.

Steve Young: I almost killed everybody a couple times.

Jim Loughlin: We were playing at one of the places on the west side. It was another one of those "You have to play this club to climb the ladder." It was probably a five-band bill. This is when Topper was managing us. So we left Buffalo a little bit late and just cranked down to Manhattan. Topper was already down there and we had to hit our time slot or you just lose it and that's it—we drove to New York for nothing. It literally ended up with the van parking illegally, making a big, huge train to get all the gear in. The drums went in first, and I immediately start setting everything up; now the bass rig's coming in, I'm halfway through my stuff, the guitars are getting set up. Al went to park the van and we started playing as he walked in the door, played our forty-five-minute set, then broke everything down, and split. There was no way we could afford a hotel room in Manhattan.

Jon Topper: We started playing the Court Tavern in New Brunswick . . . that's kind of my hometown. I wanted to be able to go home and do my laundry . . . my parents would feed us and we would all sleep on the floor.

Jim Walsh (Publicist): By the time 1995 rolled around, Thanksgiving weekend, they sold out a couple of nights at the Wetlands. They were happening.

Al Schnier: We were having conversations with several different labels at the time. That was also when Spin Doctors, Blues Traveler, Dave Matthews were all gaining traction and it was becoming a thing where jam bands were getting played on radio. H.O.R.D.E. was as successful as Lollapalooza at this point. It was this whole other thriving music scene that really had potential to blow up into this very popular mainstream thing. And we were being recruited.

Jim Loughlin: We moved to Albany . . . this was our full-time job. We had to figure out how to give everyone some kind of stipend, and then everything else went towards the band. In the beginning, it was minimal. There was community grocery money because we all lived in the same house. All that was taken care of by moe. We just needed money for cigarettes and beer.

Steve Young: They based themselves out of Albany because they could hit the Wetlands and do all the Northeast.

Jon Topper: I think there were three labels looking at us at that point.

Chuck Garvey: Michael Caplan heard about us on a Listserv—he found people talking about us. And a lot of people talking about us. He thought that was pretty impressive, I guess.

Rob Derhak: We were one of the first bands to start an internet presence or have a website. We had a bunch of computer nerds who were friends and fans. And the tapers happened to be those same people. We tapped into that and they started the moe-L Listserv as well. Caplan contacted the moe-L, thinking it was us somehow. They just sort of shit on him, immediately, as nerds will do.

Michael Caplan (Senior Vice President of A&R, Epic Records): The first band I signed when I started doing A&R was The Radiators in New Orleans. So I definitely had an affinity for the scene. The funny thing is, I don't think I saw moe. live before I pursued them. I did go up and visit with them in Albany and go see them play and they knew I worked with the Allman Brothers. So when I walked in the door with Jon Topper, they were playing "Whipping Post" just to mess with me—and they were killing it too. I went for it pretty quick.

Al Schnier: He liked the music. It felt like there was a guy here who had a very strong foothold into organic music. He had G. Love, Keb' Mo', and Anders Osborne all signed.

Jon Topper: The label had a lot of people that were out there touring. We actually chose our label by where we thought we fit the best instead of taking the most money we probably could have gotten.

Michael Caplan: My boss wasn't into it. Bands were really polished.

Al Schnier: The president of the label told us point blank, "I don't really understand you. And I'm not sure I care for your band. But Michael believes in you and that's all that matters to me. So welcome to our label." I walked away thinking, "I really like her"—I liked her for being so transparent with us. As the president of a label, there's no way she possibly likes all the acts they sign. And that's okay. I'm glad she just told us that. And then I remember relaying that to somebody else, several years later, and they were like, "Are you kidding me? And you still signed with them? That the president of the label didn't like your band wasn't gonna be a problem?"

Michael Caplan: I was CBS Records or Sony or whatever—I was real cocky . . . not that *I was,* but I'm saying what I represented was like, "Oh, we want you and so therefore bow down."

Al Schnier: Michael was also a huge prog rock fan. He and I connected on that and talked about Genesis, King Crimson, and Peter Gabriel. He liked that side of what we brought to the table. I think he saw, maybe, that moe. could bridge the gap between Americana roots and prog rock somehow.

Michael Caplan: I don't know who asked, "Why do you call us a jam band?" But I said, "Because when you come up to my office, when you leave, it smells like hemp!"

Rob Derhak: The whole bidding war thing would happen, where one guy would be like, "I found this band." And if somebody found out about it, then it's like, "Oh, well, I want them and I'm gonna give them more. And I don't even know what the hell I'm throwing a million dollars at."

Michael Caplan: moe. got a pretty good deal. They asked for a lot, and we weren't balking.

Rob Derhak: We got a pretty good deal—two-album deal, something like eight hundred grand.

Al Schnier: Now it felt like we were putting our big-boy pants on—our first major label, big budget record.

Rob Derhak: That was like a summer camp for us.

Al Schnier: We recorded *No Doy* at Long View Farms in Massachusetts. It's a residential studio on a farm; they have horses on the farm and a great location. The Rolling Stones were there to do pre-production for The Steel Wheels tour. There's a pretty long hill that was an approach that went up to the farm—they said Mick [Jagger] used to run up this hill backwards because it would make his butt look good. I remember trying, which is a lot harder than you'd think.

Rob Derhak: It was like a bed and breakfast where they served us insane meals every day. I probably gained twenty pounds recording there. And I got to ride on horses. We drank a lot of whiskey and beer. We recorded to twenty-four-track tape and we had guys cutting tape to make drum tracks fit together. It was a real art form. The producer we had for that was John Porter. Our A&R guy put a lot of pressure on us to pick him. From our A&R guy's perspective, since we're such a young band, and he was an older English guy, he could fucking tame us and make us fit in the right mold, so he could sell some records.

Chuck Garvey: He had to whip us like a rented mule.

Rob Derhak: And he did try pretty hard. And he'd get frustrated by it. The A&R guy was up his ass about getting a song. We had a single candidate that was a song Al wrote called "Guitar." That's what he really wanted to be the single and then I just remember there being a lot of clashing between us and the producer, about what we wanted that song to sound like. And I imagined it had a lot to do with him being the go-between between A&R and us. Al ended up pulling it from the record. It got to a point where we had to be done with that process. We spent two months living there—it was a summer's worth of shit. We learned, really, how you make the sausage.

Michael Caplan: One of the marketing things we did was a single for "Meat"—to make the longest single ever. I think it was forty-seven minutes or something.

Al Schnier: He came to us with a suggestion that we record the "Meat" single, and had Sony pay to press copies of this forty-five-minute single that we were then going to send to radio.

Michael Caplan: Me and Topper went into the studio—they started playing and then Topper and I left to go eat. When we came back it was like, "Okay, wrap it up."

Al Schnier: He knew that we weren't going to get a song on radio, they were not going to push a single.

Rob Derhak: They wanted their money back, or they wanted to make money on it. I mean, even though it's a drop in the bucket to them, no matter what, you're making a record and they want a single from it. They want something they can market it with.

Chuck Garvey: All of our songs always had the core part of the song, which we thought was amazing, and then we could spin it in a different way, as a jam. Well-constructed songs—Caplan and Sony thought they could actually use that stuff. We would write these things that we would think would stand the test of time, but then they would be like fifteen minutes live. We could go either way, at that point.

Michael Caplan: moe. probably sold a hundred thousand copies of *No Doy*. That's crazy by today's standards.

Jim Walsh: The album cover was a big, large bald guy and the album title was stupid. The funny thing about moe. is they did things that got in their own way . . people didn't get the joke. It went over people's heads sometimes . . . and maybe it wasn't that funny, either.

Rob Derhak: You hear these horror stories about bands that would get a huge single and people are like, "Oh, you don't want to be like them. They got massive and made millions of dollars. And now they don't have another thing." And I'm like, "Why not? That seems awesome!"

47

I Wouldn't Say Lawless, But You Could Do What You Wanted Here

Rick Farman (Co-founder, Superfly Presents): There are four co-founders of Superfly Presents. And three of us went to Tulane. So that's how we all ended up in New Orleans. We really met around Tipitina's.

Kerry Black (Co-founder, Superfly Presents): I went to the University of Vermont for a year and a half before I transferred to Tulane.

Rick Farman: The bridge between New Orleans music and jam music was starting to brew.

Kerry Black: We did not start Superfly on purpose. We weren't like, "Hey, we're gonna do this for the rest of our lives," kind of thing. In the beginning it was a one-off situation where we just thought we were going to help put together this cool show and have a good time and do something in music that we were so passionate about.

Ben Ellman: They had their first offices above a comic book store and their second office was above a laundry service.

Kerry Black: New Orleans offered a certain opportunity too, because New Orleans, at the time, was not the most business-minded. We always joked that just by returning phone calls and emails on time, that put us a pretty good leg up.

Rick Farman: Jazz Fest '96 was the year that Phish played. It was one of the catalysts that brought that jam scene to New Orleans.

Andy Gadiel (Founder, Andy Gadiel's Phish Page; Co-founder, Jambase.com): Jazz Fest had this huge incubation period of exposure to new artists and people who loved a diversity of music.

Andy Bernstein: Jazz Fest was first on my radar because of Phish.

Rich Vogel: Phish playing Jazz Fest was obviously huge.

Kyle Hollingsworth: The culture down there embraced the more hippie, improvisational jam scene.

Eric Krasno (Guitar, Soulive, Lettuce): There was this influx of jazz-influenced music, and it was more embraced by the jam band community then.

Kerry Black: They share a certain DNA so that makes perfect sense as to why it would meld together. The improvisation, the spontaneity, the players being able to come in and out and jam with each other—they both independently have those same chops.

Rich Vogel: We applied to get a Jazz Fest slot—we sent in a little press pack we had made with *Coolin' Off*. So we played our first Jazz Fest gig in the spring of '96. It was on a smaller stage sponsored by the House of Blues.

Rick Farman: The specific show I connected with my soon-to-be business partner on Superfly was Medeski Martin & Wood that he booked at Tipitina's. One of my contributions to that was booking the opening act and putting Michael Ray and the Cosmic Krewe on. I already knew of the connection between Michael and Phish a bit, and knew the fans would be intrigued by the Medeski Martin & Wood thing. And because Phish had endorsed them by letting them open up for a few dates. And what was really cool is both Michael and this guy Tim Green, who was this amazing local saxophone player, sat in with MMW during a good portion of that show. He fit in with them like a glove. We sold a lot more tickets than we were anticipating. The first set of Superfly shows were in '97. We did a Mardi Gras series and a Jazz Fest series. And certainly, we were capitalizing on the fact that so many people had come down to that '96 Jazz Fest.

Kerry Black: The first idea was at the Contemporary Arts Center—we postered and flyered like mad.

Robert Mercurio: It was basically a big warehouse—nothing glamorous at all.

Rick Farman: We ended up booking Medeski Martin & Wood and Béla Fleck, with New Orleans openers.

Kerry Black: And we did really well. We did over fifteen hundred people, made some money, and we're like, "Wow, that actually worked." That was our entrance to doing shows during Jazz Fest, which became our bread and butter for a bunch of years.

Rick Farman: Most other markets, if you had the premier venues in town and hundreds of thousands of music fans in town, promoters would be knifing each other to get in there. But it wasn't really the deal in New Orleans for a couple of different reasons related to who was in the industry down there. So we had a fairly clear lane and we started booking the Saenger Theatre or the State Palace Theatre, and finding unique venues like the *Creole Queen* riverboat.

Robert Walter: We never played Jazz Fest. We don't have the pedigree of someone like Galactic, that is a band from New Orleans and highly involved in that scene and working with artists from New Orleans and the traditions—so they have a built-in backstory. We were just some weird guys in San Diego that liked cool records.

Karl Denson: There were several promoters down in New Orleans that were taking on that task of trying to make the bread. We couldn't get any shows at clubs during the regular hours. So, it was [Erik Newson's] idea: Let's start at two o'clock in the morning. And so along with the Superfly guys, we started doing these shows at two o'clock in the morning. And they were packing out. And then the fact that we would play till eight in the morning sometimes, everybody thought that was the craziest thing, but then they're all on drugs, so it was great. They didn't have shit else to do.

Robert Walter: We were sitting in a funny place where we were too commercial for the jazz gatekeepers, and we were too jazzy for anything like the pop world, right? So it didn't really belong anywhere. We didn't really get a lot of love from jazz festivals, or critics. Because it's like homemade punk-rock jazz in a way. Most of us couldn't sit up there and play standards all night. The Blue Note world, we were not legit enough for them, not artsy enough. That was a great thing about finding this [jam band] audience. It's sort of a whole industry outside of all that.

Kyle Hollingsworth: Where we were musically was the same way New Orleans was playing. By definition, there's a giant jazz festival during the day and then the nights turned into more of a jam, improvisational scene.

Fred Wesley: A lot of kids took from funk and took the songs in a different direction. You know, it wasn't normal funk songs.

Kerry Black: You have this phonebook of incredible New Orleans songs where everyone in the city knows how to play them. Anyone can jump up with anyone at any time, and they did all the time. And it's the same thing with jam bands at the time. It was no surprise to me to see them getting along.

Andy Gadiel: One of the earliest pieces in JamBase.com, when it first started, was a guide to Jazz Fest at night. The daytime, on the fairgrounds, they had a grid and cubes. But once the fairgrounds closed, there were a hundred shows and you judged Jazz Fest not by what you saw, but what you had to miss to see what you saw.

Chris Stillwell: It's a whole different environment in New Orleans . . . this insulated hotbed. And people just freaked out.

Robert Mercurio: Superfly was one of the first to start bringing in more national acts and making that its own scene—post–Jazz Fest in-the-evening kind of stuff. I know it has been a blessing and a curse. A lot of local bands feel like it's kind of sad that they get shut out during Jazz Fest. And I agree, you know, there should be more of a focus on New Orleans music during that time.

Rich Vogel: There was another bar we used to play a lot—the Mermaid Lounge.

Robert Walter: It is a functioning neighborhood spot. And it's also not in the Quarter on Frenchmen Street . . . you have to make a trip to go there.

Stanton Moore: In the early days, there wasn't even a stage.

Rich Vogel: It was in kind of a seedy area, this back alley at the time. It was hard to find originally, but then once you knew where it was, you knew where it was. It became a hip little spot and was run by some great, music-loving people.

Stanton Moore: There was nothing around—it was kind of under the interstate. I wouldn't say lawless, but you could do what you wanted here.

Rich Vogel: They started to develop a music calendar, and have a good solid music calendar every month, like the Maple Leaf, or Tipitina's. When Jazz Fest was coming, they got the idea, "Okay we got to do some shows outside because we know we can draw more than our capacity. We're here in this no-man's-land, we can do whatever the hell we want." So we did an outdoor show at the Mermaid Lounge, so we could draw more people than it would hold—we had a huge late-night audience. It probably started at midnight. That was the night Jon Fishman was there and he sat in for a tune. We just kept playing and playing and playing. And that's where we got this reputation of a late-night thing. And it was also the beginning of people realizing,

"Oh, you can do late-night shows at Jazz Fest, and especially with this audience that's coming to town now, you could have a show that starts at two in the morning and goes till five, and people will come."

Robert Mercurio: Superfly were starting to promote these late-night shows. Some of them, like the Mermaid Lounge show, was not planned to be a late-night show. But we literally played until the sun came up. We didn't intend to play until the sun comes up, but the place was so packed, we played a third set. That became a tradition for us.

Andy Bernstein: I would never think of Jazz Fest as a jam band phenomenon. I would think of the late-night at Jazz Fest, what Superfly did, as a jam phenomenon.

Robert Walter: I was down to do every night. There's something that happens when you push your body and mind beyond what you think you can do. You start playing more in the moment, that thing becomes more visceral. You don't have time to be nervous anymore, because you're just running on fumes. And it does become sort of hedonistic, too, like we're the bad people going to do the crazy thing. It doesn't feel like the entertainment industry anymore. You're doing something that's a little more pure.

Kyle Hollingsworth: You wake up at two in the afternoon and you start watching music—then you soundcheck at nine o'clock at night and play your stuff from two to four.

DJ Logic (Musician): I started a set at one to six in the morning. We had Jon Fishman, Warren Haynes, Casey Benjamin, Scott Palmer. It was awesome.

Stanton Moore: A lot of the Jazz Fest shows for the next several years were really, really good for us because people would view us and they'd go back to their cities or towns and tell their friends about us. And then when we would show up in those towns, that really helped.

48

It Took So Much to Have My Shit Together

Ray Schwartz: Phish was one of the bands that we looked to as a role model. We had a correspondence going with Phish.

Andre Gardner: They really helped us put things together in a business sense.

Reid Genauer: That whole crew was mentoring us.

Brett Fairbrother: Small town, right? Strangefolk's got a little bit of a buzz. Here's this huge band. It's known that the people in the band are fans and their manager's beyond a fan . . . I was so into it. It took so much to have my shit together . . . to not be a fanboy in situations.

Sam Ankerson: Our first forays into going out and renting theaters on our own, producing our own shows . . .'96, I think, was the first time we tried it. We rented the Barre Opera House in Barre, Vermont, and then the Waterville Opera House in Maine. Those moves were because that's where we felt our fans were, but also we'd been inspired by what Phish had done in the early years—started just doing it themselves, and taking over theaters and putting on their own shows.

Al Schnier: The second or third time Phish came to Buffalo, they played at a roller rink. They had outgrown the bars, because those were selling out at three hundred people. Whoever the promoter was for this show booked them—it's basically a roller-skating rink so they could do like five or six hundred people, and it wasn't a music venue at all. But it was a perfect place to go see Phish. In fact, Trey put on roller skates at one point and had a wireless guitar. He was skating around and playing on the roller skates, which was fantastic. After the show, Page was hanging out, just sitting on the side of the stage. I gave him the *Fatboy* cassette. We talked about the band for a while, and I told them all about moe. and who we were and what we were doing. The story I heard, and I think Fishman was the one who told me this story later, was that tape got stuck in their tape deck and it was the only thing that they could listen to—they were doing a tour out west. So they were forced to listen to moe.

Jim Loughlin: Trey loved the song "Yodelittle."

Al Schnier: The letter went "Dear moe., we listened to your tape and we just wanted to tell you that 'Yodelittle' is the greatest pop song ever written, maybe the greatest song since 'My Sharona' by The Knack, since 'You Really Got Me' by The Kinks." It goes on and on and names a bunch of pop songs.

Ray Schwartz: We were just so excited to get any kind of feedback from them.

Brett Fairbrother: John Paluska mentored me the whole way.

Jon Trafton: Brett just hit it off with John Paluska really well and had a really friendly relationship . . . everybody in our organization had a real friendly relationship with their whole organization.

Brett Fairbrother: Remember when Phish did the Ross Sports Center for *Rift*? We did the same thing, but we hadn't been signed yet. And we sold it out about a month plus in advance. When I told Paluska that, he was like, "You need to talk to Chip Hooper . . . he needs to be your agent."

Jon Trafton: John Paluska invited us over . . . we were really interested in just understanding how they organize their organization, from the band to the office and merchandise, and how to keep it all in-house.

I lived in Waterbury, which is maybe forty minutes from Burlington. And you know, it's like *Ferris Bueller's Day Off*—I overslept, woke up, and I knew I was going to be late. I jumped in my car and happened to have the Great Went cassette in my player and I remember hearing that "Bathtub Gin," driving up Highway 89, going like ninety, to be as close to on time as possible.

I showed up a bit late, in a hurry, rushing in the door. Who's sitting there but Strangefolk, all of our organization, Trey, and there's an empty seat next to Trey. Trey sat there with us and answered every question under the sun.

Luke Smith: I wasn't at that meeting. Part of how that happened was that Ankerson played squash with Paluska. He had been a child prodigy squash champion. He played squash at Yale. He came up and lived in our house and lived under the stairs. The only way to get into Sam's little domain was through the bathroom in our house. Paluska heard about Ankerson and was like, "I want to play with this kid."

Sam Ankerson: I didn't have a role in that meeting or in the Phish mentoring of Strangefolk, which was very true. I do remember a couple of lunches with Jason Colton.

Andre Gardner: When we were in Burlington, I was in touch with Brad Sands, Phish's tour manager. We went out to dinner, and I was able to pick his brain. He showed me their tour book and gave me advice on how to do things on the road.

Reid Genauer: I remember making two records at Dan Archer's and having both Fishman and Page pop in. I met with Trey and Paluska for lunch . . . me, Jon, and Brett, and it was encouragement. And I think they were proud. At the time, I don't think there was another band that was touring nationally from Vermont.

Brett Fairbrother: One time my girlfriend and I picked up Trey to give him a ride somewhere, randomly, and I had to pretend that I didn't care.

Jamie Janover: I was in college in '87 and it was around those times that some bootleg cassette tapes were circulating of Phish. Me and my band listened to this cassette and we were like, "Holy shit, these guys are on it!" I went to go see Phish in '89 at Pearl Street in Northampton, Massachusetts. They're playing all this material I don't know, but then they go into "Good Times, Bad Times." I was like, "This is impossible. These guys are college kids and they're playing better than Led Zeppelin." One day I was at The Front in Burlington and Fishman played one of his classic trombone solos—and you use circular breathing, playing a really long note.

So I went up to him after the show and I was like, "Dude, nice work with the circular breathing. I do circular breathing too with the didgeridoo."

And Fishman says to me, "What's that?"

"You don't know the didgeridoo? It's a native Aboriginal instrument."

"Bring one the next time you come to a show. I want to check that out."

So in September of '91, I showed up at the Chance in Poughkeepsie, New York, with a whole bunch of my college friends. And I peel off from them . . . there was no security at that time, so I just walked into their dressing room with the didgeridoo and just started playing it. And they all just froze in their tracks and Trey goes, "Holy shit, man, you gotta play that with us! Do you know 'Colonel Forbin's'?" And I'm like, "Yeah, I know all your songs." He's like, "I'll say, 'Colonel Forbin climbs up the mountain and then he looks back down into the valley and he sees all the villagers playing their didgeridoos.' And then you come out."

They're like, "We need a costume."

"I don't have any costume. I'm wearing a T-shirt and shorts."

And then Fishman's like, "You can wear the Zero Man dress and I'll wear the Captain Zero outfit instead." So I took my clothes off in the dressing room, put on the Fishman Zero Man dress, put my hair in a ponytail in the front of my head, and then came out and played didgeridoo and my friends literally pointed and were like, "Holy shit."

Liz Penta: We were playing Burlington. And the band came to the show. They took us swimming . . . there was a rope swing. Then we met the whole organization: John Paluska, Jason Colton, Brad Sands. Everybody was on board. We would stay at John Paluska's house . . . we became a part of their family.

Jimmy Herring: I remember a time when Trey knew I didn't have a place to sleep. I'm like, "I was gonna sleep in the van."

"No, man, I'm not letting you do that."

He and Page had a hotel room.

"No, I don't want to put anybody out, I'm not going to impose. I'm fine out here, man."

They got me a rollaway in their room.

49

We Need a Pie Baked by Someone's Grandma

As the late '90s came into view, jam bands and the scene around them were a pure American phenomenon, alongside grunge, hip-hop, electronica, and metal. Though record sales and radio play certainly were waning, live shows were certainly not.

Derek Trucks: There's a little bit of going against the grain and trying to swim upstream. Obviously you want people to connect with your music, but you're not concerned about any mainstream part of this.

Warren Haynes: Panic was starting to get bigger and bigger. They were at the UNO Arena and I went by to say hi to the guys. I walked up on the bus and Mikey was the only one up—we hung out for a little bit.

He said, "Hey, Warren, I got to do an interview for *Guitar* magazine. It's the first time I've ever done anything like that. I never know what to say. You've done a bunch of those, right?"

And I was like, "Yeah, well, I just finished one."

"They ask all these weird questions, and I just don't know what to say. The last guy said, 'How would you describe your music?' It's music people who smoke pot would like."

Chan Kinchla: Bill Graham had this great house in San Francisco called Masada . . . beautiful place. We were up there, still just young. David Graham had a big party, a big blowout. And at the end of the night, I was sitting up there with some girl and most people had gone. I hear this rustling behind me and I turn around and it's Bill Graham by himself, cleaning up. He's got a big plastic bag, cleaning up all the cups.

Derek Trucks: When I was fifteen or sixteen years old, I played in Col. Bruce's solo band on a few H.O.R.D.E. tours. The first time I met Phish, was sitting in with them . . . and I really met them on stage.

Bruce Flohr: Dave Matthews Band and Big Head Todd did a tour together. Dave Matthews was supporting Big Head Todd. And halfway through the tour, Big Head Todd came to Dave Matthews and said, "This isn't working, we got to flip . . . too many people are leaving after your set." So Big Head Todd flipped and became the support band. Which is unheard of.

Peter Jackson (Drum Technician, Production Manager, Widespread Panic): When I came on board [in '96], we were split into a band bus and a crew bus, and one semi. Midway through my first tour, we were having to do the proverbial "shove the elephant into the back of the truck every night, and his tail was still sticking out" kind of thing. There was just too much equipment, too much merchandise. I think over the course of that tour, we had to expand to what we would have called a bobtail truck . . . a big moving van, kind of thing. In '98, we went to a third crew bus, and eventually a second full semi and it was just quick to expand at that point.

Derek Trucks: Once my solo band was on the road three hundred days a year. You're just constantly gigging, constantly playing, and there were still places to do it. There was an audience where you could go improvise, and people would show up enough to get you to the next gig.

Scott "bullethead" Reilly: One night, Doc McGhee was in Denver, and he's telling Mötley Crüe "tearing up the motel" stories—how they destroyed hotels and how he had to pay these giant bills, the whole thing. Bevo and Tomo are sharing the room. So they take everything apart in the room. They take down the towel rack, they take the shower head off, anything they can take apart, they take apart . . . instead of breaking it. Then they wake up in the morning, they feel guilty, and put it all back together. So God Street Wine to me.

Derek Trucks: I was playing in Gregg Allman's solo band in my mid-teens and I remember he took me on this ride in his car and laid out pretty bluntly about the things that you should and should not do . . . certain bumps in the road that you don't need to take. You take those things seriously.

Cody Dickinson: I was working five days a week when we were just getting started. The goal was just to stay busy. We booked weekly gigs, locally, and left the weekends open to tour. So we would do a Wednesday and Thursday and a Sunday in Memphis, but then fill in Friday and Saturday, say a couple of college towns within two hundred miles. Next thing we knew, we were playing five days a week. When we finally started to get some traction and started getting gigs, we got an agent in Chicago. We were doing residencies, but in different cities. So instead of doing a residency on Beale Street in Memphis, we were doing Tuesday night in Birmingham, Wednesday night in Atlanta, Thursday night in Tuscaloosa.

Chris Stillwell: I always kept my money in a drawer . . . for years. We did a gig in San Diego at this place called the Catamaran, which is a ritzy resort place near the beach. The place held maybe eight hundred to a thousand . . . we were pretty big in San Diego at that point. I came home with like three grand. I put in the drawer. I don't know why I didn't put it in the bank.

Vinnie Amico (Drums, moe.): My first show was at the Bayou in DC [in 1996]. We jumped into the RV to go there . . . and it was taking a long time. And our poor manager had fallen asleep in the front seat. And I look out the window and I'm like, "Where are you going?" And they're like, "I don't know, Mike's asleep." I'm like, "Get off here, we already passed our exit by like twenty miles." And I had to navigate to our first gig. We were so late . . . and we had an opener, which was Yolk, who were friends of ours. Jim Loughlin was playing drums in Yolk at the time, so I actually had to play on Jim's kit, because we didn't have time to set mine up.

Cody Dickinson: We were playing Smith's Olde Bar and Phil Walden Jr. was watching us on a Wednesday night in Atlanta. He was like, "I want you to come into the office, I want you to meet my dad. And we're interested in you guys." That was such a morale boost.

Jamie Janover: I remember sitting at the kitchen table with Kang and Travis and they opened the *Boulder Weekly*. And Kang goes, "Oh shit." And we're like, "What's up? What's the matter?" And he's like, "Leftover Salmon got two nights at the Fox. Dammit, they're getting big. We gotta get two nights at the Fox."

Derek Trucks: One of the people that I spent the most time with was Jimmy [Herring]. And that was on the road. When I joined Frogwings, I was fifteen or sixteen, and I was rooming with Jimmy. I'd play an alternate tuning, and he was really interested in that. So we draw out the neck and we dig into all the chord possibilities and all these things that I hadn't really considered. He was a great teacher that way.

Kristin Wallace: I started to really change how I looked at booking. There was money, but there was also artist advocacy. Booking MMW was trying to really step up and say, "Hey, this is really important to these guys." The measurements of instruments were often larger than the doorways to some of these loading doors. So you would have to say, "I'm not kidding, you need to go measure the door to see if they can get in . . . if not, they're playing in the parking lot." So, advocating for an artist outside of just their smaller needs. They didn't want an opening band, because they wanted to go in and have the piano tuned, and they wanted to really take their time and soundcheck. If they had an opening band, it was like something of their choosing and would have the same setup every night and know what to expect. On their rider, it said, "We need a pie baked by someone's grandma." And they often got it!

50

Hanging Around Long Enough That I Became Useful, I Guess

The scene also presented opportunities for some to get into the music business by complete accident: The love of the music drove them, and they found work at the same time.

Chris Rabold (Live Sound Mixer, Production Manager, Widespread Panic): The South was ripe with regional music, from the R.E.M. stuff, to the Drivin N Cryin stuff, to the Widespread Panic stuff. I went to go see them live and I was like, "Oh my god, what is this?" It was at the Electric Ballroom in Knoxville, Tennessee, which was a perfect rock club . . . a big black box of a room. I knew the records, I knew the songs, and I didn't know you could extend a song.

In 1995, I'd done one semester of school at the University of Georgia. And I'm like, "Man, what am I doing? I really do need to figure out what I'm doing." I'd saved up enough money from working at Rocky's Pizzeria, which is in downtown Athens, to drive around and go see my favorite band. They had a tour coming up in the spring of '95. One night in South Bend, Indiana, I had a casual acquaintance who was friends with their merchandise guy at the time. Richard was the merch guy and I went up to the merch stand and said, "Hey."

He goes, "I gotta go take a piss, will you watch the merch?"

"Yeah, sure." So he hands me a fanny pack of cash.

Then he's like, "Will you help me load this stuff out?"

"Well, sure." So I go out there, put everything on the truck with them, and then we hung out a little bit. Through the remainder of that tour, I was driving myself around, but then helping Richard out. At that point in time, they were two buses and one truck. I quickly met everyone, and everything felt so natural. I was "Young Chris"—definitely the Dennis the Menace of the bunch.

And then I left. I got a call back two weeks later and they were like, "Hey, are you coming back?"

"I don't have any money."

"Look, get out here. We'll work it out."

Then they had a summer tour coming up.

"Why don't you jump on the bus with us?" There was still no mention of salary or pay.

"We'll take care of you . . . we'll get you hotel rooms, we'll feed you, whatever."

So I jump on the bus with them.

Luc Suèr (Monitors Engineer, Medeski Martin & Wood): The first time I got to see Medeski Martin & Wood was on a festival stage. I was touring with Beck as a monitor engineer. They were on the same stage that we were going to be on . . . and I was fascinated from the moment they started. They liked to just set up as close to one another as possible and that fascinated me. A few years later, some small festival on a river that runs through Richmond, Virginia . . . I was with the band Cibo Matto. That day, Phil Harvey was sort of scrambling to get his stuff together on stage and started asking around, "Is there anybody that can help me out and set up the monitors on stage for these guys?" It seemed like the festival might have been somewhat understaffed or not quite up to the task in one way or another. So he was looking for help. And I jumped in. Shortly after that set, Phil came to me and said, "I gotta get your number. As soon as we can afford it, you're on top of the list of people to hire to come out on the road with us if you like." And I'm like "Hell yeah, take my number."

Peter Jackson: There was a band out of Athens called Allgood. I pestered those guys into giving me a job . . . offered to help load equipment as a fan, would stick around after the show and help get the gear out the door. Volunteer roadie-ism. On the H.O.R.D.E. tour that Allgood was a part of with Blues Traveler and Aquarium Rescue Unit, I got to be friendly with Garrie Vereen. He took me under his wing and took note of my services. The phone rang one day, probably early 1996. And Garrie said, "Hey, we're seeking a drum tech." After the Sit-n-Ski tour, I was brought on tour immediately after that. I toured with them strictly as a drum tech until probably late 1997 and then there was a sort of reshuffling of the crew. They promoted me to production manager.

Michael Weiss: I became really friendly with God Street Wine and started seeing them quite a bit. In early 1992 or late '91, they played a show down in Dover, Delaware, in the area that I was going to school, and asked me if I had any interest in them full time. I went from being the everyman and doing everything to really focusing on being a tour manager for a while, then I kind of moved over to production, production management, and was their lighting director for a couple of years. I officially worked for them from '92 through some point in mid to late 1995. And then went to work at Irving Plaza for a couple of years as a lighting director there. But in my three or so years, I got fired twice. I was not the easiest person to deal with on the road.

Matt Busch: Being a Deadhead in the analog years was a lot different than now because you didn't have an internet to go listen to every show the day after it happened or even to know a setlist the day after it happened. I had subscribed to *Relix* magazine and with that, you got to take out a free classified ad. So I took out some ad that was like, "Help this young kid find tapes" type of thing. A few people bit. At that time, I was expanding beyond Grateful Dead . . . Blues Traveler started to make a buzz at the Wetlands. I had seen a Blues Traveler show at the Wetlands and in the back-and-forth with someone, they had a tape of that, and so I had them throw that in with whatever trade we were doing. At the very end of the tape, they stuck in three songs . . . and this woman wrote with calligraphy, so it was hard to read her handwriting in this weird way. I eventually figured out that these were not Blues Traveler songs, this was a different band called God Street Wine. The energy just leapt off the tape deck. It actually turned out to be this woman who had produced *Bag* for them . . . I think she paid for it out of her own pocket; she was friends with the band. And so I started getting more music from her and then eventually started seeing them . . . I think the first time I saw them was in Albany, at Bogie's in '91. I just started following them as much as I could, in and around everything else I was going to see. And a good friend of mine became their sound engineer and I started hustling him for a merchandise job, because I figured that's what I'm qualified to do. I sell records and T-shirts at a music store . . . I can do that on the road. I wasn't getting in too far with it. The fall of '97, they were finishing up seven weeks in Port Chester, New York. What basically happened is the guy they had hired to do merchandise had become lighting designer over the course of the tour. And as they got to venues, they would just find and hire someone locally. And I guess that night, whoever the venue thought they found for them, never showed. And I guess Rick had gone to the band: "You know, we have no one, how about Matt? He has always wanted to do it. He can count money and sell records. Just throw him back there. We got no one else." Six months later, I was interviewing with Warren Haynes to do his merchandise.

Dirk Stalnecker: Panic came through Boulder where I was living and they did a gig for the promoter that I worked for at Red Rocks. And so I was their runner. The crew was like, "Hey, we got to go to an ATM." And then they started saying, "Hey, we got this tour manager and he's a total dick. Would you be into it? We're going to mutiny his ass." That guy got fired, and I got a call from Sam Lanier. He said he wanted me to fly down to Athens to meet with him. And they hired me for the job and in March of '95, I was minted their tour manager. I was twenty-four years old at the time and was pretty fucking scared.

Philip Harvey: I was living in Austin, Texas, and touring with this band Soulhat. We were on the last tour, and the singer decided to leave the band. Someone on the tour had MMW's *Shack-man* and *It's a Jungle in Here*. I was living with the guitarist at the time and he was like, "Hey, you should get a job with these guys since our band's breaking up." In May '95, the trio came and played the White Rabbit in Austin . . . small little shitty club. And I was completely blown away. The wheels started going off in my head: They didn't have a sound engineer.

The next time they came through was during South by Southwest at the Radisson ballroom. It was basically a conference room. It sounded horrible . . . the sound engineer couldn't care less, he had his feet propped up on the console. Chris Wood's bass was all distorted and it was terrible. After their set, I easily got to the side stage and I saw Billy Martin, and was like, "Hey man, you guys need a sound engineer!" He was like "What? We're all independent, we do it ourselves; we don't need a sound engineer."

Liz Penta walked up and said, "Yeah, you guys need a sound engineer." Billy just looks at me and was like, "So how do I know you know your shit?" I quickly rattled off a couple of things like picking up drums as a complete kit with the overheads and letting the band control the dynamic, leaving things pretty open. He said, "Okay, you're saying all the right things . . . maybe we'll catch each other down the road." Like a month later, they came back to Austin and played this warehouse called Liberty Lunch. A couple of guys I knew were in the support band, so I was like, "Hey, man, let me run your sound so I can try to get in good with Medeski Martin & Wood." I got my courage up, called Liz on the phone, and I said I'd love to have a chance to mix the band.

"Okay, who have you worked with?"

I rattled off a bunch of names from Austin and regional bands.

"Yep, never heard of them. How much do you want?"

"Well, my buddies are opening for MMW so I'll be there anyway. So fifty bucks from them, fifty bucks from you guys. I'm happy with a hundred for the night."

"Alright, cool. Let's give it a shot."

Andre Gardner: Reid, Luke, Jon, and I all went to UVM. I eventually lived with Reid and Luke my senior year . . . they had graduated from UVM and I was finishing my senior year. And when I graduated, they said, "Well, any chance you'd want to do this full time?" It was a gradual process of hanging around long enough that I became useful, I guess.

51

Why Don't We Do It As Far Away As Humanly Possible

Rob Mitchum (Journalist): In 1996, Phish was big at that point. They had won the post–Grateful Dead war of who was going to be the top jam band. The New Year's Eve '95 show [at Madison Square Garden] proved Phish could sell out the most famous arena on the biggest night of music. But it still felt like people couldn't really picture how many fans there were out there.

Pete Shapiro: It was new and fresh . . . like Grateful Dead on fucking steroids; faster, lighter. The trampolines—no one had seen that.

Nancy Jeffries (Senior Vice President, A&R, Elektra Records): But we're still in the time period when radio ran the game. And if you couldn't get on the radio, you couldn't make it. So we had Phish. Not great for big commercial radio, and alternative music. People rejected them. For some reason, the alternative world did not like Phish.

Brian Cohen (Vice President of Marketing, Elektra Records): From the beginning, there was a tension between the success that was Phish and how a major label understands what success should look like.

Pete Shapiro: It was unusual for the jam scene to cross in a cultural thing. "Cool" is not really our scene. Oasis is cool. The Pearl Jam scene, the Rage Against the Machine scene, the Roots scene. They're cool.

Shelly Culbertson: They didn't want to interfere with the things that the band were already doing organically to promote themselves.

Nancy Jeffries: Paul Fox did one of the records [1994's *Hoist*]. And I asked Paul about it, and I sent him the stuff. He listened and said, "Oh, I don't want to do that." I said, "Well, come see them play with me." So we went to a gig. And he got halfway across the parking lot and he said, "I'll do it." He's like, "Look at this. There must be something we could do here."

Tom Marshall: There was a musical peak right around the time; they were getting huge, they were at Bearsville [Studio] with this amazing producer and everyone was smiling the whole time.

John Siket (Engineer, *Crash, Billy Breathes, Tin Cans & Car Tires, The Story of the Ghost, Farmhouse*): They really wanted to produce *Billy Breathes* themselves. Sometimes they wanted input from me, and that went on for twelve weeks. And we got some good stuff done. But I think after twelve weeks, those guys realized that they didn't want to produce it themselves. They asked me, "What's it like to work for Steve Lillywhite?" And I was like, "Oh, he's great."

Trey Anastasio: I had a bunch of songs. "Free," "Prince Caspian," "Taste." I got married in '94 and then my daughter was born, and "Billy Breathes" is about the first time I ever walked outside with her. That was her nickname. All the lyrics in that song are real, meaning a pickup truck drove by—"a pickup screams." I was just writing down what it was, because it was so scary and amazing. Nobody in our scene had a kid yet. No one in our management company, or any of our band members had a kid. It was a bit of an adjustment at the time, because everybody was starting to move pretty fast, and I didn't really want to.

Page McConnell: We went around in a circle, playing one note at a time for about two weeks.

Trey Anastasio: We were doing this democratic voting thing. We like each other too much, so we're too nice to each other. So sometimes we can lose our bearings by voting to make everybody happy. We had a whiteboard, and we would vote songs off for one reason or another and "Character Zero" got voted off. It was too loud and raunchy or something, I don't know. Wasn't my idea. So Steve came in a month into this process, and he went into the control room, and was looking at the whiteboard. He said, "Play me some of these songs, and play me some of the ones that you guys weren't thinking about putting on the record." We played "Character Zero" and he came out with that British accent, and he goes, "Okay, not only is that song going on, it's going to be second. And not only is it not too rocking. It isn't rocking enough and you're going to get your asses out there right now and play it much more rocking than the polite version you just played. *[Snaps]* Snap to it boys." This is after we had all these stupid, long-winded conversations. We played it in one take, and now it's on the record.

He came to see us at the Garden, two years later. We closed the first set with a really crushing version of it, and he came backstage laughing—came into the band room and was like, "Told you."

Steve Lillywhite: I thought we had a chance with "Free."

John Siket: Steve thought that he could turn them into a multimillion-selling band. He's like, "Wow, they have tons of rabid fans, just like Dave Matthews Band. Why can't they have a hit?" I don't really think Phish had the same expectation. Their manager might have been pushing them. The label might have been pushing them. But I didn't really feel it from the band members.

Steve Lillywhite: I'm not a songwriter, so, I hate it when someone says, "Steve, I'll do whatever you want." I'm stuck there because I don't know what I want, but what I love is when an artist has so many ideas, they don't know what *they* want. And then it's a case of me going, "Okay, give me your ideas. Okay, that one's great. Let's take a bit of that, then we take a bit of that, and we do this." With Phish, they were an artist who had so many ideas and didn't know what they wanted. I helped just mold it.

John Siket: With *Billy Breathes*, we cut everything in [Bearsville Studios'] Barn. I spent a long time setting up for the first twelve weeks, so everybody was in the same room and they could all see each other. And that was a really great thing. And so, you know, everything's not so isolated on that track. When Steve came, we didn't hardly change a thing. He was blown away. I had to make it so people could move around and play each other's instruments if they wanted to. "Free" we had done before Steve came . . . and we thought we had done a really good job with it. And Steve just said, "I think we can do better." So we recut that . . . and it actually did come out a lot better.

Trey Anastasio: We had this bar—we used to go to the Pinecrest, which was basically like walking into a scene out of *Twin Peaks*. And they had a jukebox. We would work until eleven o'clock, and then we would go down to the Pinecrest before they close, and we'd put money in the jukebox and crank up T. Rex's "Telegram Sam."

Steve Lillywhite: The cover of *Billy Breathes* . . . I don't think it inspires. Mike Gordon, I love his nose, but I don't think it should be the reason for an album sleeve.

John Siket: I saw ads in *Rolling Stone* where you'd never see a Phish ad before. And I heard them on the radio a lot—I heard "Free" a lot. So, the label was behind them.

Nancy Jeffries: They did their level best to try to come up with something a few times, but that wasn't what they were doing. Authenticity was their brand. And they went along with it gamely . . . I mean I have to say, I never had a problem with them saying "Go fuck yourself."

Trey Anastasio: There was a lot of real emotion that went into that album.

Billy Breathes *came out on October 15, 1996. Two months before that, Phish threw their first-ever festival, the Clifford Ball, in Plattsburgh, New York. An estimated eighty thousand people showed up.*

Brad Sands (Tour Manager, Phish): We went to Europe in 1992—the Roskilde Festival. I feel like that was the moment where the band was like, "We gotta do this on our own in America." We saw these people camping, and they were all there for the weekend. We didn't have that in America at the time. We didn't have any festivals . . . we didn't have Bonnaroo, Lollapalooza was a touring festival. It just took a while to get to the point of "Where can we do this?" Where can we find a place that allows you to play at any hour in the day and is separated, but there's an interstate near for traffic, and you got to take all these things into consideration. The Plattsburgh decommissioned air force base was brilliant because it had four miles of giant wide roadway, where you could bring cars in and then park, and the ground was hard.

Trey Anastasio: Your mom didn't know where you were.

Andy Bernstein: We forget—as big and successful as Phish's been over the years, they were never bigger than the Clifford Ball in 1996.

Andy Gadiel: A band putting on their own festival, in a remote part of the US, had never been done before like that.

Trey Anastasio: There weren't festivals. We were all like, "Oh, my God, what is this? What is going on here?" There was Lollapalooza, but at the same time, Lollapalooza went to existing venues. That was a tour.

Nancy Jeffries: It didn't shock me at all.

Trey Anastasio: We were building cities and people were meeting and nobody knew it was happening.

Brad Sands: The thing about Phish that was great was they always took care of the little things that made them great, right? We were like, "Let's have a radio station for traffic updates," and Trey was like, "Traffic updates? Let's just play music." We're like, "Oh, yeah, duh." Thinking what sucked when I went to a concert . . . twenty porta-potties for a thousand people; so let's just have thousands of them.

Tom Marshall: I do remember, and it could be the Great Went, this incredible moment where we were hanging off the back of a golf cart. One was driven by Trey, and I forget who the other one was, and Danny Clinch was in the passenger's seat of Trey's golf cart, and he was just clicking, clicking, and clicking. I've never seen those photographs, and I have realized *that* to me is kind of the epitome of the whole thing right there. We were cruising on a runway, and then cruising through tents, and people were realizing that was Trey who was going by at twenty mph, or however fast a golf cart can go. They were running after him, and a little bike parade was happening—it was just so fun.

Dean Budnick: Although it was seventy thousand people, it flew under the radar.

Andy Gadiel: I think it was the first time everybody was in the same place feeling the overview effects, so to speak, of the Phish experience . . . many point to the Clifford Ball as being "Wow, this is really this big."

Danny Clinch: You go to those festivals, and there's kind of a lot of sitting around . . . the band might be in their room for a little bit, and then they're eating and they're hanging out with their families. They're just kind of kicking it. I was always the guy that was just looking for an opportunity, looking for a moment to pull the band aside and get a portrait. Clifford Ball was on an airstrip and I went out and wandered around and looked for a spot . . . and I thought, "Wow, this is kind of amazing . . . it's emptiness forever."

Andy Gadiel: All the people that worked on it have gone on to work in the festival scene. You can draw a direct line from the Clifford Ball to Bonnaroo and the modern day music festival . . . the people that came up on that, were cultivated in that world and learned how to do those things.

Trey Anastasio: After Clifford Ball, there was some management conversations where it was like, why don't you do it at Randalls Island [in New York City]? And we were like, "Why don't we do it as far away as humanly possible in the continental United States?"

52

Play That Ill Shit!

Billy Martin: Our introduction to Blue Note was through Craig Street. Craig Street is a producer who's worked with Cassandra Wilson and Chris Whitley—singer-songwriters that were more creative and had their own niche. Craig told Bruce Lundvall, who was the president of Blue Note Records, "You got to see this . . . this band is really special." He brought Bruce down to CBGBs Gallery and also down to Margaritaville in New Orleans. Our first gig in New Orleans was at Jimmy Buffett's club, in the French Quarter. We knew that Blue Note was interested.

Chris Wood: John was passing this enormous kidney stone and was just writhing in agony during the show, and Bruce was in the audience. The whole thing was just so surreal, but it led to our record deal.

John Medeski: I was in so much pain. I met Bruce and I went back to the camper and those guys hung out with Bruce and that's when he offered us a deal. And then we waited. There was a bidding war.

Billy Martin: And Bruce was basically like, "Hey, let's do it!" He's a yes man. Now, Liz Penta at this point had a lot of connections with a lot of big labels. Liz basically started playing the bidding war game.

Liz Penta: There was a ton of interest. Ruffhouse Records was interested and they had just had the Fugees break at that time.

Billy Martin: V2 was a new label with Virgin.

Liz Penta: I was nervous as they weren't just a running, well-oiled machine. They actually had Richard Branson call me directly. I was in my apartment and in his English accent, he said, "It's Richard Branson. What can I do, what can I say?" Of course, he knew nothing about the band.

Billy Martin: We went to Capitol Records when we were in LA. I didn't like a lot of these executives, because they always were just so egotistical and had their own ideas. "You need a singer. You need a front person."

Chris Wood: Donnie Ienner comes into the room. And the first thing he says is, "So I hear you guys want to sell some records," which none of us had ever said. We were just there to meet some people. Next thing out of his mouth was, "So get a vocalist." And then he walked out of the room.

Billy Martin: In the end, we liked Blue Note—we liked the history, the legacy. And we liked Bruce, and they're giving us what we want, which is we can do a major record every year and we can also do a B-record, which is not commercial. It was a really good deal.

Liz Penta: It was long, like six records or something. The formula for the increase of each record was significant. Yeah, it was a good deal and enabled them to build a studio.

John Medeski: It was so worth it . . . to make the records, we were able to spend a lot more time making records, spend more money. Basically, if it wasn't working for them, they could drop us . . . So for us, it was a win-win situation.

Chris Wood: We barely caught the tail end of the old paradigm. For the kind of music we were playing, we got a deal that nobody gets today . . . not playing weird instrumental music.

Billy Martin: I don't know exactly what the money was. But it got up to about $300,000 advances on the later records. Now we're an organization: managers, booking agents, bookkeepers . . . everybody's getting a percentage that we're sharing all of a sudden.

Liz Penta: John Scofield's record *A Go Go* . . . we made that record right as we were signing to Blue Note. And he had just left Blue Note and went to Verve. So it was a little tricky.

On 1998's Combustication, *their first album for Blue Note, Medeski Martin & Wood did something revolutionary: They threw a DJ into the mix.*

DJ Logic: I was doing shows downtown and in the Village. And I was playing with a wonderful musician and great friend, Vernon Reid, in one of his projects called My Science Project at CBGBs Gallery, right next door to CBGBs. MMW happened to be playing alongside us. I met them and I thought they were a great group of guys . . . and the music was awesome.

Chris Wood: Vernon Reid had a band and we saw them play a show. And it was like, "Wow, this is a DJ and he's improvising with these guys!" We were really attracted to that in the same way that Billy would play hip-hop and Brazilian music and all these other styles, but he can improvise like a jazz drummer. DJ Logic was similar. He could interact.

Alan Evans: Logic was the bridge.

DJ Logic: I got a call from their manager, Liz Penta. They were doing a release for the *Shack-man* record at the Knitting Factory. They asked a few DJs to come down and spin before the show and I was one of the DJs. At the time, I didn't know the following was that big . . . so I came down and brought a few records that I thought would be fitting for the environment—a little bit of hip-hop, a little bit of acid jazz, a little bit of funk. Just something eclectic. And they asked me to sit in with them, from seeing me play with Vernon Reid. They thought I had very good ears and knew how to improv.

Chris Wood: He had the rhythm and the openness to pull it off.

Scotty Hard (Producer, *Combustication*): I'll be completely transparent with you: I knew virtually nothing about the jam scene. The first time I saw them, [Lounge Lizards bassist] Erik Sanko took me to see them at the original Knitting Factory on Houston Street, between Elizabeth and Mulberry. I remember going there the first time and I'm like, "Oh my god, there's actually sweaters on the ceiling . . . old knit sweaters." The bottom part of the club became a bar called Botanica, which I think is still there. You went upstairs through the staircase full of knit sweaters and I saw them play for the first time . . . I was pretty blown away because you don't hear something like that very often. Not long after that, I did a record with my friend Michael Blake for his first record called *Kingdom of Champa.* Billy played percussion on that. I had John play on the second New Kingdom record—he played organ and Clavinet on a couple of songs on *Paradise Don't Come Cheap.* New Kingdom was a band that I was heavily involved with. That was right after *Shack-man* came out . . . I remember listening to the CD in the van, when I was on tour with New Kingdom. Shortly after that, they asked me to work on *Combustication.*

I was like, "Oh, did you hear the Sex Mob record . . . was it because of that?"

"Oh, no, we didn't know you did that. It's because you make hip-hop records."

John Medeski: It was kind of a big turning point for us to be able to start using the studio as part of the creative process. We brought in DJ Logic, which was a first for us.

Scotty Hard: They brought in an enormous amount of equipment.

Billy Martin: It was so easy . . . everything was paid for . . . food, dinner.

Luc Suèr: That also took a little bit of figuring out. On the one hand, what was really good about the music, was that it was already really layered in a way where they always experimented with having new, interesting textures that were somewhat unusual. Combined with DJ Logic with his turntable, because of the kind of musician that Logic is, he would quickly figure out how to add his layers and textures to it. So sonically, it worked really well.

Chris Wood: We recorded *Combustication* in a whole week at the Magic Shop in New York City, with Scotty Harding as the engineer. And then we did a whole other week with David Baker as the engineer, so two separate week-long sessions. It was just an incredible luxury, after all the sessions we'd done in the past, to have that much time to experiment with two different, very unique engineers. When we are working with them, they're like a fourth member. But they're very different people. So when we work with David, he brings out different things in us, Scotty brings out the things. Scotty was definitely versed in jazz, but also hip-hop . . . he'd worked with the Wu-Tang Clan, but also mentored by Teo Macero, the guy who did all the amazing Miles Davis stuff. He had the hip-hop vocabulary and the jazz or the improvisational mentality. We'd even record the same song with each of them at different sessions just to see what would happen. And sometimes we'd have one of the guys mix a song that the other guy engineered.

Scotty Hard: I had met Logic when I was mixing and recording Vernon Reid's record *Mistaken Identity*. Logic came into the fold through Melvin Gibbs. He had started playing around the scene with some people after he was with Vernon.

Philip Harvey: When there's different players sitting in, there's a different aptitude or different face that's shown with a trio. I didn't feel that with Logic. He pretty much belonged there—it was just like the icing on the cake with their vibe and musical signature.

John Medeski: We were actually interacting with Logic . . . not just the turntable in there for a sound or color.

Chris Wood: Seeing DJ Logic work with Scotty Hard was just hilarious. Every style of music has its own vocabulary, and I'll just never forget DJ Logic came in and he was going to overdub over some of the stuff we recorded already and Scotty Hard just kept yelling into the talkback, "Logic, play that ill shit!" And then Logic would know exactly what Scotty was talking about.

53

Something Big As Stravinsky but Euphoric As Little Fluffy Clouds

Pete Shapiro: Whenever you are part of something new—and it's hard to happen, it's hard to create "new"—you feel fucking great. That whole sound of Disco Biscuits, the New Deal, Sound Tribe Sector 9 . . . there was light, live instrument–based stuff that takes you in another zone mentally.

Benjy Eisen: The musicians who were concurrently creating this new movement and subgenre were all heavily influenced by Phish who, at the time, were destroying America.

Jon "The Barber" Gutwillig: We thought we were the best of all the jam bands out there. We were like, "Of course you're gonna listen to us . . . why would you listen to anything else, frankly?" That's how we felt. Those are the kind of blinders that you need to make art. Picasso thought he was the best. Is he better than Monet? A lot of people would say no. Art is very subjective, but to the person making the art, you have to really, really believe that you're at least capable of doing the best in the game.

Marc Brownstein: In New York there were a ton of club nights—house music was hot, drum and bass was super hot.

Sam Altman: There was a period of time we'd spend in people's basements to practice. We were practicing in Jon's fraternity basement and a lot of kids in his fraternity were from the UK, or from Hong Kong—they were into electronic music and we started hearing it and hanging out with those guys. They would go to raves in New York on the weekend sometimes.

Jon "The Barber" Gutwillig: We were doing esoteric jazz. I just don't think we were educated enough to do that kind of music. Maybe Marc, maybe Aron, but me and Sammy didn't really care that much about the difference between this chord and that chord. And if you're in Philadelphia, Christian McBride was around doing his thing, I think Branford Marsalis was even around in those days, Joey DeFrancesco was around . . . the scene didn't need a bunch of guys who didn't quite know what they were doing.

Sam Altman: Planet Dog Records, in the '90s, had this sampler and it was minimalist techno. I used to listen to it all the time. And when Jon's fraternity brothers started listening to more trance music, it was a little more flowery. Those two styles kind of mixed. And that was the nucleus of the electronic music that became what the Biscuits started to improvise over.

Benjy Eisen: They were listening to DJs and to electronic music, and they were doing the raves almost as homework, but also because they were genuinely interested in it. Sammy Altman would spend hours on his laptop with this early electronic music program that was generative, where he could just push a few buttons and have a change.

Marc Brownstein: There was this guy named Jizz who was a friend of ours in Jon's fraternity. And he was DJing at our college parties and playing a lot of psychedelic trance—Hallucinogen, GMS. He was from London so he was tapped into the psychedelic trance scene. And we would create these parties at Barber's fraternity where the Biscuits would play from eight till twelve and then we would stop and Jizz would go on immediately and he would DJ from twelve till six.

Sam Altman: An often-touted moment is when Aron got a digital synth—a specific kind of digital synth that could make sounds that we were hearing in some of that electronic music. I don't know when we started doing it, but I started playing four kick beats on the floor, like we were hearing in trance music, and Aron started using that keyboard like some of the DJs and producers we heard. And there's delayed drums playing delay pedals. And that's kind of how it started. It was just another way to improvise. It wasn't over a rock beat or rock groove.

Marc Brownstein: When we started out, we were playing Grateful Dead, Allman Brothers, Phish, Santana songs . . . all of the classic rock and jam bands that existed.

Jon "The Barber" Gutwillig: We were seeing Phish all the time. I didn't see Phish as much as the other guys did. But they saw them a lot. They were using harmonic tension and release, timed with the lights. People were going bonkers over that stuff.

Marc Brownstein: At one point we were playing "Antelope," and we are in an "Antelope" jam, and it's a Phish song and it was so Phishy sounding and I remember thinking to myself while we were playing it, "How are we going to ever not sound like this? How can we get out of this?" I was going to Phish shows, listening to Phish all the time.

Benjy Eisen: The Disco Biscuits were businessmen that wanted to be successful, and wanted their own identity and did not want to be an offshoot of Phish.

Jon "The Barber" Gutwillig: We were on more of a visceral level . . . can we make our hair stand on end using just music? Phish was doing that. DJs were doing that. Orbital were doing that.

Marc Brownstein: One time I was sitting in a friend's apartment, and there wasn't music on. And a Phish jam was playing in my head. But it wasn't a Phish jam that they had played. It was just like the *sound* of Phish. And I was creating a jam in my head as we were sitting there. And I said to the kid, "Man, I've got the sounds of Phish in my head at all times." And so that would translate to the instrument. So I'd start playing and it would just start sounding like that. And so there was a moment where we were like, "We got to stop listening to this. We have to stop listening to jam bands, or it's never going to change what we sound like." And we started listening to Hallucinogen and other electronic music acts. Little by little, that started becoming the soundtrack to our day.

Benjy Eisen: They would have endless conversations about how they were never going to be a successful longterm band, if it was just, "Well, Phish isn't playing tonight, so let's just go see the Disco Biscuits."

Jon "The Barber" Gutwillig: I was looking for something big as Stravinsky but euphoric as little fluffy clouds.

Marc Brownstein: Halloween of 1997, we showed up at the Phi Sig fraternity house. There was a band called the Mad Hatters at Penn that had been playing this party every year on Halloween. And it was a huge party and they graduated and we got the gig. I was like "Man, we got the biggest party of all time." And we showed up and nobody came. Fifty people came to this legendary, yearly Halloween party. But I remember so clearly . . . Magner had this new synthesizer called the JP-8000. And during the show, Magner was playing some synth sounds and it triggered Sammy to go to a four on the floor. And that was it. It was like, "Oh my god," we're in the middle. We played a "Run Like Hell" and "Morning Dew"—I remember an hour-and-a-half jam where Sammy was just playing four on the floor the whole time and Magner was emulating electronic music. It clicked. We had our sound, overnight.

Jon "The Barber" Gutwillig: There was Biggie Smalls, which was to me very much cerebral hip-hop at the time. Those rhymes are some of the most genius poetry ever written. But it wasn't like rap got to big beat stuff. Musically, there wasn't much going on. It was like the same loop the whole time. You take the Geto Boys stuff from back then and you're like, "This poem is a movie; the level of poetry is outstanding." But if you were going for musical experiences, that was a different type of thing. It wasn't really quite what we were looking for. Miles Davis had gotten there with *Bitches Brew,* twenty-five years earlier.

Marc Brownstein: Kraftwerk was playing electronic music in Europe . . . but nobody had ever done this in the United States. And certainly nobody had ever done it over improv. It was just such a pivotal moment in our career. The question had been answered: "How are we going to ever sound like ourselves?" And so we started to develop it.

Jon "The Barber" Gutwillig: I would try and play muted trumpet on guitar and figure out a way to get the band into some grinding, pulsating, undulating rhythms. That was basically what we did a lot of the time. I would loop what I was playing, to get the band to loop—we would all loop together to get into these big undulations. Then I would play a kind of blues solo, almost . . . like a three, four note arpeggio over the top of undulating music and try to recreate *Bitches Brew.*

Pete Shapiro: I remember Marc Brownstein being like, "Hey, we have a new sound we want you to hear." It was the first time hearing "jamtronica"—live electronica. That hadn't really been played before, melding the extended jams of the Grateful Dead and Phish with electronic beats.

Marc Brownstein: And what was funny, we didn't figure out how to make legit electronic-sounding music, we just kind of played over a four on the floor beat and just improvised. It was just kind of feeling it, mimicking it to the best of our ability and trying to compose songs that played into this new sound.

Jon "The Barber" Gutwillig: When you're done with your show, you talk to the people who saw the show and you like them to be happy. And when we were doing dance music, people were happy.

Benjy Eisen: On the surface, the Phish phenomenon looked like a burgeoning counterculture fueled by drug-enhanced danceathons . . . which, coincidentally, could also be said of rave culture at the exact same time. One was happening on distant shores; the other, in the Northeast. The two different scenes had a lot of parallels and they were both exploding on reasonably concurrent timelines. If they could somehow merge the two together, the music's appeal would form a Venn diagram with enormous potential for growth. Livetronica wasn't a happy accident; it was very intentionally forged. It took effort to figure out. And expensive equipment to create.

Marc Brownstein: It wasn't until we ran into Sound Tribe Sector 9 that we had found another band that, under the premise of the collective unconscious, happened upon the same concept.

Hunter Brown (Guitar, Sound Tribe Sector 9): We were in Atlanta. I grew up knowing about Widespread Panic because my cousins were going to the University of Georgia and were way into Panic, giving me live tapes of them when I was in high school. Phish, the same thing. But the actual music scene in Atlanta was incredibly eclectic. I grew up in high school following Medeski Martin & Wood anywhere I could afford to go. I was literally outside of shows because I was too young to get in. They would find out how far I'd come and let us dance or just listen right outside the front door, right by the bouncer inside the front door. I saw probably six or seven Medeski shows like that—being chaperoned by the bodyguard. I went to see Phish in Boston when I was fifteen . . . I got a ride with people I barely knew, my parents didn't know where I was going or where I was. I didn't have a ticket, and got miracled in.

Zach Velmer (Drums, Sound Tribe Sector 9): We were taking in as much as we possibly could.

Hunter Brown: Atlanta's really good at bringing a bunch of different people together to create something new. We used to hang out at a place called the Yin Yang Cafe. And there were people there like Tria de Luna, who were studio musicians at the time and playing some of the biggest scores at the time . . . they'd come back home to Atlanta, and play at the club. They played a lot of drum and bass, house music, soul, funk, and jazz influenced stuff. And they welcomed us with open arms. The club is right underneath the big Centennial torch. And that's where we hung out a lot and really cut our teeth on what was possible musically.

Zach Velmer: We were experimenting in front of people, real time. It was full-on experimentation, to further what we were hearing. You could not live in Atlanta and not be influenced by OutKast and Dungeon Family. In high school, the Aquarium Rescue Unit . . . they were gods. One night, Oteil Burbridge came and sat in with us. And then we got to meet his brother, Kofi Burbridge . . . that was our introduction, more or less, into the Atlanta scene.

Hunter Brown: We lived in Atlanta and Athens during the last half of the '90s. Warp Records was one of the biggest influences on us . . . if we could be on any label, that would be it, no questions asked.

David Phipps (Bass, Sound Tribe Sector 9): It was more inspiring to us to create our own label. And that's what we did with 1320 Records—not only release our music, but we tried to create that same community around a label.

Hunter Brown: We got a ton of early support from local promoters, clubs, and bands. Panic was so cool to us. I think they took us under their wing a little bit because they were the big dogs and we were the little puppies coming out of the same place.

Instrumental in our success and coming up was Gary Gazaway, a.k.a. El Búho, the trumpet player. He played with Bob Marley, the Beach Boys when they played in front of a million people in DC back in the '90s, Phish . . . he was the trumpet player when they covered *Remain In Light* in '96 in Atlanta. A promoter that we met in Florida, the first show that we ever did outside of Georgia—we played right on the beach at this little shack—he was bringing all kinds of people down there and one of those was Gary Gazaway. We met Gary and he took us all around the South and pushed us beyond our limits. Gary took us around as the El Búho Acid Jazz Experience for a year. We followed that up just going back to all the clubs we played and said, "Hey, we're STS9, we were El Búho's band, can we come back up and play?"

Zach Velmer: We knew the club owners, and we met the club owners, and then they knew this person, and then that person was connected to this person. It kind of started snowballing in the Southeast.

Hunter Brown: We pulled up to this frat house, and it's during Christmastime. It was the most decorated thing you'd ever seen in your life. And we were kind of making fun of the whole situation—did these kids' moms come and just set up? You went inside and it was like a museum of Christmas . . . everywhere you looked, there was just crazy shit.

Zach Velton: The yard had all the light-up Santa Clauses . . . and five of the same one.

Hunter Brown: Towards the end of the night, police come in and it turns out they had stolen all of those things from the town that they were in. They stopped the show so we radioed our front-of-house and I say, "Hey, put on Jane's Addiction's 'Been Caught Stealing.'"

54

It Feels like a Blur to Me

Jon Trafton: '97—that was when things were heating up for Strangefolk.

Reid Genauer: Labels started coming. We were skeptical.

Brett Fairbrother: Throughout the country, all the clubs were pretty full.

Russ "In the Bus" Weis: We had a number of notable offices here in Burlington: one small one above a recycle/reuse facility, another in a big apartment in what's called the Woolen Mill, and perhaps the most dramatic was in another mill, literally on the bank of a river, right near some raging rapids.

Luke Smith: Michael Luoma was a DJ at WIZN, which was a big radio station in Burlington. He started playing "Lines and Circles" and "Sometimes," which was broadcast to upstate New York and across northern Vermont. And that was a really big deal. You could turn on the radio and have a good chance of hearing Strangefolk.

Jon Trafton: We signed with Monterey Peninsula and Chip Hooper, who was Phish's agent at the time, [along with] Dave Matthews and Metallica.

Andre Gardner: He knew the strategy.

Jon Trafton: John Alagía came to see us about producing.

Reid Genauer: Our MO we took from Phish and the Grateful Dead mode of thinking, which is have them come looking for you. You don't need to pimp your soul.

Luke Smith: We weren't as organized as Phish.

Russ "In the Bus" Weis: It was a bit of a mishmash. And in a way, it reflected the personalities and the convergences and divergences of the two principals, Reid and Jon.

Brett Fairbrother: Our first tour was '97—we worked the New England and mid-Atlantic area for three years before we went anywhere.

John Moore: Many of these jam bands were selling more tickets than all the bands on their label.

Reid Genauer: We weren't overly anxious, because we had made two records and made money on them. We were distributing them ourselves. At first, we're just literally doing them on consignment. Bull Moose, which has three or four stores around New England, were like, "Who are these guys? Okay, well, we'll do it." And then they were calling a week later to get more because they were selling.

Sam Ankerson: I think we all felt that while the first love was playing live, the band's sound was also conducive to a crossover appeal.

Luke Smith: It feels like a blur to me, how many people took us to lunch and dinner . . . wanted to be friends and make a deal. Some of it was comical. All they wanted was money. Some were better at disguising it, or they were more authentic.

Andre Gardner: I remember it was the Cat's Cradle. All of those [Mammoth Records] guys were there. They were based in Carrboro. The saving grace of

Mammoth, at the time, was John Moore, the A&R guy. He was another guy that was first and foremost about the music.

John Moore: I did a lot more concerts than I did schoolwork. I graduated college in '95. I decided I wanted to try and make a go of it in music, in the business, but not performing. I learned about the labels in Carolina and I got an internship at Mammoth, for free. I convinced my dad to sponsor me for a year, to go down, and I kind of called it "grad school." I mean, I wasn't lying. I told him what I was doing, but "instead of grad school, I need to go work for free to get into this crazy business." It took only six months of working for free and then I was offered a job to move to New York. My day job was to be the assistant to [President] Jay Faires. You can picture a big square office, with a bunch of important folks with offices that have windows, and then a pit of assistants, and open floor plan. I would answer his phone, I would Xerox, walk his dog, get lunch. Somebody gave me some advice: Read everything and learn. At night, Jay wanted me to be in the music scene—going and seeing new bands. I didn't have an A&R title, but it's definitely what he wanted me doing. I was at Brownies, Mercury Lounge, Wetlands, Don Hill's. I got to see Elliott Smith at Brownies. I got to see Creed at Brownies. I was going to Knitting Factory and seeing Grandaddy and Death Cab for Cutie—I needed to for work but also loved it. I was the guy that could talk Merge Records and indie bands—then they would make fun of me for wearing a Phish shirt, or talking Grateful Dead or Widespread.

Reid Genauer: Mammoth had sold a million albums out of a dinky little office in Durham, North Carolina.

John Moore: Mammoth partnered with Atlantic and it was a time when indie labels were popping up. The idea was these indie labels would become an A&R source for Atlantic. Everyone wanted to find the next Nirvana. I remember Sublime demos being handed around. Things were coming out of the indie world, so I think Atlantic wanted to capitalize on that and see if they could get hit bands and records. Seven Mary Three was the first one really happening for Mammoth, who had been getting rock radio in Florida. Around the time I got to Atlantic, Hootie and the Blowfish started to happen. They were not a jam band, but they were a southern touring band. And they'd been at it for what seemed like a bunch of years. So I just thought bands toured and toured until they got a record deal. But then when I got to Atlantic, I saw bands were getting signed off of demos, and some of them hadn't even done concerts before. It was weird.

Reid Genauer: Pete Shapiro flew to Burlington and wanted to start a label around Strangefolk.

John Moore: I gotta believe that Pete turned me on to Strangefolk.

Pete Shapiro: I was going to do a label around them . . . or management. One of those.

Luke Smith: We knew what we had, too—we had something that people wanted.

Brett Fairbrother: When I gave John the green light to start being serious about this, I think we'd sold out two nights of the Great American Music Hall, for Halloween.

Sam Ankerson: When Mammoth came along, it just felt like a good fit with their roots in independent bands and bringing them to a national audience.

Brett Fairbrother: I said, "Let's do this. Put some stuff together and set up some meetings." And he did.

Reid Genauer: Disney bought the label . . . I remember hearing the number was twenty million dollars.

John Moore: I felt like they could have a hit song.

Pete Shapiro: I did too.

John Moore: Their harmonies were much better than many of the other bands in the scene. I thought they could make a very good record and be accessible and then jammy in concert, and it would be two different things.

55

A Lot of Guys, Their Whole Life Has Been a Mess Because They Can't Stop Playing Music

Tomo: We were our own worst enemies a lot of the time.

Jon Bevo: The five of us could not go on.

Lo Faber: I was hard to work with, sometimes.

Aaron Maxwell: I don't know what separates a band that gets stardom and one that almost does.

Matt Busch: It surprised me to learn that they were really a struggling bar band because what I saw from the audience was just this kick-ass, unbelievably successful, dangerous band that could do anything at any moment.

Lo Faber: The only time we were really mindful about trying to make a commercial record was the last one, *Hot Sweet & Juicy,* which never came out. Basically, at that point, our manager told us if you can't get a radio hit on this record, it's over. The irony was that when our manager said that to us, it was already over because they were never going to put that record out.

Tomo: I officially left in May '98. But I'd been itching to go for a while. I had watched the arc. We went from a bus back to a van . . . people sharing hotel rooms again. All the signs were there.

Dan Pifer: These things often have something to do with money. And there was definitely a financial element of it, where we had this debt, and we had to work in order to pay it off. We had personal assets, especially Lo and myself, that were on the line that the bank could have come after, if they'd chosen to.

Lo Faber: Labels are guilty of many things. But I don't think I can hold the success of my career just on the labels. Ultimately, it's up to the artist.

Dan Pifer: We were of a mind like, "Hey, you know, it may not be that fun, but we have to get out there and work. We still have an audience, we can still make money playing gigs, and we just have to tough it out and do this."

Scott "bullethead" Reilly: The band couldn't just call it quits. There was no way all five members could have said we can walk away from this financially—they couldn't say that. And some of the guys could, and it was really uncomfortable.

Dan Pifer: Tomo and Lo were at a point where they were just like, "I don't want to tour . . . can we just take a break, can we just make another record?" And we were like, "No, there's bills to pay, where's the money gonna come from?" It's a business and you have people who work for you who are dependent on you to pay them so they can pay their rent, and you're trying to pay your own rent. At that point, living together was not really feasible anymore. People had moved out of the house and gotten their own places. So there was a financial reality to what we needed to do to keep the band and the business going, because of these obligations. And I think in a lot of ways, Tomo and Lo were right, but there was a reality they weren't really willing to look at either. That, to me, is probably what drove the split more than anything—they were sort of done in terms of the constant touring and exhausted by it, as I think we all were.

Lo Faber: It wasn't necessarily what the mass wanted to hear.

Tomo: At that point, we were doing these college gigs where we'd all arrive in separate vehicles. We'd meet backstage, do the show, and go our separate ways.

Jon Bevo: Tomo and I were putting out this vibe, "How much longer can this go on?"

Dan Pifer: I don't think we were playing as well as we had in the early days, because we were somewhat jaded at that point by all the horrible record company experiences.

Aaron Maxwell: We weren't moving forward . . . we needed to reassess what we were doing.

Tomo: Not being a prima donna at all, but I was going, "Hey, guys . . . you see this? Come on . . . what the fuck?" And I just got tired of being that guy. And I think they got tired of me.

Lo Faber: I had a relentless energy. And I wouldn't necessarily be very sympathetic to hearing about how he was feeling burned out. Unfortunately, my reaction might have tended to be something like, "Oh, poor you."

Jon Bevo: It was a decision that should have been made probably even a year before that.

Tomo: So, there's me wanting to leave and then them going, "We're tired of you. You should go." It kind of happened around the same time.

Scott "bullethead" Reilly: The whole thing was horrible. It was just really horrible.

Dan Pifer: It was really sad when we ended up parting ways with those guys.

Jon Bevo: After I wasn't going on the road with them, I did do the last record.

Scott "bullethead" Reilly: I gotta say I love the *God Street Wine* record. Bevo came into his own as a songwriter. Sometimes when you only get a few bites, you don't realize how rare and great it is.

Lo Faber: Tomo and I have been playing music together since seventh grade. And I love him, he's like a brother, or more than a brother. And that's true of all the guys in the band.

Scott "bullethead" Reilly: A lot of guys, their whole life has been a mess because they can't stop playing music. And then there's other people where when they hit that hard wall, they stop playing music, at least trying to do it full time. If you're not one of the people who's gonna just let you play music, and mess up your life, and you don't get along great with the guys that you're touring with . . . you're gonna have to have huge success to hold the band together. And God Street Wine didn't have huge success.

Aaron Maxwell: That was a difficult, yet exciting, time for me personally, as I was excited to connect and play with other musicians. But I was also a bit fraught with frustration, and a sense that this thing that I had poured my entire being into, for over a decade, was on the brink of completely falling apart. Mainly because of personality conflicts, fatigue from being on the road so much, frustration from two record deals that ultimately went south, but really it came down to the fact that, even with all of this, various members still wanted to go on the road, play gigs, try to move in an upward direction as a band, and others felt that going on the road, back in the van, slogging it out, was not something that made sense for them, and that we were not moving upwards, but downwards. Both ways had their pros and cons.

Lo Faber: If I was an A&R person, I don't know if I would have picked God Street Wine as the most likely to succeed commercially. I probably wouldn't have, to be perfectly frank. We were much better suited to be a cult favorite than to ascend the pop charts.

56

Just Do It So We Can Get You Out of Here

Jim Walsh: David Fricke, in 1998, yelled at me because I kept calling him at *Rolling Stone.* And I was like, "Look, David, I'm sorry I keep bugging you, but I think you're really gonna like this record." And it was *Tin Cans & Car Tires.* And it ended up in the "Albums That Mattered" in 1998. He loved it and gave it four stars.

Vinnie Amico: That was my first record ever.

John Siket: I didn't really know moe. at all. John Alagía hired me, even though Sony paid for the whole thing. And we did that all up to BearTracks, not to be confused with Bearsville. BearTracks was in Rockland County, New York. It was built into an old stone Huguenot farmhouse.

Rob Derhak: That turned into a pretty good party.

Al Schnier: There was a lot of debauchery.

Vinnie Amico: A lot of debauchery.

Steve Young: I didn't really track anything. I brought all the gear down and set up all their stuff.

Al Schnier: It all felt very rock and roll to be drinking whiskey every day and recording a record in the studio.

Vinnie Amico: John Siket, I think he had just come from recording *Crash* with the Dave Matthews Band. Alagía was also in the Dave camp. They were guys that, in my mind, were way above my paygrade.

Jim Walsh: The guys asked me to sing backup vocals on a track. We were drinking in the studio, and I think it was Siket who threw me in the live room. It was me, Vinnie, Rob, and Al all around one U47 microphone. And then they pulled me out really quick because we were pretty toasty at that point. And I didn't know what I was doing.

Rob Derhak: We did some pre-production beforehand and got a lot of stuff done with Alagía without Siket there . . . we did some really good work.

Vinnie Amico: The recording session wasn't too strenuous with the drums and bass because we had written a bunch of that stuff for that record.

Rob Derhak: The *Tin Can* sessions, we had some fucked-up things happen. I'll tell you the story, but I'm not gonna give any names. We were staying at this guy's house, a friend of ours who was an agent. He wasn't our booking agent, but he was a friend who was going to potentially be our booking agent at one point. He moved from the New York area to California to start working out there. And he was trying to sell his house, which happened to be close to the studio. It was a tough market, so he's like, "Alright, I'll rent the place to you guys. You can live there while you're going to the studio." We just basically turned his house upside down. And it was a nice home. We finally took a break from the studio, and we're like, "Let's take the weekend off," and everyone kind of left early. He didn't tell us that he had a showing . . . he's like, "Just keep the house up, because people are still trying to buy my house." We did a massive party the night before, with just shit everywhere. A guy I was friends with made his bedroom in a walk-in closet with a blow-up mattress. And he was naked in there, passed out, a pile of puke on the floor next to him. And they're bringing people through a showing. And they go up into it, open up the door, and the dude's just laying there in his own sick, naked.

Al Schnier: Everything kept moving along at the same pace, but nothing changed significantly for us. We found that super frustrating. We felt like we were doing all the work. And I'm sure that's a very common experience for acts that don't get a priority treatment, which is probably 99 percent of them. And so it's not unique and nothing that we should feel too precious about.

Ken "Skip" Richman: There was one point where Michael Caplan, who signed them, was screaming and yelling at them: "You'll never be anything and you guys are useless. You're not doing anything."

Michael Caplan: [*Laughs*] I don't remember that. But it sounds like something I'd say.

Ken "Skip" Richman: At the same time, our agent was at a conference, and the president of Sony, Jimmy Iovine, was talking about how Sony is going back to working grassroots and working with bands that are about doing it the hard way, working on the road and building a relationship, and he's talking about moe. the whole time.

Jon Topper: I knew we were gonna get dropped.

Michael Caplan: It was alright. I kind of lost interest afterwards. I thought *No Doy* was so fucking fabulous, it paled in comparison to me.

Al Schnier: We found ourselves in what felt like a one-way relationship.

Vinnie Amico: They canceled after two albums because they only sold a hundred grand.

Jon Topper: The greatest thing we got out of our relationship with Sony was that they introduced us to the retail world. So moe. was in a position that when we got dropped from Sony, we already had a distribution deal, because we kept *Fatboy* and *Headseed* . . . we didn't give those to Sony when we did our record deal. I did a separate distribution deal with RED Distribution. When they put out *No Doy*, we put *Headseed* in the bins too . . . we just piggybacked off their marketing. When we got dropped, my first phone call was to Chip Hooper, and Chip's reaction was, "I don't really give a shit. You know, I don't make anything off your records anyway." Then I called Howie Gabriel and Alan Becker at RED . . . they were mentors to me . . . and their reaction was, "Who cares? If an indie band can sell five thousand album units they're doing amazing. You guys can sell twenty-five to thirty-five thousand units. So just do it yourselves."

Al Schnier: They weren't investing anything into it at the time, and so we asked to either option the next one or release us from the contract. They released us at that point. You don't want to wind up in a dead-letter office, but that's where we found ourselves. We sold out two shows at Radio City Music Hall after they dropped us. Which is crazy when you think about it. Why wouldn't you get behind a band like us and make sure that we get on *Conan* again or put a song on the radio? Rob writes these great songs that could easily be on a soundtrack or on the radio. Somebody should get behind that shit. But it's not my job.

Jon Topper: It was like, "Here's your first album. Nothing happened. Here's your second album, just do it so we can get you out of here."

57

We Were Like the Beverly Hillbillies on This Tour

In the summer of 1997, the second Furthur Festival tour hit the road, a post-iteration of the Grateful Dead sans Jerry Garcia. This tour featured nightly sets from Bob Weir and RatDog, the Black Crowes, Bruce Hornsby, Arlo Guthrie, and the newcomers of the bunch . . . moe.

Al Schnier: I saw all the SPAC [Saratoga Performing Arts Center] shows the Dead played.

Vinnie Amico: Six months before I started playing with moe., I was in a Grateful Dead tribute band. It was a really good one, but I was just covering Dead music. Six months later, I was playing nightly on the stage with those guys. I was playing in the all-star jam every night . . . I was the drummer that knew every song.

Rob Derhak: It's a core memory that everyone has. Everyone's in a tour bus, we're still driving our camper.

Ken "Skip" Richman: We were the young guys on that tour, but everyone really seemed to like us and take care of us.

Al Schnier: We couldn't afford a bus yet at this point. Everything we did still very much had this DIY attitude. We didn't work beyond our means. When I think about it, we were like the Beverly Hillbillies on this tour.

Jon Topper: We're playing at five o'clock in the afternoon—it's not like millions of people were seeing us.

Rob Derhak: We had a forty-minute set that we were allotted . . . the first gig, we went over by five minutes. So we got punished . . . all the old Dead crew, these guys were fucking salty. Some of those people we're still friends with, but they were like, "Alright, well fuck you guys. Let's teach the kids a lesson."

Chuck Garvey: Robbie Taylor. He hated us at first.

Rob Derhak: He used to scare the shit out of us.

Vinnie Amico: Bob and the Dead guys were pretty fresh off Jerry's passing.

Chuck Garvey: It was a really long day, with a half hour of music.

Rob Derhak: They did a tour practice for a couple days where they set up in Florida. We went and we were like, "Oh my god, how can we even be part of this?" We were total rookie scrubs. I don't remember any of the playing at all. It's all the extracurricular stuff.

Ken "Skip" Richman: We weren't making that much money back then. But it wasn't like we did it for the money. We did it for getting out there and being seen and being known.

Vinnie Amico: Just being around the Black Crowes in a time when they were going through a bunch of shit that you didn't really know about . . . they were completely imploding. And they were also at the top of their game.

Jon Topper: The total rock and roll moment: I think it was in Philly, and moe., the Black Crowes, and all the Dead guys and all the crew guys were all around the TV watching the Mike Tyson–Holyfield fight and he bit the ear. Everybody's like, "Ahhhhhhhhhh!"

Al Schnier: They would do an encore every night, where different musicians from the bands would play. They said, "Well, you know, we're gonna start out with a core band. And then maybe down the road, we'll see if we can start to squeeze you guys in and see how it goes." And after the first night, we were in West Palm Beach, and I think we wanted to leave before the crowd left. So we had packed up all of our gear and just as they were starting to get ready for the encore, we headed out to the RV. We were about to leave and John Scher, the promoter, came out and was knocking on our RV. He's like, "Where's Al? You know 'Truckin'' . . . get your shit, come on, let's go!" From the very first night, they started including me. And then from that night on, I got to play the encore every night with these musicians—with Mickey, Bobby, Arlo, Bruce Hornsby.

Vinnie Amico: I had seen the Grateful Dead a few times. That was the first time I played at SPAC. And I'd seen hundreds of concerts there at that point. And here I am on that stage for the first time, which was my dream when I was sixteen, on acid and watching the Dead, or Elton John, Peter Frampton, whoever I saw. I mean, I saw everybody there. And that was my dream to play on stage one day, and here I am, on that stage playing with one of my idols. We did "That's It for the Other One," which the Dead hadn't played in years. Had my career gone no further than that day, I would have been fine. My dreams were realized.

Al Schnier: We played in Forest Hills [Queens] at the tennis stadium the day before and we got Bobby to play "Mama Tried" with us during our set. And it went well, and he liked it. And so we asked him if he wanted to go with us again and he said that he would. So we busted out "That's It for the Other One." And we thought, "Well, we'll just make that the whole set."

Ken "Skip" Richman: One day we played the San Francisco show and Al got to sit in for the encore. It was him on stage with Mickey and Kreutzmann, and Phil was there and Bruce Hornsby was on keyboards. And Bobby was there, of course, and Al was standing there in Jerry's spot during the encore. What a thing for a young guy, who's been a fan of the Dead his whole life, to have that experience. The next day we show up and there's a moe. dressing room, and then there's an Al Garcia dressing room.

Jim Walsh: I think we were in . . . I want to say Raleigh or somewhere in North Carolina. Or, you know, it could have been Michigan too. It's a whole fucking blur, man. Somehow we got some cigars. Al and I walked all the way up to the top corner [of the venue], and sat back and had a cigar and we were kind of like, "Wow, this is fucking cool."

Ken "Skip" Richman: There was a lot of bullying . . . where we learned to stand up for ourselves. Al had gone into the production office and asked what the encore was going to be because he was always excited to see if he could get in on the encore. So he had stopped by the production office, and they yelled at him—told him to get out of the damn production office. And he came into the band room and was visibly upset to be yelled at. I walked into the production office, and said, "Listen, you can treat me any way you fucking want, but don't talk to my artists that way. He's still an artist. He's still working his ass off, and you don't have any right to talk to him like that." And they apologized. They were very cool about it. It was a big step for us, too—to make that point.

Al Schnier: Bobby and I shared this whole experience over our adoptions with one another that summer. He had just gone through finding his biological parents and I was going through that on the tour during that summer. And he ended up mentoring me through the process.

Jon Topper: We were able to bump up in the venue size.

Jim Walsh: Later, when moe. toured that fall and they were in San Francisco at the Fillmore for the first time, Bob came and sat in that night.

Jon Topper: We knew he was coming and I was waiting for him at the door. And he walks through the front of the Fillmore . . . doesn't go around back, and I'm standing there, and I'm like, "Hey, Bobby, the guys are waiting for you in a dressing room. You want me to show you where it is?" He's like, "I think I know where it is."

58

They Thought We Were All Black

Ben Ellman: In the beginning, it was really acid jazz, a different hipster scene. And New Orleans—people who just like New Orleans music.

Robert Mercurio: Widespread had us open for their summer tour. We aligned ourselves a lot with them at that point. Every time we played with them, more and more people were coming to our show. So it was a great combo, even though to me we're not that similar. But it just connected with their fan base. Halloween '97—we opened up for Panic at the UNO Lakefront Arena. And it was a sold-out show.

Rich Vogel: We obviously were enough of a buzz band that we got that gig.

Robert Mercurio: They definitely covered their share of Meters and New Orleans songs. And there was definitely a nod to the funk in their music. And we played probably on the more aggressive side that didn't really show up on *Coolin' Off*. I mean, one of the main reasons we called it *Coolin' Off* was because it had this relaxed feel to it. But live, we always put a lot of energy into our show, so that's where I think we connected—the energy.

Rich Vogel: We were like, "We need to do something . . . visually, we have to be something more than five guys at the Mermaid Lounge."

Robert Mercurio: We all painted our faces silver, we wore painted silver ball caps, and we had these costumes that we made and we ran battery-powered lights on them. In '97, that was high-tech. We were just silver-looking, bald-headed guys up on stage. Widespread Panic's tour manager, as we're getting off stage, asked if they could borrow our costumes.

Stanton Moore: That was a shot in the arm for us.

Robert Mercurio: Our crowds started doubling after that show. All these Widespread Panic fans started coming. And we would meet them and they thought we were all Black—because they couldn't see us and our singer [at the time] was Black.

59

Don't Hurt My Town

On April 18, 1998, Widespread Panic threw a release party in Athens called "Panic in the Streets," celebrating their first-ever live album Light Fuse Get Away. *The show was free and set up in downtown Athens—just a stone's throw away from the old Uptown Lounge where they cut their teeth just ten years before. It was one of the biggest jam band events of the decade, a testament to how the band had grown its fan base through relentless touring. A hundred thousand people showed up.*

Buck Williams: Phil and I came up with this concept and the band always wanted to do something like this—have the biggest release party ever. They had no idea who was going to show up.

Ted Rockwell: It coincided with a lot of different events—just having enough of a fan base in the Southeast, that had enough free time, and were of the right age, to be able to just drop everything and get there.

Dirk Stalnecker: There wasn't a promoter. It was the band that put it together as an album release party.

John Bell: We're planning to have this party. City's on board, then they start catching wind people are interested.

Buck Williams: The only way to ensure that a lot of people showed up was to make it free.

Domingo "Sunny" Ortiz: The whole concept of it being free did not go over good with Capricorn Records.

Ted Rockwell: With the internet, word spread a lot faster than I think they realized it was going to. I don't think they had any idea that once they got the word out, people from five, six states away would come.

Peter Jackson: I was the production manager at that point. It was kind of a terrifying experience.

Mary Dugas: The band was in Europe, so between myself and Dirk from Europe, we worked with the city, the mayor, and the Downtown Development Authority to organize the concert.

Chris Rabold: Everything from '95 to 2000 . . . the beauty of them is it was a linear path. It might have had not the steepest incline in the world, but if it wasn't a purposeful trudge, it was an obvious destination where it was going. It was obvious that they were moving forward with every gig. Every bit of passage of time, they just kept getting bigger, and also better.

Buck Williams: I was talking to the chief of police and the mayor, Gwen O'Looney. I said, "They have football games with eighty thousand people in there—how can they think that this thing is going to be out of hand?" The cost of security kept going up and up.

Peter Jackson: She was super passionate about Athens and the culture and music scene. And she saw that for what it was . . . R.E.M. had certainly hit the national radar at that point. It was not hard to get excited about the music scene in Athens. But Gwen was a very dynamic political leader. She would be out in the bars and stuff—engaged with the electorate.

Dave Schools: The mounted police force was making us buy feed for their horses because they were scared that our fans were gonna dose the horse feed.

John Bell: They're starting to worry about it: Wait a minute, there's a lot of interest in this. We might have security issues and travel issues. The town started getting really spooked about it.

Domingo "Sunny" Ortiz: The glitch was the city wanted to make sure that their town was not going to be destroyed. And of course, we couldn't guarantee that.

Buck Williams: The city of Macon reached out. They said, "We hear you're having trouble up there. And we'd like to tell you, you can play here and you'll have no problem with police or anything else. We'd love to have it."

John Bell: They said, "Screw it, we'll have 'em. Just throw the party down our way."

Dave Schools: "We'll pay for everything."

Buck Williams: Capricorn didn't back out, they just didn't put the money up. They took out some ads, but it was word of mouth and it spread like kudzu.

Domingo "Sunny" Ortiz: As great as the city of Athens is, it's still a business. And there were issues that weren't being resolved at the last minute. If Capricorn wasn't going to pay a nice chunk of change, then it would have to come from somewhere, right? So it came from, let's say, an anonymous donor.

Peter Jackson: We were pretty heavily under-resourced in terms of production, budgets, staging, and stagehands. Behind the scenes, it felt like it was hanging on by its fingernails.

Dirk Stalnecker: We had delays going all the way up the street. Mobile stages were a new thing and we got a hold of one of those and brought it in first thing in the morning.

Domingo "Sunny" Ortiz: Everything that we could think of was being taken care of, except for realizing that there's a church where our stage was, and there was a wedding going on, when we were about to get on stage.

Peter Jackson: The wedding thing was a huge dustup ahead of time.

Mary Dugas: It was actually a girl I knew getting married. And her mom was a writer at one of the newspapers, and so they kept it on the front page of the paper for a long time with lots of questions.

Domingo "Sunny" Ortiz: The groom came to us at the stage, dressed in his tux, and said, "Fellas, I know this is a special moment for you guys. This is a special moment for me and my future wife. I was wondering if you can just hold it down or not start until after the nuptials?" We had a representative dressed in blue jeans and a T-shirt at the ceremony and as soon as the nuptials were over, we kicked it.

Dirk Stalnecker: We took over the 40 Watt Club as a dressing room.

John Bell: I wasn't really nervous. I was most nervous earlier in the day, because I was doing the national anthem at one of the University of Georgia baseball games. I really just started getting all sweaty palms and stuff.

Dave Schools: I remember walking out there and seeing that immense crowd and thinking, "Okay, we got to keep them focused." You know, that was my thing. We have to really just do our job and keep them focused. If some ripple of consternation is out amongst this crowd, and then they got unfocused, it could be crazy. It could be really bad. And I think Mayor Gwen O'Looney felt the same thing when she introduced the band and said, "Don't hurt my town."

Dirk Stalnecker: I heard reports that people were really getting pressed up against the glass on some of the establishments on that street. I went to check that out and it wasn't as dire as it was projected to me.

David Blackmon: I was at the 40 Watt Club, behind the stage. Allen Woody was playing bass with Warren at the time, before he passed away. I was friends with him when I used to live in Nashville. We were catching up and Warren Haynes apparently heard my fiddling several times live and he immediately knew who I was.

He said, "Hey, man, you wanna sit in the whole night with us?"

"I don't know anything you do."

And he said, "Don't worry about it. You'll figure it out in two seconds."

Steve Fleming: Just before they started the second set, Garrie Vereen came over to me and was like, "Steve, Steve, the guys in the band want to talk to you, they want to ask you something." They were using the 40 Watt Club as the dressing room area, and I walk over with Garrie, and all six of the guys come out and basically encircled me. And they're like, "Oh, we got a song we want to do. We want to check with you first before we do anything. We're calling it 'One Arm Steve.' We're just going to make sure it's okay." I just laughed and said I have no problem with it. I went back over to where I was standing with Michael Stipe. And they opened the second set with "One Arm Steve" and Michael turned around and looked at me and just sort of smiled.

Dirk Stalnecker: There really wasn't anything super dramatic that was going on with the crowd. People were getting high and there were open containers out there but just like the mayor said, "Don't break my town," and it was okay.

Mary Dugas: Phil, Phillip, Buck, and Sam all huddled around this little weather radar machine. And there was this huge storm coming across Alabama, towards us, but that storm came to right outside of Athens and stopped. It just lingered outside of Athens. We were all just waiting, people looking for lightning . . . are we gonna have to shut it down? And then it finally did come towards us as the night was ending. And it started to pour during the encore of "Ain't Life Grand," which couldn't have been more perfect.

Buck Williams: I got an aerial count—they had a picture and you can take a square inch and figure how many people are in that square inch, and then multiply it by the number of square inches. And you get a rough number; that's how they do crowds anywhere. It was over a hundred thousand people.

Dave Schools: The show was over in a flash. I walked around town with my buddies. Every bar in town was sold out, every band was playing their best.

Buck Williams: The city made a fortune out of it. And the cleanup . . . it was the biggest mess.

Peter Jackson: I have this memory of walking around as the sun was beginning to come up, and it's just devastation across the moonscape of downtown Athens. I'm with Art Jackson—he was up in senior level staff—and we were just sort of surveying this *Mad Max*–looking landscape. We rolled up the garage door on this city facility that was close to the stage and it's floor to ceiling with fifty-five-gallon drum trash cans. None of them had been deployed out onto the streets, and we're looking at just trash everywhere. Well, someone forgot to put the trash cans out.

60

Who Are These Guys Who Promote Harder than Anybody?

Marc Brownstein: There was a flood of jam bands. We just wanted to be the one that people heard about the most.

Rich Vogel: We'd go "flyering" as we called it. We had some big, heavy-duty, "swing like a hammer" staplers, and we'd go out at night, and it was technically not allowed, and they could get ripped down . . . but they usually weren't.

Steve Eichner: You'd go to a gig, get a flyer, and you'd say, "Okay, these guys are playing over here."

Michael Travis: We were self-booking and self-flyering, making them up and then going to Kinko's, printing them out, and putting them all over town.

Chris Wood: Early on, Billy's dad had a Xerox machine; we could make posters and flyers. Billy was very artistic.

Chan Kinchla: We made these "Gigs at a Glance," which were these early little flyers with a calendar on it, where we're playing at the time. We had a rule that anyone we met needed to know the name of the band, when we were playing next, and get a flyer within five minutes.

Tomo: We played the Cat Club, which was a real rock and roll, pay-to-play sort of place, where you handed out flyers and as many flyers came in, you'd get a dollar for each one.

Cody Dickinson: The staple gun on the telephone poles, just paper and the flyers. Then cassettes . . . we'd make one hundred to five hundred copies, and either give them away or sell them for next to nothing.

Dave Schools: Steve Fleming made a comment after one of the Monday nights: "You guys should raise your price." We'd been charging one dollar. "Raise your price. You guys are starting to draw a crowd. Now's the time to do it." So we thought about it and we went back to the band's house. And we drew a flyer for a dollar fifty. That's not doubling the price. It's just a good little step up. We thought we were smart—brilliant marketing geniuses. We put the posters up and Steve was fucking incensed.

"What? You're the one that said we should charge more!"

"Yeah, but remember, I only have one arm."

Steve had a system so that he could make change at the door with one arm—tens in one pocket, fives and ones in another.

"I've never ever had to deal with change in my life. You guys are idiots."

Jane Tower: I was a student at UVA and I went to work for the summer in Richmond, Virginia, where Coran owned the Flood Zone. I would buy rider requirements for bands that would come through—I heard you could get into shows for free if you did that or hung flyers. They didn't need anybody to hang flyers back then so they got me to start buying the rider requirements for the greenroom.

Keller Williams: There was definitely the trading of tickets for folks that hung up flyers.

Rick Farman: We were doing hardcore street marketing—posters, flyers. A buddy of mine, we went up to the Panic in the Streets show with a duffel bag of flyers to our Jazz Fest shows. I probably gave out ten, fifteen, twenty thousand flyers at that.

Hunter Brown: I remember living in Kinko's.

Sam Altman: My job was to make the flyers. I was the computer-art guy for some reason. I tried to make them in the spirit of all '80s hardcore and punk rock posters. We'd go around Penn and Philly on the days leading up to the show, with a staple gun and a bunch of flyers we printed at Kinko's. The band would approve them; we'd fight over them because I was attached artistically to the flyers I would make. Marc would say, "That's really good. But you didn't put the time of the show." And I'd say something like, "Well, artistically, it doesn't fit." So we'd have to put the time of the show. And we'd take these flyers around and staple gun them to all the telephone posts around school . . . I would take a certain quadrant, Marc would take another.

Marc Brownstein: If Phish came to town, we would print ten thousand flyers. And then we would go to the lot early in the day with a box of flyers, we would meet up with some of our friends who were our street team, and we split up the lots.

Sam Altman: It was a lot of hours walking around Phish lot.

Marc Brownstein: Every car got hit. Every single one. We would talk to every single group of kids that was going to the Phish show. We got to a point, after the Phish show, that when people were coming out, they'd be like, "I got one, thanks. I talked to you earlier, thanks."

Jon "The Barber" Gutwillig: We would see who's playing where, and could then advertise to their audience. We didn't have a record out. We didn't have a hit song out. So how are people going to find out who we are? Well, there's word of mouth. And then there's finding audiences that you think might like you.

Aron Magner: I've always thought since day one that it's about the ticket sales.

Marc Brownstein: There was a show we had at this place called Downtime on 29th Street in New York City after a Phish show. We had these eight-by-ten green flyers and we printed ten thousand of them. At set break, at Phish, when the lights went up, we had people waiting at the bottom of every single section of the Garden—fifty people working. We would take the stack, and go up to the first seat with the stack and say, "Hey, can you just take one and pass it down?" Within five minutes, the entire arena turned green. You could see, as it fanned out, every single person in the whole arena reading the flyer. You know, like 180 of them came to the show or whatever. But it didn't matter. That wasn't what it was about. It was about name recognition.

Jon "The Barber" Gutwillig: We got a gig at a dumpy bar around the corner from the Wetlands called New City Cafe. We talked them into giving us a show and then we flyered the Wetlands every single day for a month. Honestly, we wanted the Wetlands kids to come see us play. We didn't realize what Wetlands was going to think of it. We didn't think of it that deeply and Wetlands was cleaning up these flyers for the Disco Biscuits every night. Eventually, the club promoters were like, "Who are these guys who promote harder than anybody?"

Marc Brownstein: We put down a thousand flyers just everywhere: outside, before the show, after the show, inside the show, on every bathroom, everywhere. But here's the thing. Before that show, we had called the Wetlands every single day for like a month.

"Hey, is Chris Zahn there?"

"Who's calling?"

"It's the Disco Biscuits."

"Hold on. No, Chris isn't available."

A full month of every single day calling the Wetlands and having the guy not take our call. Then we littered the place with flyers. And then on Monday, we called.

"Hey, is Chris Zahn there? It's the Disco Biscuits."

"Yeah, hold on one second. Hey, this is Chris. Alright, Disco Biscuits. What was that? If you're gonna promote your shows that hard, you can play here whenever you want. That was a beautiful effort."

Joel Cummins (Keyboards, vocals, Umphrey's McGee): We sent out tons of tapes and CDs to different people in advance of us playing anywhere. That strategy seemed to work pretty well. We played in Boulder, Colorado . . . we were playing a two-hundred-and-fifty-person wine bar called Trilogy and we sold it out our first time in Boulder.

Alan Evans: One time, I was cruising around, and kept seeing these posters for Phish at Nietzsche's. This is before I knew who Phish was. I'm thinking, "Oh, shit. Fishbone playing at Nietzsche's? I can't believe this." I got over there and I'm like, "What in the world is going on?"

Sam Ankerson: Through our newsletter we would encourage people to get in touch with us if they wanted to help us put up posters in advance of shows.

Kerry Black: We always were about having a super cool poster. We were doing silkscreen posters, getting artists to do them. Everyone else in the city was doing the paper block writing thing. And that works. We were always wanting to be something more—an ode to Bill Graham.

Ken "Skip" Richman: One great thing about moe. is the logo and poster artists get really confused on what to do. Since it's lowercase, they always want to make it as big as everything else that's uppercase, therefore it gets larger and more bold. So when you look at festival posters, moe. always stands out.

Jon Topper: The great thing about the moe. logo is you could be at a Phish show and be on one side of Madison Square Garden, look all the way across, and just see the yellow moe.

Rick Farman: We started our CD sampler, *The Sweet Sounds of Superfly*. We would give out a sampler at all of our shows and charge the labels to put a track on. Because we knew we had such a specific audience . . . this jam audience was so burgeoning at the time. We had this national audience that we could put into the hands of a kid for free. If Derek Trucks was putting out his record and his label would buy a track on the record, all of a sudden, these thirty or forty thousand people who got the samplers would be exposed to that song.

Andre Gardner: I remember sitting in our kitchen with Reid and we would send demo tapes out, unsolicited, trying to get gigs.

Marc Brownstein: A little box on Andy Gadiel's Phish Page said, "One of my favorite bands, the Disco Biscuits, is going out on tour. Here's the dates, go see it." We had already done one run around the country and played to nobody. And then this next run, we went out with Gadiel behind us and it was like three hundred, every single show, sold out. That was some of the most profound word of mouth . . . we couldn't do that with flyers.

Cody Dickinson: It was all word of mouth.

61

We Didn't Even Know We Were in a Tidal Wave

Chris Bowman: There wasn't a lot of radio stations back then for this scene. And a lot of the first wave of the jam bands that were formed in the '80s like Phish, Blues Traveler, and Widespread Panic—they were smart in that day. That's the Grateful Dead culture, the tape trading.

Bruce Flohr: The cassette tape, at the time, is now what the internet is: the first case of music going viral.

Benjy Eisen: Taping culture was the original social media for music fans—the analog version. Instead of a post, it was a post office.

Alan Evans: Taping was huge.

Karl Denson: The taper scene was just insane.

Chris Barron: The tapers sprung out of the Grateful Dead scene . . . it was more of a testament to the ephemeral nature of music than it was a shift to the idea of everything being available to be recorded all the time.

Andy Gadiel: I wasn't following Phish as closely at the moment, however, all that their Halloween '94 show did was lead to this "Oh my god, this story I have to catch up on . . . and look at all this incredible archive of material they have that is being traded freely by people who are willing to mail blanks and postage to someone else, to hope to get back a tape."

Marc Brownstein: If we're taping and putting it out, it's promo, right? If the fans are taping and putting it out, it's word of mouth. And there's a big difference between promo and word of mouth. Word of mouth is the best marketing thing that can happen to any product. Nothing is more effective at getting your brand out there than people talking it up to other people. So taping and disseminating music through a scene can be promo, or it can be word of mouth, and it's definitely better if it's word of mouth.

Vinnie Amico: Tapes were ninety minutes or whatever and you had to fill space at the end. And so there'd be a moe. song or a couple moe. tunes. They were "fillers" on Phish tapes or Dead tapes.

Reid Genauer: It cross-pollinates.

Dean Budnick: One of the beauties is you would get twenty minutes, maybe thirty minutes on the B-side of a tape where you can drop in whatever interests you and so you can proselytize about another band to your friends. You would trust certain tapers' tastes. Or certain people that you trade with, you'd trust their tastes.

Jeff Cook: What record company wants to miss out on potential sales?

Sue Drew: Phish set aside these sections that they called taping sections and tapers came. And that was extremely unusual and difficult for a record company to swallow. Like, "Wait a minute, you're encouraging bootlegging? This is something we absolutely fight against every day." And Paluska said, "This is how we increase our fan base. This is super important to us. So you must let us do this. We're not stopping this particular aspect of our marketing plan." And Elektra got down and said okay and that was really difficult to come around.

Brian Cohen: In many respects, it was the right place for Phish to be because Elektra had to understand multiple cultural bottles for pop music and be good at all of them. We were working everything from Metallica to the Sugarcubes to They Might Be Giants to Missy Elliott. We had to become students of each genre, and each marketing culture. Phish was just a new marketing culture that we had to understand. At the same time, they were introducing new aspects to music marketing that no label was prepared for—like downloads. That immediately became a tension. I wanted to do what I could to have that rub off on record sales, but you know, most of it didn't.

Trey Anastasio: We had so much good original music already, and that was before we signed to Elektra. We were kind of like, "We don't need you to break us or tell me what to do." Because I don't believe in your mentality, anyway, I know what kind of music I like and I'm writing it on a regular basis and people were really into it. The shows were explosive.

John Bell: We were taping our own shows and trying to get it out there as early demos.

Marc Brownstein: We were taping early shows and if we found good material in it, we would let it out.

Eric Krasno: I was sending tapes to people. I used to send tapes that were recorded in my dorm . . . we would set up in this tiny little dorm room and I had an eight-track tape machine. And we would record the whole band. Eventually, we recorded ourselves live at a show and that was our representation.

Reid Genauer: There was never any question that we allowed taping. It was clear that that was part of what was driving us.

Cody Dickinson: We always encouraged taping. I was always wary of the soundboard feeds for whatever reason. So we always allowed mics. And, man, the archives that are out there are incredible. In a way, taper culture invented message boards . . . they were the first ones that I ever saw use it in any sort of meaningful, practical way. The word spread so fast. If we were on fire, you could see the momentum . . . you would gain momentum in real time, because people were sharing the music.

Dave Matthews: We used to let people plug directly into the soundboard, but that became a spaghetti mess.

Marc Brownstein: From the very first day of Disco Biscuits touring, the fans took over the process of taping . . . they're much better at taping than us. We would give them a patch into the soundboard when that made sense. We went on a ten-show tour in the Northeast, March of 1997. And there were tapers that did all ten shows.

Bruce Flohr: You'd go to the show and see all these towers of microphones by the soundboard. And the Dave Matthews Band really noticed the impact of that. The first time they went to Colorado, I believe they played the Fox Theatre with The Samples. And everybody in the room knew the words. That was an "aha" moment for the band.

Vinnie Amico: The way we sold out the Fox, when we got to Colorado, was through tapes. Everything has been done through people hearing our music in advance. It was the same with the Fillmore in San Francisco.

John Medeski: The fans were trading tapes.

Chris Wood: That's how people would pass around new stuff they were excited about.

John Medeski: And we were not into that at first because our mentors were the jazz guys and they were really against taping. Jazz guys were used to European promoters recording gigs and making records and putting them out and then seeing their records and not getting any money.

Vinnie Amico: Sony wasn't psyched about it. They had never dealt with anything like us. And they ended up not knowing what to do with us either. They were kind of bummed about the taping, but the whole reason that they signed us in the first place is because we were selling out so many shows because of those tapes. People are trading tapes, they're still gonna buy the records. And they saw that once we sold records.

Eric Krasno: Blue Note wasn't really into it. But they weren't fighting it. Taping helped bands like us expand our audience at that time.

Brian Cohen: We didn't even know we were in a tidal wave. And we were in the middle of the tidal wave, and we had no fucking idea. Remember, this is the early internet. It's everything at the same time and Phish was at the forefront of it. When you realize you were in the middle of the zeitgeist, and that you didn't understand it at all . . . it's interesting and fascinating, but it also makes you feel powerless. I was told in no uncertain terms, "You are fucking this up because those motherfuckers are selling out Madison Square Garden and we cannot get past gold."

Eric Krasno: It was kind of a lost cause to fight it.

Benjy Eisen: The Phish winds were whipping college students like me into a frenzy over a band that the record label couldn't profit from, even though they were in the middle of it.

Nancy Jeffries: It was the subculture. You don't want to inflame the base, and to me it was never what was playing on the radio anyways. So we lost ten sales or something?

Jon Topper: One of the biggest lessons I learned, it was from Paluska, Coran Capshaw, Scott "bullethead" Reilly, and Dave Frey. When we were negotiating our Sony deal, something came up about us doing our live recordings. And I remember that was the first time I ever called any of those guys, I cold-called all of them. And if they didn't pick up the phone, they called me back within minutes. And I was just like, "What did you guys do on your contract for this?" And most of them were just like, "Just let it go. Your fans are going to do what they're gonna do, and you're not going to stop them." And I don't think it ended up in our contract.

Alan Evans: I have discovered so many bands, who eventually you would hook up with and become friends, because someone would hand you a tape at a gig. The tapers would always show up with other tapes that they wanted to share, because they figured you might like this or you should check these guys out. That whole community was really huge in blowing all of us up and bringing us together.

Benjy Eisen: I turned on countless tape trading friends to the Disco Biscuits by adding them as filler on Phish tapes, and I think the first "live" Phish I ever heard was the song "Possum," which some old head put as filler on a Grateful Dead set for me.

Eric Krasno: My thing, more so than anything, was: Yes, get a good recording, but enjoy this show. We're all here together. Let's not focus on your microphones being in the right position.

Buck Williams: The fans really self-policed themselves against bootlegging—meaning selling tapes. They would shut them down . . . the fans would, not us.

Kyle Hollingsworth: We went to Connecticut for the first time ever and thirty-five people showed up because their friends had sent them tapes in the mail.

Buck Williams: The records were selling. We were doing three hundred thousand units, they just weren't getting to the units of gold and a lot of it had to do with tapers—which also expanded our audience. You give and you take.

Benjy Eisen: It was not a failure of the record label . . . it was a misunderstanding of the entire structure of the jam band culture and a gross miscalculation of the consumer's demands. They demanded tickets and access to free recordings of the live shows. No matter how much the band themselves wanted their albums to sell, studio albums just weren't important to most fans. They were for completists or newcomers too green to know that *Hoist* was not the best thing to listen to if you wanted to hear "Wolfman's Brother,"

"Down with Disease," "Julius," "Scent of a Mule." The live versions were simply superior, even when the quality of the recording wasn't.

Reid Genauer: Sure, it was a way of sharing music, but if you were at the show, it was a way of reliving it. The key to all this stuff was it built community.

Marc Brownstein: Labels are such idiots. Haven't we seen the Grateful Dead movie? We've all seen the fucking Grateful Dead movie, we know who wins this battle. The tapers win the battle, the music gets out there, the band becomes gigantic. This conversation was solved by Jerry.

62

Nuggets! Nuggets! Nuggets!

In 1998, Brad Serling, a taper who had been working in the budding tech industry, had an idea to start distributing live shows over the internet. Nugs.net was born. These days Nugs is the Spotify equivalent for the jam band community, where thousands of live shows are available for streaming for a yearly subscription fee—and in a lot of cases, shows that just happened the day before. Here, he discusses the origins of Nugs.

I graduated high school in 1990 and then went on tour with the Dead and started taping. And those were analog tapes. The reason I was taping is so that I would be able to listen to the tape on the drive to the next show. The Grateful Dead taper section was very welcoming, very warm, and willing to bring you under their wing. The six-night run at MSG in September '90, I was wearing a "Steal Your Face" shirt with the Cornell logo in it in the taper section. Some dude yelled out to me after the show: "Hey, you're at Cornell? Are you on the Dead net? It's a thing where we trade tapes. David Gans will be on there talking about shows and people swap tickets." It was the rec.music.dead Usenet group. I was a freshman at school, and it gets gray and cold pretty quick at Cornell . . . it's not like I was out there making a lot of new friends. I was sitting in my dorm room on the Dead net twenty-four seven, trading tapes. So I built up this whole community of friends that were all virtual, who I didn't know, and then I'd go chat with my friends in my dorm, play a tape or whatever, and tell them about all these people I met.

There was this one guy at Cornell, a postdoctoral student who was maybe ten years older than me. He had the greatest tape collection I'd ever seen . . . second- or third-generation cassettes of Fillmore shows from the '70s; a lot of that stuff that's now classic Dick's Picks. I would come back from the Garden with fresh tapes of the shows that just happened, then he would spin me tapes of 2/13/70 that were just unbelievable-sounding recordings. Through that whole process, it made me think there's got to be an easier way to trade tapes. So what really started as Nugs.net was not a business . . . I was looking for a way to more efficiently trade tapes.

I had this flash of inspiration when I did my junior year abroad, '92–'93. I was at King's College London and I would use their computers and it was the fastest internet I could get to. Back then, you could convert audio with what was called uuencode—you would take a digital media file, and it would convert it into ASCII, and you could post it. It was a very primitive way of doing what Nugs.net does now. But I had this flash . . . here I am, sitting in London, the morning after the show that happened in Oakland, California, and I'm listening to a clip of this brand-new Grateful Dead song.

My first real job was working for Adam Curry, who was the big-haired VJ who hosted MTV's *Headbangers Ball*. He was my first boss. And the company was called On Ramp and what we did was we built the first generation of websites in the mid-'90s. I built the NFL's first website, Budweiser.com, I built woodstock.com for Woodstock '94. Through that, I got the number of the Grateful Dead office and called them up and said, "Hey, can I put my tapes on a website?" This was fall of '94. They were like, "What's a website? Do whatever you want, just don't rip us off."

Fast forward, I was flying back from the Great Went and I was looking out the window and thinking of this network of tapers . . . I have a core of friends in New Orleans, in San Francisco, Denver, and New York, where I was still living at the time. And it's like a network of nugs. Of course, I just spent the whole weekend walking up and down the Loring Air Force Base, hearing people say, "Nuggets, nuggets, nuggets!" . . . you know, slinging their nugs. So I thought, "Wow, that's clever. Nugs.net." The Monday after the Great Went, I registered the domain Nugs.net and I put up this homepage that said, "Nothing but Nugs. A site by Heads for Heads."

By summer '98, my DAT deck had been on tour. I did a couple of shows at the beginning of the tour. I didn't do the whole tour, but my tape deck did. By the time I got to the Lemonwheel, I pick up my DAT deck, and I've got a stack of tapes. That was first time for me that I had recordings of every single show of the tour. I immediately transferred those DATs, put them up on Nugs.net, and built this interface that you could scroll left and right and "go on tour" and listen to every show . . . stream it, download if you wanted to. That was really a breakthrough moment.

In 2000, I got a call from the lawyer that represented the Grateful Dead and Phish. He said, "We either need to shut you down or go into business." At that point, we were doing three million downloads a month of free MP3s from my tape collection. I took all the download stats from Nugs.net and I started attaching dollar signs to them, saying this is what it would look like if you just actually let me do this for real. Next thing I know they hired me. My very first day on the job for Grateful Dead, I'm in a meeting with Bob Weir, Mickey Hart, Jeff Ament from Pearl Jam, both bands' archivists, their attorneys, their managers. Sitting and having Heinekens with Bob Weir for a couple hours after that meeting on the first day was pretty impactful to me. The most impactful thing was about maybe a week or two later, when they flew me back up to take a tour of the vault. It was like seeing the Dead Sea Scrolls. The Rosetta Stone. That moment in *Raiders of the Lost Ark* when they take the lid off the ark and everyone's faces melt.

63

Out of Self-Defense, Not Out of Any Real Genius Plan

Keith Moseley: Too many artists get caught in this trap of recording an album for a major label, and then tour and how the band is marketed. A lot of bands ended up dying by that—getting bogged down in the record company process; not being able to put out a second album when and the way they wanted and finding their touring dictated by the record company. We knew early on that we didn't really want to go that route.

Mike Luba (Manager, The String Cheese Incident): I became a booking agent right out of college and it saved me from going to law school. I showed up and they handed me an old-school Rolodex and it was for all the frat house phone numbers in the Southeast. In 1994, it was Dave Matthews, Edwin McCain, Gibb Droll, Hootie and the Blowfish . . . these are bands I couldn't get a gig for a thousand bucks to save any of our lives.

Jeremy Stein (Manager, The String Cheese Incident): I was in Telluride . . . myself and Jesse Aratow. Madison House started in Athens with Mike and Nadia [Prescher], and they were a booking agency only at the time—small bands. Mike and Nadia always had fabulous taste and they picked the right ones. There was a lot coming out of New Orleans at the time, a lot of jam bands, a lot of that scene. And I was running a venue called the Sheridan

Opera House and Jesse was running the door and operations for a bar in town called the Fly Me to the Moon Saloon. We are the two spots for music in Telluride. The ski band in town was this cool string band, The String Cheese Incident. There was a show at a place called the One World in Telluride—New Year's '93. I said, "Hey guys, let's do a show. We're doing Fat Tuesday—like the New Orleans Fat Tuesday—at the Opera House. And that was a big step up for them out of the bar into the Opera House.

Mike Luba: I moved to Athens, Georgia, in 1996 and we started Madison House.

Jeremy Stein: We teamed up to start doing more and more shows with them there.

Mike Luba: The way I have it in my head was that Keller Williams had sent me a cassette of the String Cheese guys' first time at Telluride Bluegrass, which must have been '95. They used to do a bluegrass version of "Walk This Way" by Aerosmith and you can hear ten thousand people gasping in horror. And I was like, "Wow, I can help these guys." And I booked their first gigs east of Colorado in '96.

Keller Williams: The Grateful Dead tour that I was accustomed to . . . I did many shows from '87 to '95. By '97, when I started with String Cheese, all that just kind of came back to me in that way. The parking lot scene, the smells, the styles, the beautiful people singing along, the dancing, the vibe. And you could definitely feel the scene happening, especially in the winter of '96, when I got to open for them at the Fox.

Jeremy Stein: We were the first ones to say, "Hey, here's eight shows around Colorado—Aspen, Telluride, Durango." That hit a peak where we had the first late-night shows ever for Telluride Bluegrass Festival at a place called the Quonset Hut in Telluride. It was a gym with a stage in it. And somehow they let us run late-night concerts in there—we got the idea of late-night concerts from Jazz Fest.

It turned into the first sold-out show that was over a thousand people for

The String Cheese Incident. That was a tipping point for the band. And a funny thing in the Quonset Hut . . . it was also a roller-skating rink for kids. And so there's like four hundred pairs of roller skates backstage and everyone runs in there, steals all the things, and starts skating around. It was just a madhouse. Right after that was when I started talking with Mike and Nadia more and said we gotta team up. And the band said we can't just live in Telluride . . . it's too hard to tour from here. We brought everything to Boulder.

Bill Nershi: We started talking to Luba and Nadia, and ultimately asked them if they would take over management.

Kevin Morris (Founder, SCI Fidelity Records): I was a big jam band fan . . . into the Dead a lot, Phish a lot. A friend of mine, who I used to go to shows with a lot in the '90s, had told me about String Cheese and I started to get tapes and listen to them. One day, I was at South by Southwest, and I'm walking down Sixth Street going back to my hotel, and it's very late. And I walked by a venue and see people in the street who are hula-hooping. I walked in, I went to the merch table, and was like, "This is String Cheese, right?" When they were finished, I went up to them afterwards. Gave Kyle my business card. I said, "Hey, if you ever need a lawyer, you know, I'd love to work with you." I was in law school. I would go to the Bayou a lot, in Washington, DC. My uncle was managing Big Head Todd and the Monsters and then Leftover Salmon. Fast forward to December and Jim Lewi started the Aspen Artist Development Conference. My boss was like, "Hey, do you want to go to the Aspen Music Conference?" I didn't know anyone. So I fly there. Everyone would ski during the day and then at night you would have the conference and shows. We're sitting in the hotel lobby, while everyone else is out skiing the first day, and then all of a sudden, this guy walks in and my uncle sees him and goes, "Do you know Mike Luba?"

"No, I don't think so."

"He manages this band The String Cheese Incident."

I went back to Nashville and then I started to hit up Luba about representing the band. At one point I sent him a fax and said, "Dear Mike, I'd love to represent the band, this is my last effort." And then he immediately called me and said yes. I became the band's lawyer at that point.

Keith Moseley: We were talking to as many other bands as we could—new, up-and-coming bands—about their record deals and what worked and what didn't work.

Mike Luba: We took a bunch of meetings.

Keith Moseley: We'd already been slogging it out on the road, trying to build a fan base.

Mike Luba: One day, Donnie Ienner, who at that point must have been the president of Columbia Records, flew out to meet us. He was a genius and did incredible stuff. But the band kind of looked at us and was like, "We'd rather be poor and broke for the rest of our lives and never have to deal with shit like that."

Bill Nershi: I remember having a conversation with Butch Trucks from the Allman Brothers about record labels. Nobody had anything very good to say about how they can help their career. So we started thinking twice about that.

Kyle Hollingsworth: Capricorn came to us and at that point, as goals were concerned, it was to keep everything in-house.

Michael Kang: We're getting approached by labels, looking at deals, and we realized, "Oh, we've done everything ourselves up to this point, what would be the benefit?"

Kyle Hollingsworth: We knew that we weren't necessarily going to be commercially viable.

Keith Moseley: We had a couple of offers and we decided to start our own label. We probably weren't going to see the income that we might have seen from another label, but we had the feeling that the most important thing would be to control our own creative destiny.

Michael Kang: I don't think any of us really looked at it and went, "Oh, wow, we kind of made a mistake by not going with somebody."

Keith Moseley: Maybe we would have sold more records if we'd gone with a major label. It's hard to know. But certainly the idea of maintaining creative control was at the forefront of the decision.

Michael Kang: Having some A&R person telling you that they do or don't like your music or don't like the album, giving you an advance, which at the time might seem like a lot of money, but at the end of the day, they're recouping it anyway . . . it was a total no-brainer for us to do our own thing.

Mike Luba: moe. signed to Sony and I think we were all kind of jealous of that. And then they had such a terrible time, we were like, "Thank God, we managed to dodge that bullet."

Jeremy Stein: A lot of these acts shied away from that kind of situation, because there wasn't true support. It was support if you had a hit, but there wasn't support to get you there.

Bill Nershi: I think we were starting already to realize it was becoming a thing of the past.

Mike Luba: I think we knew, at least in the String Cheese world, that we had no chance. So we were just going to just do it ourselves. I don't know if it was a depressive "We had no chance," but we just didn't, I really knew that. What we were going to do was not really meant for that kind of thing.

Michael Kang: We launched our own label right when the music industry really took a turn. It's hard to say whether or not it was a good thing or a bad thing.

Mike Luba: We realized that anytime we farmed anything out to a third party, it would get fucked up. So we might as well just fuck it up ourselves. That's how it turned into the label and a travel agency and the ticketing company and the graphic design part of it. We basically took everything in-house just out of self-defense, not out of any real genius plan.

Jeremy Stein: Triple A radio . . . that's the format that any of the jam bands could get into, because it was kind of an Americana mix of rock and roll, a singer-songwriter kind of thing. The AAA summit every year was at the Fox Theatre in Boulder. During the summit, we'd put the new jam bands and New Orleans bands in there, and then wow, look at that—they're getting played on the radio suddenly. There are all these alternative ways to make it happen that it used to be just the labels could do.

Mike Luba: Each time we ran into someone who knew how to do something. We ran into Lisa Pomerantz, who ran Madison House travel, because she wanted to be a travel agency. All of a sudden, we had a travel agency. Kevin Morris was an entertainment lawyer at that point and hated being a lawyer but knew a lot about how labels work. So, he started SCI Fidelity Records. And then when the String Cheese guys were all going to gather in Boulder, we all moved to Boulder together.

Jeremy Stein: Without knowing it, we were innovators at the time of what became called the "360 deal" in the industry. We were just doing what we thought was right. And so we ended up starting seven or eight companies. We had Madison House Travel Agency for fans, we had String Cheese Incident merchandise, we had the first online ticketing. You couldn't even order it online, you could just say I want to order and then you had to call with your credit card. We had our own record company. We had management. We had our own design firm that was designing websites and stuff and creating emails. We created this suite of companies that could surround a band: "Here's eight of the things that everyone needs." You can pick all eight of them or you could pick two of them, it's up to you. I don't know if we had a person over thirty years old at the time.

Mike Luba: There was no separation between work and life.

In May 1998, The String Cheese Incident staged their first shows abroad in Negril, Jamaica. These shows would be a precursor to the modern destination festivals.

Kyle Hollingsworth: It kind of came together fairly quickly.

Jeremy Stein: We were calling that "The International Incident."

Kyle Hollingsworth: Seventy-five people showed up . . . we saw them on a plane. We played out on the beach and stayed in a little compound with broken glass at the top of the wall so no one jumped over.

Jeremy Stein: It brought the core community together in a way nothing else did. You spend time with everyone for a week, on the beach, and there's huge deep memories. It enriches the fan base and the connection.

Bill Nershi: That was the fateful weekend we visited Miss Brown's tea house.

Jeremy Stein: Miss Brown was around for a long time, at that point—decades.

Bill Nershi: They make mushroom tea. And you can just go in and give her a couple of jays and they'll give you a cup of hot mushroom tea. All these Jamaican dudes were out front playing dominoes, slamming dominoes on the tables. Me and these other whiteys walked in and went to the back.

Jeremy Stein: Eventually, up comes Miss Brown, and she's an older lady at the time.

"What you boys want?"

"With all respect, we're here to see you. We've heard many stories and we're musicians."

"I've three options for you. You can get small, medium, or whammo."

"If we don't order whammo, are you gonna be mad at us?"

"Your choice, gentlemen."

"Alright, whammo."

After that, we went into a very long night.

Bill Nershi: Of course we said we want the strong. We just got really high on the beach that night and were listening to the local reggae bands playing, up and down the strip there.

Jeremy Stein: The first show, to be honest, was kind of a technological travesty.

Jon O'Leary: The gear was just horrible. Barely anything worked. It's all great, except for, you know, the stuff that is in Negril is the stuff that you can't do anything about.

Jeremy Stein: They're advertising String Cheese Incident Band—that's what it said on the sign there. And we get out there, day of the show, and there's a rickety stage, no PA, no gear. And somehow, we ran all over the town in Negril finding every piece of gear we could to put together a concert. Because the guy there who promised us everything, you know, had nothing.

Kyle Hollingsworth: We were definitely tripping out a lot of the locals. They were very open to it. When we left, two weeks later, there was a huge riot in the town.

64

You're Too Crazy to Be the Headliner

Joel Cummins: By the mid-'90s, festivals started happening that were featuring this music. There weren't many big music festivals that were happening, like the Bonnaroos or the Coachellas of today. So once those started popping up, there was this big summer scene that was happening along with it.

Andy Bernstein: You had a circuit.

Jon "The Barber" Gutwillig: Then it was still the wild Wild West. You could put up a stage in the middle of a field, park people in the cars in the middle of the field, throw up a couple porta potties and go. And people did that. Somebody ran power to a wagon. Like an old rickety-ass wooden-wheeled wagon with hay on it . . . they put the drums up there and a pair of speakers. We played a show called the Woodser which was like a sorority party, where guys went to hook up with chicks.

Jon Topper: High Sierra Music Festival . . . I would say it's a five rites of passage in the '90s for a jam band.

Kyle Hollingsworth: The early festivals, like High Sierra Festival, would be like, "Oh, go to this big barn . . . when you finish watching your favorite jam band, and you're still high on LSD, go into the barn and we'll shut the door, and this guy's gonna play music."

Dave Watts: High Sierra would do different workshops where the bands would show how they build a song, that sort of thing. They were doing a workshop and there was a Q&A at the end . . . it was a poolside workshop and everyone's just kind of lounging around the pool and they're like, "Will you guys go skinny dipping with us?" String Cheese just took off all their clothes and jumped in the water.

Kyle Hollingsworth: High Sierra would get these cargo vans, and you could sneak in your friends. After our show, instead of putting on our gear in it, we put like forty people in it. You'd go to the back row and you open it up and everybody would run in.

David Phipps: High Sierra Music Festival was like, "Here's an offer in California. Do you guys want to take?" We had to figure out small shows across the country . . . High Sierra really pulled us out of Georgia.

Drew Emmitt: We saw the potential for getting out of state and actually starting to really make a good living doing this. And the more we did, the more festivals were interested in hiring us.

Hunter Brown: That was the halcyon days, where before ultra-corporatization of the mass of the festivals came to be a thing. We would go to these festivals, and they felt incredibly authentic, and regional. And you might be from all over the country or even the world, but you're into these kinds of things. You had people from those towns, selling the things they make.

Reid Genauer: We held an annual festival, and people would come and camp for three days. And that's how the community really felt itself.

Jon "The Barber" Gutwillig: The origin of Camp Bisco was we were playing all these music festivals and they wouldn't let us headline.

Aron Magner: It was not my idea. I was more of "show me where to set up the keyboard."

Jon "The Barber" Gutwillig: We would be playing the 2:30 a.m. tent, most likely, and we were the biggest band on the festival by far. We would get relegated to this set that we didn't think we deserved. We were playing all the other cities and knew how big everybody else was. We literally were playing bigger rooms and doing better numbers than the other bands that were getting the cherry spots.

Aron Magner: It never really felt like we had the ability to demonstrate what we were able to.

Jon "The Barber" Gutwillig: We would have arguments with the promoters.

"We are the biggest band at your festival. We want to be the headliner."

"You're too crazy to be the headliner. Your music is too nuts to be the headliner, you guys are a 2:30 a.m. band, you always will be."

We took it personally. And we're like, "Okay, well, why don't we play our own festivals."

Aron Magner: The first Camp Bisco, it was the first time that we were seeing the effects of carving out our own path.

Sam Altman: It was a lot of Marc and Jon pushing that kind of stuff.

Zach Velmer: It was as crucial as crucial gets to our scene—the festivals. It brought these likeminded people together to celebrate live. And it was exponential.

65

We Were Nowhere Near There When the Shit Hit the Fan

Woodstock '99 featured mega-acts like Metallica, Limp Bizkit, Red Hot Chili Peppers, and Kid Rock. The first two days, Thursday, July 22 and Friday, July 23, 1999, jam bands moe., Strangefolk, and The String Cheese Incident played too.

Jim Loughlin: It was unbelievably surreal.

Reid Genauer: Woodstock was like, "Let's take a brand name, market it, and make a lot of money."

Ken "Skip" Richman: When we originally showed up at Woodstock '99, we were all very excited. We were psyched to play, psyched to be part of it. We get to spend the whole weekend there camping, all the bands we get to see. So we got there and the first thing they do is hand you out your all-access passes. And what they say to you is, "Make sure you don't wear these out in public. People may rip them off your necks." And I was like, "Alright, that's not a good sign."

Reid Genauer: It was kinda like Altamont. It didn't feel good.

Jim Loughlin: There was an unreal disconnect between the bands and the general public.

Steve Young: I remember walking into that and getting the mix together. The first song was cool, where I wanted it. And I'm looking around and I'm like, "Oh, wow, there's a lot of people here. This is a big show." And then I turned around and saw all the people behind the front-of-house tower. I'm like, "Oh, shit, it goes on forever!"

Ken "Skip" Richman: We were backstage in the morning, eating lunch and getting ready for our set and whatever else. You could just feel this is the first day of the festival . . . you can feel the tension in the air. It was not a comfortable place to be. So we went and we did our set. The way it was set up was there were two stages: a main stage and a second stage. And they were across from each other; you could hear the music from each other. There probably was seventy-five thousand people watching our set and probably two hundred thousand people watching James Brown perform. But you couldn't tell that it wasn't one crowd.

Kyle Hollingsworth: It was a Thursday night pre-party. We're playing goofy calypso white-boy Boulder pseudo-Latin music. "Hey, we're these guys, we go skiing!" People were like, "Show us your tits!" with girls on their shoulders.

Reid Genauer: We were fish out of water. We weren't going to make fans at that place—it was a shit show.

Vinnie Amico: They cut so many corners . . . the infrastructure was soft . . . charging too much for water, and food. And then the security they hired didn't do anything. So they had no control.

Jim Loughlin: The artists' compound, where it was located and how it was set up, was so removed from the general populace, that there was no way that any of those bands had any idea what was happening out in the crowds.

Vinnie Amico: There's Insane Clown Posse on one side of us and Sheryl Crow on the other.

Jim Walsh: Insane Clown Posse was running around on these little motorized scooters.

Jim Loughlin: We're next to Insane Clown Posse. We watch them show up in two tour buses, full security entourage, all their props, they have wrestling masks on. They go into their trailer, they come back out, and they're all face-painted. But all their guys are wearing black denim and Timberlands. I'm like, "These guys are dying. They better have fifteen cases of water back there or people are gonna start to drop."

Steve Young: Our trailer was right next to their trailer and there was something wrong with their gray water. It wasn't sewage, it was gray water and just leaking out of the trailer. So there was like this whole swampy area of gray water that smelled. ICP was in the trailer next to us and they just came out and they had all their pomp and circumstance. Our friend Shelley comes running right out of our trailer and just kind of jumps down on the ground and sprays them with gray water.

Jim Loughlin: And then Parliament shows up. Parliament is marching through the whole backstage and George Clinton is wearing a monk robe with the hood pulled up. And he's sneaking all around, the whole time—walking behind all the trailers.

Ken "Skip" Richman: After we did our set, and we came back, I looked at everybody and I'm like, "Man, I don't know about you guys, but I want to get the hell out of here." And everyone agreed. We went back to Al's house and camped in Al's backyard and watched the fires start.

Jim Loughlin: As we're walking to the lot where our car was parked, there's a bunch of kids and they're diving and sliding through all these mud puddles. And I'm thinking, "It hasn't rained in several days." And I started looking around, and they're at the bottom of a hill, and the top of the hill is a whole bunch of porta-johns.

Luke Smith: We were nowhere near there when the shit hit the fan.

66

Us Against the World

Dave Frey: I got a call from New Orleans police. They needed a living relative of Bob Sheehan's to call them at once. I knew what that meant. So I had to call Bobby's mom and tell her. She called the police. He was dead. And she called me back. And I had to call everybody and tell them that he had died.

Grant Cowell: As soon as that happened, I got a phone call from his mother: Can I quickly fly down there and take care of things?

Chan Kinchla: I was at a family reunion in Maryland on the Chesapeake Bay. Just a happy little family reunion. I kind of ruined it.

Cree McCree: Early in the morning of my birthday on August 20, 1999, the phone rang at my apartment in New York City. It was Jimmy MacDonell, the Louisiana-born leader of the New York zydeco band Loup Garou. But he wasn't calling to wish me happy birthday. He was calling to tell me Bobby Sheehan had just been found dead of an overdose at his home in New Orleans, where we were about to become neighbors when I moved there the following year.

Brendan Hill: It hit me so hard. I was driving back from Whistler and we were waiting in line to go back through the border; it was like two hours, a slow stop and start. And we'd already been there an hour when I got a call from Dave Frey.

He said, "You know, I've got some really bad news for you. What are you doing? Are you safe?"

I said, "Yeah, I'm in my truck."

"Bobby was found dead this morning, in Louisiana, in his house."

I pulled the truck over, and my wife and I were both crying. It was just like a bubble had burst. This thing that we created—it felt like us against the world—and all of a sudden, it just popped. All of a sudden reality took place.

Chan Kinchla: We just decided to take a year off . . . well, semi-off. And that's when Bobby happened to pass away. We were burnt out, but there were no huge tumultuous cracks in the foundations of the band.

John Popper: I think there was certainly some excess. But really, we spent that time working. In our mind, playing was not just a living, it was a reason to do things. We enjoyed the playing so much that it was a perfect storm of suddenly now we had way more gigs than we could possibly do, and a lot more money. We played and played, and we never really got lives. I think half of us got lives. Brendan and Chan both got married and got pregnant almost at the exact same time. It actually kind of fucked up a tour.

I was getting into Bulls games and hanging out with Dennis Rodman. And it was fun. But I was pretty solitary. Bobby was having fun with his friends. And they were pretty solitary. I was just gaining weight, because that was my drug of choice. And Bobby was doing other drugs. We had each other as codependents: "I might be shitty, but look at you."

Grant Cowell: When he started living down in New Orleans, I was very leery of it. We had some good long conversations about being down there and the people he was hanging out with. I didn't like them. I thought they were hangers-on.

Chan Kinchla: We'd have friends come backstage and bring stuff if we wanted. We also would just get a big amount [of drugs] in New York before we left. Me and Bobby were the worst. The worst partiers. There was always pot around. It always strikes me as interesting when people are like, "People were forcing it on you." It's like no, we made sure that we had what we wanted. Me and Bobby rode hard for a while.

John Popper: I knew that if I didn't stop touring, if I didn't do something for me, that wasn't for the band, I felt like I was going to die. I had a real feeling that if I stopped touring, Bobby was going to die.

And when you're confronted with that, what you ultimately come to—the conclusion that you have to make is choose yourself. And I did. And I made my solo album *Zygote* and ten days before it got released, Bobby died. And before that happened, I had to go to the hospital because I was having chest pains, and I was 436 pounds. The doctor said, "Yeah, you're 95 percent blocked, you're going to die if you don't get into a bed now."

Chan Kinchla: John's health was really bad, because of his weight. I got married and had a kid, so I kind of veered off. Bob moved to New Orleans, which was not maybe the safest place for somebody who liked to party to move. Drugs and alcohol are dangerous, as we all know—but we were partying our ass off in sophomore year of high school.

John Popper: The band came to me to have an intervention. They all came to me and said, "John, we're really worried about Bobby." And he wasn't there. He was two hours late for my intervention. He showed up after everybody and he looked blue. I mean, physically blue. And he was like, "Dude, you gotta get your life together." And that was the last time I saw him alive.

Cree McCree: The last time I saw Bobby he'd gone full New Orleans native at a neighborhood second line, where I'd run into him by chance a few days after he'd given me a tour of the mini-mansion he was fixing up right off St. Charles Avenue, just a few blocks from where I ended up living. We'd stayed up late talking about the spirits that haunt a lot of the old houses.

Brendan Hill: The next three or four months, we went to Bobby's wake, his funeral, and his memorial. I had this newborn, and I didn't know how I was going to make money. But it's also the loss of a brother that I knew from the age of seventeen. Sure, it was twelve years. But it was a long twelve years. It was cutting our teeth, the ups, the downs, John's accident, fights, record deals, good times, bad times, everything. It's never been the same since then—that kind of rosy-eyed vision of a world that we had back then.

Cree McCree: The church where we gathered to celebrate his spirit was full to overflowing. My most vivid memory of the day was Jono Manson making his way up front with his acoustic to sing one of the few songs Bobby ever wrote: "The Mountains Win Again."

John Popper: Bobby and I were so ready to die when we were young. We were making no plans about what we were going to do with ourselves. We were thinking, we have one mission: to succeed at this.

I remember those days following his death, I was looking at my Jimi Hendrix poster. This is another guy who died young. That's when I just started being very aware of the grace. The real act of courage is surviving. Then you have to compromise, you have to actually live in the world. And that's what most people do. Bobby and I needed to learn that, and at the end of the day, he couldn't break loose of that.

Brendan Hill: I still have dreams about Bob, usually right before we go on tour. We're about to go on stage at a big shell. My drum set isn't quite set up properly. The other dream is walking up, and then Bob will be walking up, and then Tad [Kinchla, current bassist] will be walking behind him. And Bob's putting his face on.

John Popper: There was always this structure to keep us in place. And so we looked for bass players within a month. And Chan's brother really was the best option. I really wanted to get Oteil but he was just starting out with the Allman Brothers.

Dave Frey: Bob was kind of the heart of the band. He was the one guy who could stand up to John. John's thing was to win: It doesn't matter if he was right or wrong. Winning is the mission. He's also going to fight every single battle. So that was a massive change in the band dynamically, for me—to not have him there politically. And that led to me quitting.

Brendan Hill: Every day I wish that he was still with us and this musical thing that we did together, he could have experienced it longer. When you think about long summers that never seem to end . . . you go to the pool or go to the beach with your friends. It was only three months of the year, but it felt like this eternity and that everything was good. That was how the '90s were up until Bob's passing.

67

Stranglefuck

Reid Genauer: It's very difficult. It takes work. It's hard enough to keep that together with one individual, let alone a group of men. The example I always use . . . it's so crude, but it's true: Someone would fart, and you'd know who it was by the smell of the fart because everybody had a unique flavor. That's how well we knew each other. Do you want to really know, or be able to identify people, by the scent of their gas? No.

Sam Ankerson: The first album of new material that Strangefolk did with Mammoth was produced by Nile Rodgers. That came about as sort of crazy set of circumstances engineered by Pete Shapiro.

Luke Smith: Pete, god bless him, brought in Nile.

Sam Ankerson: The label was happy to pay for Nile Rodgers . . . maybe in some other situations, it would raise some eyebrows because he wasn't cheap. But they went all in on it.

Reid Genauer: There was some pedestrian stuff that I think we could have done a lot better handling. Many musicians don't come from playing team sports. We didn't do that. We were in our basements, geeking out on *Spinal Tap* and playing guitar.

Luke Smith: Nile was like, "You guys are gonna be huge." He was giving us numbers. At the time, he had sold like two hundred million records and he was like, "You guys are gonna sell a million records in the first ten days, and you're gonna sell another two million in the next thirty days. I'm gonna give this to my friends who are DJs in London and Paris, and they're going to chop it all up before we even release it. We're gonna have dance tracks." He was really telling us that it was all just about to happen.

Jon Trafton: It was stressful.

Reid Genauer: Internally, we called ourselves Stranglefuck.

Luke Smith: I knew to some degree that Reid was unhappy, I had no idea that he was going to leave.

Reid Genauer: I was kind of shot.

Luke Smith: Working with Nile, I think it just became kind of crazy. I know that for Reid, part of the heartbreak was that Nile really saw us as a band, which for me, was always the deal. The alchemy of Strangefolk was always in the four of us. No one of us carried all of it. I don't mean that as a diss to Reid, but I think he had just a different vision of himself as a frontman, and that Nile really saw us as a band. He was interested in hearing everybody's songs and everybody was gonna get even representation for songs. That was a big disappointment for Reid. If I had known that was how it was gonna go down, and that was gonna drive Reid to leave the band, I would have been like, "Fine, let's give Reid more songs." Reid quitting the band at that time remains one of the greatest heartbreaks in my life.

Jon Trafton: By '99, it was clear he was headed for the exit door. It felt like we had our arc—you know, beginning, middle, and end.

Reid Genauer: Part of what made us work, like the Rolling Stones, was the tension. I never felt deep friendship. I felt a lot of competition, I felt a lot of unnecessary angst. And it's really hard to be out there, feeling at war with people you're living that closely with. It wasn't like we were always like that, but as things got bigger, egos flare, there's revisionist history.

Brett Fairbrother: The end of my Strangefolk story was finishing up the record with Nile Rodgers.

Andre Gardner: I stopped in 2000 . . . I think it was the end of '99. Reid was about to take off.

Reid Genauer: I don't feel like history really painted us accurately. There was a lot that was working for us and there was stuff that wasn't. And the conversations that I remember acutely was trying to raise the issues of what wasn't working. And nobody wanted to engage in it. Look, it's hard to be in a relationship with one person . . . doing that in multiple ways, with multiple personalities . . . if I were to summarize, and I would include myself, we just didn't have the maturity to attack the parts of us that were unhealthy. Nobody could quite say why, and I'm not sure I could today, except that there were unhealthy dynamics, and activities, that were stifling us creatively.

Jon Trafton: We all had been working so hard, and we'd gotten so far. I felt like we fell apart on our first speed bump, instead of just weathering it. You're going to go through a lot of rejection and some moments of adulation . . . you just have to believe in what you're doing. And I felt like we got knocked off that course.

Brett Fairbrother: Young guys, egos grinding, you're not putting a bunch of W's on the board all the time. And sometimes certain L's are harder to take than others.

Reid Genauer: I have lots of critiques of Strangefolk's music, our interpersonal actions. But, man, I will tell you—all four of us poured ourselves in.

68

That's the Moment and That's Where It Lives

John Popper: There was a feeling in our little scene where we felt musically superior to a lot of the music that was out there at the time. We knew more and we were capable of more than most people even wanted us to do.

Aaron Comess: We were all these self-made machines.

Dave Matthews: There was a scene, and we were kind of against what was viewed as the legitimate rock music of the time. "Jam band" was pejorative, you know? It was never "the critically acclaimed jam band." We were dismissed. But that also made what we were doing feel like a response to something and that made it exciting.

John Medeski: "Jam band" was created by the audience.

Eric Schenkman: Human success is a funny thing. When you get really successful, fast, it's a lot to handle. Very few people make all the decisions correctly in life.

Chan Kinchla: Everyone was free to develop in their own local scene in their own way. Everyone came up with really unique shit because they weren't listening to what anyone else was doing.

Al Schnier: The end of the '90s was a little bit strange. Because that was our coming of age into the digital age and not everybody was on board yet. Not everybody was tethered to a phone. Not everybody had internet in their homes.

Benjy Eisen: It wasn't reaching that commercial peak that I think a lot of people in the industry had hoped for, because they invested in it.

John Bell: Attendance was great. We were still hoping for over-the-top record sales and radio play, but then we weren't playing some of the games that you needed to play. Our touring was cooking. That was all going into Widespread Panic's bank account. We weren't dependent on the record company.

Dave Schools: We had a deal with Sanctuary Records. It was a moderate deal . . . I think it was a 50/50 deal. And it worked out great for us. We could go record records whenever we wanted to. They weren't like, "You guys were late with your product." I don't think there was any talk about extending with Capricorn, and Sanctuary really wanted us. We didn't necessarily need a record company to pay for our studio efforts. We never gave away our merchandising rights. Out of necessity, we learned to do things our own way.

Buck Williams: Capricorn could have kept us, but I heard that they were going to sell out and they did.

When the turn of the millennium came, Y2K was on everybody's mind, yet the show was still going to go on. Widespread Panic booked the Philips Arena in Atlanta, while Phish threw the Big Cypress festival, the biggest New Year's concert on Earth, in the swampy Everglades of Florida. They would play from midnight to sunrise, around seven straight hours.

Mary Dugas: There were all sorts of rumors going around about what different precautions bands were taking at these big venues for Y2K. People's imaginations kind of went crazy.

Al Schnier: It was becoming widespread that something was going to go incredibly wrong once we flipped over the calendar. The banks and utilities would fail and it would become chaos.

Dave Schools: I think we sold out three nights at Philips Arena in Atlanta in minutes.

Mary Dugas: That's when Dottie Peoples was with us. It's the only time I've ever cried. The music made me cry. What Dottie did with "All Time Low," and the band, was chilling.

Andy Gadiel: Phish had talked about doing a "long gig" and just playing until people left.

Trey Anastasio: I was like "New Year's Eve, 1999, we got to play outside, all night."

"Dude, it's not possible."

That was the first reaction.

"It's gonna snow, and you're doomed. And you put so much money into these things—you have to build the venue. You're so in debt and your career is gonna be over on January 1. You cannot do this."

"It's the millennium, planes are gonna fall out of the sky, there's gonna be no money. So let's just play all night long."

The first place we started looking was Hawaii. It was gonna be called the Big Kahuna. And we looked, and John held all these airplanes, whole airplanes and then found out, for one reason or another, this is completely impossible. It'll never work. We were in an airport and I wouldn't let this idea go. We're in this airport, and Jon Fishman is sitting there reading this book, and it's called *Abandon Ship*.

And I'm looking at, and I say, "Oh my God."

And he's like, "What?"

I go, "A Band on Ship. Let's do it on a cruise ship, and we'll call it 'A Band on Ship!' " And then I called John, and he started holding cruise ships for A Band on Ship. Well, that didn't happen, because then we ended up finding Big Cypress.

Brad Sands: Big Cypress was sort of the granddaddy of them all. The challenge was we were out of our comfort zone in the Northeast. We were on a reservation. But the band always rose to the occasion. I remember thinking, "How are they going to play all night? That's crazy. People are going to get bored." It was some of the greatest music I've ever seen.

Rob Mitchum: Big Cypress felt like if you were a Phish fan, you had to go—mandatory attendance. We were completely cut off from the world.

Steve "The Dude of Life" Pollak: Traditional police weren't allowed there. And it just enabled everyone to have a really fun time without being bothered.

Andy Gadiel: There was just a revelry in going somewhere remote and embracing that notion: Well, if the world's gonna end, where would you want to be?

Rob Mitchum: I was in traffic for ten hours in the Everglades. Every festival got bigger and bigger, and they almost started to become routine.

Brad Sands: It was about experience with all those people. You're all there for one thing, you're all staying up . . . it was a journey, and you're on the journey with all those people.

Steve "The Dude of Life" Pollak: I stayed up for 90 percent of it. I think I dozed off a couple of times, but then I woke up.

Benjy Eisen: It was a marathon. But then, when we realized the sun was coming up, and we're in the end of it, there was a triumphant joy. You felt bonded with everybody.

Brad Sands: I have a photo in my office of that moment when they came off stage . . . the four of them and myself. My natural reaction was, "Are you guys going to do an encore?" to tell the crew. And they kind of looked at me like, "Are you fucking kidding me?" Backstage, it looked like a bomb had gone off . . . it was fucking trashed. The band left right away. There was a treasure trove of items backstage . . . nitrous tanks and champagne and all this stuff. And you could just see the scavengers out there gathering everything and putting it in their cars.

Rob Mitchum: The band had nowhere else to go after that. Big Cypress was a huge success, but also the thing that probably caused the hiatus [after October 2000]. I don't think they knew how to top it, and they had spent the whole decade trying to top themselves.

Andy Gadiel: When the sun came up, it was like a wave of awe that permeated through the crowd. The moment was real . . . we survived to the next millennium.

Brad Sands: I always felt like, and I think the band might have felt this way, that's when we should have taken the first hiatus. But we had a new record and all that.

Trey Anastasio: I'll never forget it. I don't think I've ever listened to it. I don't even want to listen to it.

Dean Budnick: They weren't quite sure how to reorient. So that's why they took the first hiatus.

Trey Anastasio: We made it over the finish line . . . that first finish line, and then we had some good shows, but it was cracking at the seams all over the place. Obviously, there was the tempo and the pace and then also the partying that went along with it. I still can't figure it out. I've been sober for almost eighteen years, and I still can't figure out which came first, the chicken or the egg. I don't know if all the drug use was a solution or the problem. It was the problem. But I don't know what the exhaustion and the confusion and the self-doubt and the fraud complex, or whatever the heck it was at the time came before it, and it was the off switch.

There was an internet, but it certainly wasn't in everyone's pocket yet, before Big Cypress. It was getting darn close to a whole different world of interconnectedness, and, you know, access to criticism and judgmental talk.

But still, it was the last vapors of being somewhere that you actually really were when we all went down there.

But for many others, the end of the '90s was a culmination of a long decade on the road and finding a very enthusiastic, almost insatiable audience.

Chris Wood: Literally the end of the '90s, with Y2K, we're back in Hawaii. We figured, well, if all the planes fall out of the sky, like they said they might, I guess we'll just be stuck in Hawaii. Back at the Shack.

John Medeski: This band was really a democracy. And democracy is difficult . . . it requires patience.

Billy Martin: Suffering is learning.

Chris Wood: The way that success messed with us was a tension where we were on stage thinking we're doing this one thing and yet we have this audience out there seeing us in a completely different way. And being very aware that we could easily make some musical choices that the audience wanted, that would appease them. I think there was a certain side of us that was attracting all the people. If we kept the balance between the more accessible part of what we did, with the more challenging part about what we did, then there was the appropriate tension and release that kept people coming.

John Medeski: We could have very easily just done an obvious move.

Chris Wood: We could have so easily appeased and become much bigger, I believe. I mean, we had the ability to play into that. We couldn't help but be so self-conscious about the fact that they wanted mostly this part of us, and being the sort of contrary and young punks that we were, we couldn't help but rebel against that a little bit. It just felt like if we go with that, and we're not being true to ourselves, then we're just doing what we need to do to be even bigger and more successful, instead of making the music the priority and keep pushing the envelope. We wanted to keep experimenting. So that created a challenging tension between us and the audience, and even within the band. It was hard to reconcile that. I talked to Bruce Hornsby about this, because he did the same thing. He had his huge hit and that's all anybody wanted to hear. And he did not want to have his whole career be all about that. So he purposely got weirder and weirder, for lack of a better way to say it . . . he didn't do what people wanted him to do. And he purposefully alienated his audience so that he at least felt like he was in control of his own destiny. And I feel like we kind of did our own little version of that. Our records started to become more and more challenging.

Rob Derhak: By the time 2000 rolled around, we were still hitting the road really hard. From 1993 to 2000, we were playing almost every single day of our lives, either practicing or playing a gig or driving somewhere. We were doing three hundred shows a year at one point.

Ken "Skip" Richman: We were on the road 280 days a year at least, doing hundreds of shows, drinking a lot, smoking cigarettes, not eating well. I'm pretty sure I came home from every tour and would crash on someone's couch and I'd be sick for a week.

Brad Sands: When you're working on the road, and especially in that scene, when you're out there, and you're in that little world, you're somebody. You're the most important person in this city of a hundred thousand. And then you come home, you have to fit back into normal life.

Trey Anastasio: We were either on the cusp or actually living the role of the character in Allen Toussaint's song "On Your Way Down." I felt like round one crashed into the wall. It's really weird. I've never said that out loud before, but it's true in my heart.

Al Schnier: Things were going well for us. We just needed to focus our energy or decide what it was we wanted to do.

Al Marks: *Straight on till Morning* was a difficult record for us because it didn't have anything on it that really stuck out that radio wanted to get behind and push. We had to go back to marketing the way we originally did with them, which was through in-stores, press, and doing retail marketing campaigns. We spent quite a bit of money on that record. I think it went gold, but I don't think it went platinum. We weren't getting airplay, we couldn't get radio guys to come out to the shows.

Chan Kinchla: By 1998, we were just burnt out . . . it literally had been five to seven years of just nonstop.

Reid Genauer: It felt like the passion had been pounded out of me.

Al Marks: After '99, when we got sold to MCA, I left after that. The A&M artists that went on to Interscope really never got worked: Suzanne Vega, Sheryl Crow, maybe Blues Traveler had one Interscope record. It basically all fell apart. That was the heyday of jam bands. They really were just everywhere.

Marc Brownstein: We got into a fight on tour in October of '99. We were like, "Get to the end of the tour, play the New Year's show, and be done." In the six months that I was out of the band, I wrote fifteen songs, and they wrote fifteen songs. So when we got back together in July of 2000 we had like thirty-something new songs. It just took off from there.

Dave Frey: I was exhausted. We were working on next year's H.O.R.D.E. before the one we were on was over. So that was an endless cycle. Putting out records was an endless cycle. Touring Blues Traveler was an endless cycle. And we didn't stop. A&M Records was sold to Universal Music Group, so suddenly everybody in our label was fired, and it's all new people. I was like, "I don't think I'm the best guy for you. I think you can do better and you deserve to do as good as you can."

Billy Martin: Their castles crumbled due to the internet and really digital technology, but also due to a system that was corrupt. We were bringing back that spirit of getting on the road and playing for people. That was the thing that really worked every time—people need to see you up there as a human being, actually sweating, and doing crazy shit.

Liz Penta: Touring is hard on people, and it happens to a lot of bands. Once you have this infrastructure, you feel compelled to keep it going.

Chris Rabold: Forget any machine, any push, any grand ideas, revisions, plans. Widespread Panic just played and they played and they played and they played, and were relentless about it.

Jono Manson: The conditions have to be right. For every band that has become well known, there were dozens of others who were just as talented who didn't wind up becoming famous. Most of them wound up splitting up. A lot of those people are still in the music business, doing one thing or another, doing touring bands, or running recording studios. And then some of them stopped playing music and went back to their day jobs.

Tye North: I just wanted to figure out how to not have to travel constantly. My last gig was Planet Salmon, this big cool festival that was at the Planet Bluegrass site. I had to get off the road. I was burned out.

Scott "bullethead" Reilly: It's a long hard slog. Nobody on the planet can know if they're going to like the road until they're on the road.

Billy Martin: I was getting burnt out at the end of the '90s.

John Medeski: I wasn't burnt.

David Precheur: We did not sit around talking about how rich we'd become someday.

Robert Walter: We just toured it into the ground and we got kind of burnt. If I look at my old calendars, we're on tour for three weeks, then we would come home and there's a gig two days after. I think we were all wanting to stretch out in different ways. It just started to fray at the edges. And instead of breaking up, we were just like, "Let's just take a break."

Mary Dugas: David and I talked early on when people were starting to get riled up about Napster . . . the labels . . . if they had only jumped on the bandwagon and done what Napster did early on, we'd be in a much different space. They were just locked into that formula.

Rich Vink: The whole industry just evaporated . . . all of those big A&R guys, all the showcases, it just went away.

Matt Busch: Late '99, God Street Wine did their quote-unquote "final shows." And I worked all those and then two months later, I was on the road with Gov't Mule and have been on the road ever since.

Oteil Burbridge: All of my friends had become really big and famous. You have everybody basically struggling with success . . . struggling with "Now I can do whatever I want." And that can kill you quite quickly, sometimes. Then it's about what are your wants? What's good for you and not good for you? It doesn't matter what kind of fame, or if you're not famous and you just have a shitload of money . . . it doesn't matter. It all reduces down to what are your wants. Hopefully, you want to live, have healthy relationships, and play music, and that outweighs the wants that are unhealthy.

Lo Faber: In recent years, I realized that I really did take for granted how relatively easy it was for God Street Wine to attain a certain level of success. There were a lot of bands that did that same grind and didn't have the same success or get any record deal. We were very fortunate.

John Bell: I really don't think I've experienced fame like other people. I think for some people, it's part of the price, you know? For me, it's the relationship and making music together. If you're outside of the business, you really don't have firsthand knowledge of what playing in a rock and roll band entails. I would think that's where the fame is recognized . . . people seeing you through that lens.

Brendan Hill: You walk through Walmart or Home Depot, and you hear a Muzak version of "Run Around" or you hear the real thing . . . you're in that fabric of the '90s. You know, there is a certain amount of fame you know you've achieved, but is that something I brag about? I don't brag about it. I was so lucky to meet John, to be in this band and be in the right place, be in New York right after they canceled the cabaret law so that every bar in New York became a venue . . . we took advantage of that.

Dave Schools: I'm an only child. And so my status quo is finding some time to be alone and quiet. But also, as an only child, it's like, I wish I had this loud, boisterous family. And that's what being in a band gave me.

John Popper: When you're younger, it's the first time you're dealing with stuff, so it's a lot harder. But really what we're describing is just how life goes. There's always going to be something. There's always a bus crash. There's always somebody having a baby. There's always somebody's parents dying. When you travel a lot, there's more stuff that can happen to you. For every time that we lost somebody or had a huge setback, there was another time when something magical happened.

Dave Schools: That's the thing about Athens . . . it's never the structure of the town, it has nothing to do with the city council. It has everything to do with the people that choose to stay there. I can remember being very young there and seeing people who were members of the existing Athens music scene and thinking, "Why are they still in a college town? These oldsters should get the hell out of here." And then I found myself being one of them. Because this town is amazing. And because of the people that live here. You can't have a place that could break the B-52's, R.E.M., Love Tractor, Pylon, Widespread Panic, Drive-By Truckers, Apples in Stereo, the whole Elephant 6 collective . . . it's such a melting pot of creativity.

Chan Kinchla: I always wonder if we had never had those hits, what direction would we have gone?

Brendan Hill: Every little thing that happens brings you to where you are. As long as you tried, along the way, did everything you can, were a good person and treated others well . . . I think I can look back and be proud of that.

Lo Faber: I went on to teach college and teach students about the music industry. Often they would ask me, "Why did you let it go?" And I would say, "I let it go pretty easily, because I just assumed that I could build something like that again, when I wanted to." I really didn't realize what a special thing it was and that I couldn't necessarily build it again so easily.

Jon Bevo: The highs are really high and the lows are really low. Which is a way of living and it's a good way of living . . . I wouldn't trade it for anything.

Aaron Maxwell: It just wasn't meant to be . . . but at the same time, what was meant to be was that we're honored to be known for being part of that beginning . . . the building blocks of this scene. So, you know, I'll take it.

Domingo "Sunny" Ortiz: We just love music. We just love each other. We love playing and that's what we do.

Chris Barron: I love my guys. I love the music that we make. I'm proud of the songs we've done and the commercial success.

Eric Krasno: I embrace the community because the community loves music, loves creativity. They want us to give them something different every time, which is what we want to do as well. That keeps it exciting for us.

Jon "The Barber" Gutwillig: A lot of the Biscuits made it through the music business by making the people who would work with us succeed. And then getting the people who we wanted to work us with almost jealous, and then they would work with us on terms that we found were okay. And that's how we got leverage.

Jimmy Herring: I look back on it now at sixty years old and go, "How did I ever do that?" Well, you did it because you had to. It wasn't about money. You did it because the universe demanded it; it was musically important.

Chan Kinchla: At the heart of it, can you play instruments where there's a certain amount of improvisation, and an interplay between the fans and the band? And if that's going on, it's a special magic that you don't find in a lot of things. That's what we always loved to do when we were playing in our basement and Brendan's basement in 1985. When we got signed, that's what we liked to do. When we were having huge hits on the radio, that's still what we liked to do. And that's why we kept going . . . that special magic is something that is hard to find anywhere else in the world.

Cody Dickinson: One true virtue of the jam band world that I feel doesn't get a fair shake is the audience. They're music aficionados, man. The people who love live music, they appreciate virtuosity. These excellent bands—say your Aquarium Rescue Units, Widespread Panic, Phish, the list goes on and on—that doesn't happen in a void. It's not an anomaly. There has to be a fertile ground for that to grow, and that's what the audience created.

Eric Schenkman: I suppose that's really what we're really talking about . . . the jam band scene was authentic enough and real enough that when it dropped in the bucket, it made enough of a ripple . . . and it was undisturbed, largely left alone, to ripple for a moment, which is a wonderful thing in our society.

Marc Brownstein: That's the cool thing about live music: You have a moment and then that's it. That's the moment and that's where it lives.

Jeff Sipe: It was a tremendous decade of exploration and development. I'd do it all again.

Trey Anastasio: Maybe it was just a magical time of life.

Acknowledgments

This book was made possible because of numerous people, and I'm incredibly thankful for all of them.

Marc Resnick at St. Martin's Press believed in this from moment one and had valuable insights whenever I needed them. If he was a Dead song, imagine the sickest "Dark Star" you've ever heard and multiply that by a hundred. That's Marc. I also want to thank the St. Martin's jam band crew Lily Cronig, Rob Grom, Lisa Rivlin, Martin Quinn, Kathryn Hough, and Michael Clark for their fantastic work on getting this book into its finished form and letting the world know about it.

Special thank-you to David Dunton at Harvey Klinger Literary Agency for the extra-special guidance and thoughts, from the gestation of this to the finish line.

Of course, this book would not be possible without the help, insights, and time dedicated by all the artists, managers, road crew, producers, and more. Shoutout for helping facilitate numerous interviews: Ben Baruch, Lindsay Brown, Kevin Calabro, Jason Colton, Phil Einsohn, Benjy Eisen, Dana Erickson, Brian Heisler, Maria Ivey, Patrick Jordan, Andrew Kaplan, Bari Lieberman, Ellie MacKnight, Oz McGuire, Kevin Morris, Benton Oliver, Carla Parisi, Ross Peterzell, Paddy Scace, Dylan Sklare, Joya Wesley, and Karen Wiessen.

This book is also indebted to the advice and support from Dean Budnick and Mike Greenhaus at *Relix*.

During the '90s, I spent countless hours with the OG road crew from Blacksburg, VA: Becki, Lyle, Mike D, and Matt Fine. Up I-81 in Harrisonburg was Marty Z. Thank you all for going to and listening to so many shows with me, talking about jam band minutiae on long car trips around the country, and experiencing this fabled decade with me.

Thank you to my parents, Doug and Elaine, and my sister Laura, for having my back even when I was packing it all up to go somewhere to see a band.

Thank you to my kids, Liam and Emma, for listening to an endless stream of jam bands and listening to me (still) talk about jam band minutiae and act like the trivia facts I spew are interesting.

Lastly, but never least, thank you to my loving wife Diedre—the best road partner I could ask for, ever.

Notes

The interviews featured in this book were conducted between December 2021 and October 2024 by the author, except for the following:

Chapter 1: It's Not Horrible, but I'm Stoned

3 I think my parents were worried that I was starting to hang out with the wrong crowd and sent me to private school: Jambands.com, December 12, 20213, https://jambands.com/features/2013/12/02/tom-marshall-on-phish-it-was-30-years-ago-today/.

3 Many of our friends played instruments and wrote original songs and recorded them in homemade studios: The Mockingbird Foundation, October 1999.

Chapter 4: We Had This Vibration Around the Band

34 Phish had already been together for two years: Fan interview conducted July 11, 1996 in London, England.

34 We had six or seven Dead songs in our repertoire at one point, like our first year, in a college band, playing for parties: Interview with Shelly Culbertson conducted on April 22, 1992 and posted on rec.music.phish, July 19, 1992.

36 We'd get three-night stands: *Phish: The Biography*, De Capo Press, 2010, 59.

38 The first session we did was in winter of '87: WIZN, Burlington, Vermont, interview conduced May 1989.

Chapter 5: You Had This Great Art School and Clubs Willing to Try Anything to Sell Beer

42 The only southern rock I'd heard, because I started playing the guitar in Delaware, was Lynyrd Skynyrd: *Relix*, 1997, https://relix.com/articles/detail/mikey-houser-the-relix-interview/.

44 [Mikey] graduated high school in 1980 and he went off to the University of Georgia: *Swampland.com*, 2008, http://swampland.com/articles/view/title:down_in_the_groove_with_widespread_panics_todd_nance.

45 He'd been driving like for three days or something: *Relix*, 1997, https://relix.com/articles/detail/mikey-houser-the-relix-interview/.

47 We were the black sheep: The Independent Florida Alligator, November 12, 1999, http://widespread-panic.blogspot.com/1999/.

47 People had . . . called me "Panic" for a while because I used to get those anxiety attacks, so that kind of became my nickname: *Relix*, 1997, https://relix.com/articles/detail/mikey-houser-the-relix-interview/.

49 They tried to hire me to enforce underage drinkers and I said, "I ain't that guy": *Swampland.com*, 2008, http://swampland.com/articles/view/title:down_in_the_groove_with_widespread_panics_todd_nance.

Chapter 8: Hit the Record Button and Get Out of the Way

65 It was just a two-minute walk from the "band house": The Independent Florida Alligator, November 12, 1999, http://widespread-panic.blogspot.com/1999/.

65 He started to come and see us and he saw something in it and he offered us a deal, on one condition, and that was that we stop playing "Nights in White Satin": *Swampland.com*, 2008, http://swampland.com/articles/view/title:down_in_the_groove_with_widespread_panics_todd_nance.

Chapter 12: We Were an Alternative to the Alternatives

90 I remember sitting in the studio on the couch playing the same guitar Scott Boyer played on "Midnight Rider" for Gregg Allman: *Swampland.com*, 2008, http://swampland.com/articles/view/title:down_in_the_groove_with_widespread_panics_todd_nance.

90 We played the frat houses during the week to make money and buy equipment and then play the clubs and lose the money on the weekends: *Swampland.com*, 2008, http://swampland.com/articles/view/title:down_in_the_groove_with_widespread_panics_todd_nance.

Chapter 15: The Gossip on This Band Was Like Wildfire

107 When I moved there in the mid-'80s, it felt like such an enlightened space: *Vulture*, May 14, 2018, https://www.vulture.com/2018/05/dave-matthews-in-conversation.html.

108 The first gig we had, that we ever played, was on Earth Day: *The Tape Archives Podcast*, Episode 14, published February 12, 2020.

108 We all come from different musical backgrounds . . . the result is a big stew: Darcy's Music, VH1 broadcast, January 16, 1995.

111 There was not a lot of saxophone and violin and acoustic guitar happening in rock and roll at the time—or now: *Vulture*, May 14, 2018, https://www.vulture.com/2018/05/dave-matthews-in-conversation.html.

112 We just played . . . that's all we did: Darcy's Music, VH1 broadcast, January 16, 1995.

Chapter 21: An Emaciated Third-World Exodus, Run by a Few Homeless People and Coyotes

139 In a lot of ways Popper was driving the boat: *Relix*, May 25, 2012, https://relix.com/articles/detail/h-o-r-d-e-stories-mike-gordon-and-page-mcconnell/.

144 I don't know if the term jam band was really thrown around much: *Relix*, May 25, 2012, https://relix.com/articles/detail/h-o-r-d-e-stories-mike-gordon-and-page-mcconnell/.

Chapter 34: We Were Just These Hippies, Running Around Half Naked or Sometimes Fully Naked

219 My mother played guitar and piano, and eventually we had a family band: *Banjo News*, December 2000, https://www.his.com/~vann/LoSstuff/BNL_article.htm.

220 The picking hadn't been that great that particular night: *Banjo News*, December 2000, https://www.his.com/~vann/LoSstuff/BNL_article.htm.

220 The first gig was literally an accident: *Banjo News*, December 2000, https://www.his.com/~vann/LoSstuff/BNL_article.htm.

Chapter 39: No Offense to You, but I'm Going for It

240 One of the reasons we chose Steve Lillywhite for the early sessions was when he spoke about recording, he said, "I just want to get what you do on stage": *GQ*, May 19, 2023, https://www.gq.com/video/watch/gq-iconic-dave-matthews-band.

242 "Crash" is odd because it was a love song: *GQ*, May 19, 2023, https://www.gq.com/video/watch/gq-iconic-dave-matthews-band.

Chapter 51: Why Don't We Do It As Far Away As Humanly Possible

300 There was a musical peak right around the time: *Jambands.com*, July 24, 2007, https://jambands.com/features/2007/07/24/the-high-watermark-with-tom-marshall-and-trey-anastasio-part-i/.

300 We went around in a circle, playing one note at a time for about two weeks: *Rolling Stone*, February 20, 1997, https://www.rollingstone.com/music/music-news/phresh-phish-120559/.

304 I do remember, and it could be the Great Went, this incredible moment where we were hanging off the back of a golf cart: *Relix*, July 6, 2011, https://relix.com/articles/detail/tom-marshall-gathers-steam/.

Chapter 61: We Didn't Even Know We Were in a Tidal Wave

352 We used to let people plug directly into the soundboard, but that became a spaghetti mess: Voom TV interview with Dave Fanning, November 22, 2007.

Chapter 68: That's the Moment and That's Where It Lives

381 There was a scene, and we were kind of against what was viewed as the legitimate rock music of the time: *Vulture,* May 14, 2018, https://www.vulture.com/2018/05/dave-matthews-in-conversation.html.

About the Author

Zachary Maxwell Stertz

MIKE AYERS is a seasoned music and culture journalist, with work published in *Billboard, The Wall Street Journal, Rolling Stone, Time, Reuters, Uproxx,* and *Relix*. His first book, *One Last Song: Conversations on Life, Death, and Music,* was published in 2020 and picked as one of *Variety*'s Best Music Books of the year.

About the Type

This book was set in Adobe Garamond Pro, a typeface inspired by Claude Garamond (1510–1561). He is considered one of the leading type designers of all time, known for creating elegance while mimicking handwriting with a pen. Adobe Garamond Pro was released in 1989 by Adobe and was the company's first historical revival of a typeface, with the design process taking place over a year.